# CHEATING OUR KIDS

# CHEATING OUR KIDS

## How Politics and Greed
## Ruin Education

## JOE WILLIAMS

First published 2005 by
PALGRAVE MACMILLAN™
175 Fifth Avenue, New York, N.Y. 10010 and
Houndmills, Basingstoke, Hampshire, England RG21 6XS.
Companies and representatives throughout the world.

PALGRAVE MACMILLAN is the global academic imprint of the Palgrave
Macmillan division of St. Martin's Press, LLC and of Palgrave Macmillan Ltd.
Macmillan® is a registered trademark in the United States, United Kingdom
and other countries. Palgrave is a registered trademark in the European Union
and other countries.

ISBN 1–4039–6839–X

Library of Congress Cataloging-in-Publication Data
Williams, Joe.
Cheating our kids : how politics and greed ruin education / Joe Williams.
     p.   cm.
   Includes index.
   ISBN 1–4039–6839–X
   1. Politics and education—United States.   2. Public schools—Political
aspects—United States.   3. School failure—United States.   4. Educational
change—UnitedStates.   I. Title.

LC89.W54   2005
379.73—dc22
                                                                    2005045961

A catalogue record for this book is available from the British Library.

Design by Letra Libre, Inc.

First edition: October, 2005
10  9  8  7  6  5  4  3  2  1

Printed in the United States of America

# CONTENTS

*To my wife Bridget*

# PREFACE AND ACKNOWLEDGMENTS

Most education reporters at American newspapers get "The Call" on a regular basis. This is how it usually works: A well-intentioned person on the other end of the phone line pitches a heartwarming (but not particularly newsworthy) school event that she is sure our subscribers would like to see covered in the news pages. The pitch ends with the all-too-familiar knockout punch: "Wouldn't it be nice if you put something positive about the schools in the newspaper for a change?"

Many of us come to dread these conversations, not because we don't think the multicultural nights and science fairs and band concerts are as wonderful as the callers, but because we find ourselves face-to-face on a daily basis with the grim reality that is public education in America today. We get just as choked up as the next person as we sit in a crowded auditorium listening to a children's choir sing about peace, love, and understanding. But when the bell rings at the end of the school day, we have to go back to our news rooms and write about an education system that by any honest measure is failing the very kids who need it most in order to have a sliver of a chance in life. Despite the hard work of many individuals who dedicate their lives to helping prepare children for a productive life in our democracy, the system itself continues to stumble, and too many kids pay the price.

This book looks at how the political structures of our modern school systems give short shrift to the needs of students, who by any sane reasoning should be the focus. There are courageous stories of heroic educators and parents who buck the system and help their kids defy the odds; yet because the system itself has become rigged against the interests of students, those stories are the exception rather than the rule.

The concept of *Cheating Our Kids* is based on more than a decade of reporting on both successful and struggling schools, primarily in New York City and Milwaukee, but also in places like Miami, Chicago, Cleveland, Jersey City, and elsewhere. It also relies on research I conducted in 2004 in San Diego as part of a critical review of that city's Blueprint for Student Success under school superintendent Alan Bersin. Other information contained here was gathered at multiple National Education Association Representative Assemblies in the late 1990s and from a daily reading of education news throughout the country.

As an education reporter on the nation's largest school system, I've observed firsthand some of the best and worst that public education has to offer. As a parent of two boys in New York City's public schools, I've felt the joys that fill a family's home when things are going well at school, along with the utter frustration that comes when conditions are less than perfect.

By any reasonable standard, these are gloomy days for public education, but it doesn't have to be this way. My hope is that this book will contribute to the ongoing discussions about how the public can take back its schools in a way that puts children first in line for the system's attention. I believe our kids deserve nothing less, even if we have to fight for it.

I wish to thank all of those parents, teachers, administrators, and policymakers who entrusted me with their tales. I am grateful to my editors, including David Pervin at Palgrave Macmillan; Kirsten Danis, Linda Hervieux, and Michael Goodwin at the *New York Daily News;* George Stanley and Marty Kaiser at the *Milwaukee Journal Sentinel,* and Bruce Gill and Jim Slocum at the *Milwaukee Sentinel* for giving me a chance to observe up close what I consider to be one of the most important public services in our democracy. I also am indebted to Rick Hess at the American Enterprise Institute for assisting me with my research on San Diego's schools, as well as Alan Bersin both for generously setting aside so much of his precious time for me and for his willingness to be so brutally honest about his observations of the modern school system. I am convinced more than ever that this sort of transparency and honest dialogue will be necessary if we are to solve the systemic problems within public education.

I am particularly thankful to those friends and family members who assisted me in crafting and editing this book, particularly, but not limited to, Joe and Diane Williams, Anthony and Mary Jo Ricci, Anne Bower, Leslie Mitchell, Beryl Ament, Abby Wilson, Andy Rotherham, George Mitchell, Juli Kaufmann, Marty West, Elizabeth Hays, and Whitney Tilson.

Finally, I also wish to thank all the newspaper readers who ever offered feedback to my stories over the years—positive or negative. You helped me learn more than you will ever realize and showed me that there are enough people out there who care about putting children first to make radical solutions possible.

# 1

## CHILDREN LAST

Tiffany Schley wasn't in a mood to be overly nostalgic about her four years of high school. A feisty 17-year-old from Brooklyn's rough-and-tumble Bedford-Stuyvesant neighborhood, the largest predominantly African American neighborhood in New York City, Tiffany was the newly crowned valedictorian for the Class of 2004 at the High School of Legal Studies when we first met. Like most young people who achieve that level of academic success, she already had an impressive resume: She had served as editor of the school newspaper, had chaired the yearbook committee, had been elected to student government, and had been accepted to attend the prestigious Smith College on a full scholarship. On paper, her four years looked wonderful. Her reality was quite different.

The high school Tiffany attended was a small "school within a school" located inside the old Eastern District High School in Bushwick, Brooklyn, an economically depressed neighborhood adjacent to her own. As was starting to happen at many large dysfunctional high schools around the country at the time, Eastern District in 1999 was converted to several smaller, theme-based schools in an attempt to remedy longstanding struggles with violence and academic failure. But the experiment had seen less than stellar results. By the 2002–03 school year, only 63 percent of the students who started school there four years earlier had managed to graduate. Even worse, nearly 90 percent of the students who *did* graduate did so without earning a New York State Regents Diploma—meaning they didn't pass the mandatory tests in such basic subject areas as math and reading and were forced to settle for a virtually worthless "local" diploma. With eight out of ten of her classmates poor enough to qualify for a free lunch, these were clearly students for whom a good education might have been a ticket to a better life, if only such an education had been offered to them.

Tiffany, voted most likely to succeed by her classmates, originally intended to focus her graduation speech on what it took for her to overcome a lisp earlier in her life. When she sat down at her computer to write it out, however, she changed her mind. Thinking of how many of her classmates from four years earlier wouldn't be graduating with her, she decided instead to focus on what it was like to attend a public school that had sent every possible message to its students over the previous four years that their education didn't matter.

The way Tiffany saw it, she had put up with 12 years of substandard education, provided by what was supposed to be the greatest city in the world. The least the school administrators could do, she thought, was allow her, as the valedictorian, to shine a spotlight on her school experience. Her written speech was rejected beforehand by an assistant principal, who took the liberty of writing a new speech for her, one that glorified the school and its staff for their hard work and dedication.

When graduation day came, Tiffany decided the assistant principal's speech would be both dishonest and inappropriate. She knew she deserved a better education than the city's public school system had given her, and she decided to use the bully pulpit that is afforded to class valedictorians to let the world know about it. When it was her turn to speak, she swallowed hard, bravely threw caution to the wind and delivered her original, unedited version of the commencement address to shocked classmates and guests.

Among the complaints she highlighted: Classes were overcrowded and textbooks and other basic materials were hard to come by. The school, its staff, and its students were victims of extremely unstable leadership, with four different principals running the school over the course of her four years there. She said students were taught by incompetent teachers, some of whom had trouble with the English language. Fewer than one in four teachers at the school in 2003 had worked there for more than two years and the overall atmosphere was unpleasant. To add insult to injury, Tiffany said in her speech, uncaring school administrators refused even to meet with students to discuss these kinds of problems despite repeated attempts on the part of students to do so during the school year.[1] "They always want to keep the problems hush-hush, but what goes on in this school is real," Tiffany told me at the time.

Many students and teachers cheered in approval at the speech, but some school staff members bristled, viewing Tiffany's public airing of her complaints as being completely out of bounds. When Tiffany and her mother showed up at the school the following day to pick up her diploma, they were told she wouldn't get it unless she formally apologized to school officials for what she said. The mother and daughter then were promptly booted out of the building by school security guards. "We've been living with this for four years," a frustrated Tiffany explained to me on the telephone, moments after the class valedictorian and her mother were escorted out of the school building.

I wrote about Tiffany's situation for my newspaper, the *New York Daily News*, and the story took on a life of its own. Red-faced school officials eventually caved in after Mayor Michael Bloomberg called the decision to deny Tiffany's diploma "boneheaded" and referred to the offending educrat as a "bozo" at a press conference. Tiffany's proud mother, Felicia Schley, was shocked by the response of the grownups involved. The kids who managed to stay in school from freshman year through graduation, she told me, did so in spite of the obstacles the school created over the course of four years. "She busted her behind to get there (to the podium as valedictorian), she kept it clean, and she was honest," her mother said. "Sometimes the truth hurts."[2]

The truth, as it is increasingly clear, is that our once-heralded system of education in America has lost its way. Almost everyone agrees that the education system *should* exist to serve children like Tiffany, but it has been captured by groups—teachers and other employees, politicians, philanthropists, higher education institutions, vendors, consultants, et cetera—whose interests and egos are protected and advanced through competent and powerful organizations, including unions, lobbying firms, and even the major political parties themselves. Children don't have such representation or political pull, let alone the right to vote. Their parents often are treated more like opponents of the system than the actual customers, especially when they have concerns or complaints.

It has become a dirty little secret within public education. Despite the fact that the system as it now exists does not meet the needs of many students like Tiffany, our society is often unwilling to talk in stark terms about the gravity of the situation. Everyone knows there is a problem, but we prefer to speak of public education as an institution in glowing terms. We prefer to see the glass as half full, even when the vast emptiness inside the glass translates into the dashed hopes and dreams of so many of our young citizens who most need the institution. We often say we are pro–public education, yet we allow the system we supposedly support to continue chugging along unobstructed, while by almost any measure, the job of educating children isn't happening the way it should.

Among the world's major industrialized nations, the United States had the poorest student outcomes per dollar spent on education, according to a 2004 comparison of math and reading scores conducted by the Organization for Economic Cooperation and Development. Of the 40 countries whose scores were analyzed, the United States ranked twenty-eighth in math and eighteenth in reading.[3]

Even our best and brightest are getting a substandard education. Many of our students who leave high school and head for college do so without having mastered basic skills necessary to complete college-level work. "Free and open to all, the public school system tricks students into believing they've been well-educated," wrote former *Los Angeles Times* education reporter Richard Lee Colvin in a 2005 opinion piece, noting that the California State University system in 2004 required 58 percent of its freshmen to take remedial classes in math, writing, or both.[4] And remember, those are the students who do make it to graduation day, the kids we consider the lucky ones. The Children's Defense Fund estimates that every school day in America, 2,539 high school students become dropouts.[5] Often, these students report that they have simply grown tired of school violence and pointless lessons that don't seem to be getting them any closer to a diploma.

The statistics in New York City alone are shocking: Only 18 percent of children who begin high school graduate with a Regents diploma four years later.[6] For black and Hispanic students, the Regents graduation rate is less than 10 percent.[7] Despite years of curriculum and other reforms, fully two-thirds of the city's eighth graders are not capable of passing the New York State math and reading exams.

Put bluntly, the nation's schools are in a crisis, a reality understood best by the same people who work in school systems every day. New York City school chancellor Joel Klein notes that most people who work for him within the bowels of the school system would never dream of allowing their kids to attend schools like the one from which Tiffany Schley graduated. "When I meet with people in the department, I ask them how many schools in the city they'd feel comfortable sending their children to, and no one has ever said more than 20 percent," Klein said. "That means that, at best, 80 percent of our schools aren't good enough for our own people to send their kids to."[8] And yet the grownups keep cashing their paychecks, consultants and other experts keep getting fat contracts, and the public sticks its head in the sand, or at best, wrings its hands while the cycle continues. The kids always come last.

Public education has long been viewed romantically as a distinctly American way for the underprivileged to pull themselves up by their bootstraps. As Americans, we value individualism and stories about rising above the odds, so much so that we sometimes fall into the trap of unfairly blaming students for the lousy education they are getting from adults. We like to think that it is up to the students to rise to the occasion, often turning a blind eye when our American public education system neglects these same kids year after year by failing to provide the kinds of tools and incentives they need to beat the odds.

Take the example of comedian Bill Cosby, who in 1992 joined New York City mayor David Dinkins in visiting Public School 113 in Harlem to give the students a pep talk about the need to stay in school and get an education. The school, located in one of the toughest and economically depressed parts of New York City, perennially had the lowest reading and math scores in the five boroughs. But Cosby's message was delivered to the wrong people. When less than 5 percent of the school's students are reading at grade level, it's a safe bet that there is an entire cast of adult characters who should have been lectured on the "importance of education" before the students.

These adults had for years failed the children who met with Cosby and Dinkins that day. The long-time principal, who blamed the problem on budget cuts, had been denied tenure in the 1970s because of poor performance but was ultimately allowed to keep her job after her union sued on her behalf and won. Parents and students complained that the principal would spend her days getting drunk in her office, while reports of teacher assaults on students at the school piled up. When confronted with accounts of her drinking, the principal denied the charges, saying, "I know nobody came here and smelled alcohol on me."

In the 20 years before Cosby visited the brick school building, a dozen school superintendents had come and gone with no success in turning things around. Chancellors at the central office came and went, too, while the principal kept her job and hundreds of students moved from grade to grade without getting an education. In 1987, only one third grader in the school was able to do math on grade level. In the 1987–88 school year, teachers at P.S. 113 racked up 328 absences, less than half of which were covered by substitutes. Students told a *Newsday* reporter at the time that they frequently were asked to sit in classrooms unsupervised because there was no teacher around to supervise them. A 6th-grade girl said she was frequently asked to teach children in younger grades when their teachers were absent. For her work, she received a certificate and was given a mailbox with the rest of the faculty in the school office.[9]

Considering how badly public education had failed those young people, a pep talk about the importance of education from Bill Cosby amounted to kicking the victims while they were down. In addition to possibly tearing into the powers that be who had allowed the school to get to that point in the first place, Cosby might have also considered a pep talk to the parents who ever let their children step foot inside the school. Considering the lack of any real education that had been made available to these young people by the system, their parents clearly would have been better off keeping them home in front of a television all day, where they at least might have had a chance to learn something.

## MONEY IS POLITICS, POLITICS IS MONEY

As long as we continue to spend tax money on public schools, education will inherently be a political operation. Politics at its core involves the conflicts that arise over the distribution of public resources. As political scientist Harold Lasswell defined it, politics is the everyday fight over who gets what, when, and how. We spend more on public education than any other industrialized nation, making education spending one of the most sought-after pools of cash in the public sector. In the 2003–04 school year alone, local, state, and federal taxpayers ponied up more than $500 billion[10] for public schools—more than the entire military defense budget.[11] On average, only 60 cents on the dollar go toward "instruction," including teacher salaries and benefits, and supplies such as textbooks.[12] That the other 40 cents go toward something other than teaching children—on expenses like legal fees, lobbying, transportation, and administration—shows how far off track our system has gotten. Often, as education professor Martin Haberman notes, the 40 cents of noninstructional spending shows "the highest priority is always the protection and growth of the district system" rather than the education of young people.[13] We don't get what we pay for in our schools, but we get what we deserve because we simply don't insist as a society that the resources be used in ways that benefit our children.

The list of people and institutions fighting over the billions of dollars in school funds nationwide on a daily basis is dizzying: local colleges and universities that earn millions a year to train (and then retrain) teachers and principals, book publishers and test makers, bus companies, food vendors, et cetera. All claim to have the interests of children in mind. Even if the system that keeps them in business fails to do its job of educating kids year after year, these grownup interests still get paid.

Sometimes we even crank up the intensity with which we write these checks, but because the system is built in a way that puts other needs ahead of children, our students don't benefit. In Kansas City, Missouri, where tumultuous conditions wore out 20 school superintendents in 30 years, a court ordered that an extra $2 billion be spent over a dozen years (between the mid-1980s and late 1990s) as a supplement to the district's $125 million per year operating budget to improve education for minority students. School officials used the unprecedented cash infusion to boost teacher salaries and build 15 new schools. They included pricey luxuries like an Olympic-size swimming pool with an underwater viewing room, television and animation studios, a robotics lab, a 25-acre wildlife sanctuary, a zoo, and a model United Nations chamber with simultaneous translation capability.[14] Unfortunately, after a dozen years very little had really changed and the district still failed to meet any of the state's performance standards.[15] Structure matters in education, particularly when school systems are configured in ways that assure that the needs of adults are addressed first and foremost.

There is simply no shortage of adults, however well intentioned they may be, who are willing to stand in line looking for handouts while our children suffer. When a special court-appointed panel in New York City recommended in 2004 that the city's public schools should get an additional $5.6 billion per year on top of its $13 billion operating budget to remedy a funding adequacy lawsuit, Chancellor Klein said he was bombarded by offers of help on how to spend it. "I never had so many friends before," Klein joked.[16] Many people benefit from the billions of dollars spent on education in America each year—our task is to make sure students are at the top of that list.

There is no way to avoid the political nature of public education, but understanding that fights over money and power rule the day is the first step toward regaining control in a way that puts the needs of kids and parents first and foremost. As *New York Post* columnist Bob McManus once put it: "This is the New York City public school system, after all, where power comes first and kids come last—but where money matters most of all."[17] The trick, of course, is making sure the money is being spent in ways that benefit children first and foremost. And while New York City represents the largest school system in the country (one out of every 47 American public education students attends a school in New York City), the same structure that shoves children to the back of the line exists in urban, rural, and suburban public education systems nationwide.

To be sure, most people who make a career out of trying to teach our children how to read, write, and do math—and even those who support them by driving buses, serving food, and waxing the floors—are fabulous, caring, and decent individuals. The irony is that good people often find themselves stunted and obstructed by bad systems—and those bad systems are in turn created by people protecting their own interests. There are also fabulous, caring, and decent individuals who tolerate (and often perpetuate) incompetence, fraud, and shameful displays of adult arrogance at the expense of young children and their families. They cannot be expected to do otherwise, as the system is set up to minimize responsibility and accountability. It is easier to go along to get along.

Everyone knows that things could be a whole lot better in our schools and school systems, but major change is something that seldom takes root because all the incentives for those on the inside are aligned in ways that reward them for maintaining the status quo. Why stick your neck out if doing so has more risk than keeping your head down and collecting your check? Far too often, it is the needs of schoolchildren that get left behind in the public school culture. Public education is about politics. Politics is about power. Parents and students have no power.

Parents and the general public often are so disenfranchised from the schools that school leaders easily can get away with glossing over real problems that stand between our children and a decent education. Sadly, it often appears that to have your needs met by the system, you either have to belong to a union or be somehow politically connected to the people who control the purse strings.

Employee unions, vendors, and other groups will always be fighting over their piece of the pie. There is no way around that fact. This book argues, however, that the *right kind* of politics, driven by parents who have decided once and for all that their children deserve better, can save a public education system that is losing supporters by the hour. As we will see in later chapters, it is parents who can ultimately save the system, but they need help from a public that understands the gravity of the situation and appreciates the long-term implications for our society if we don't radically alter our current path.

## REFORM AT THE MARGINS

Public education is at a crucial juncture in America. In its current state, it doesn't get the job done for the students who need it most. Its survival as an institution requires a return to the notion that students should come first, and that their parents are the real customers of school systems. When a blue-ribbon panel appointed by the Reagan administration released the report *A Nation at Risk* in 1983, declaring that American schools had been caught in a "rising tide of mediocrity,"[18] it served as a wake-up call for a nation that had been lulled into thinking all was well in its classrooms. It was treated as a national crisis, and wave after wave of reform was introduced to improve schooling. But two decades later, very little has actually changed, raising serious questions about the American public education system's ability to survive into the future.

None of this came as a surprise to the groups that do control what happens in schools. They have understood for years that they are steering their ship into an iceberg. "Time is running out on public education," the late Al Shanker, president of the American Federation of Teachers, said in 1995.[19] "The dissatisfaction that people feel is very basic." In the decade that has passed since Shanker's remark, public support for alternatives to the education system—like charter schools, or public schools that operate outside of the traditional public school system, and even the use of vouchers for students to use at private and religious schools—has continued to increase. Cities, including New York City, have looked to their mayors to try to break the grip of special interests on the school system, and nontraditional superintendents hired from outside of school systems have become commonplace. These outsider school leaders often are brought in specifically because they have no allegiance to any of the internal forces within the public education framework. Often they begin their jobs with what they think is a mandate and a blank slate, only to discover later that the special interests are so entrenched in the form of labor contracts, legal precedents, and other agreements that there really is no such thing as a blank slate in public education reform.

Two decades after *A Nation at Risk*, it's difficult to find a single major metropolitan area that has improved its public schools to any widespread and measurable extent. Meanwhile, even our best students have trouble competing with their counterparts worldwide on math and science tests. What we need in this country is more along the lines of an educational revolution.

True reform of our education system will require honesty on the part of everyone about what we have on our hands—the good and the bad. It requires real governmental transparency so that parents and the public can see that school dollars are being spent in ways that benefit students first and foremost, and so that reforms can be properly evaluated based on what students get out of them, rather than merely on what school leaders put into education systems.

The clock is ticking and we must get it right. When baby boomers begin to retire at the start of the next decade (2011), and more and more of our tax money is earmarked for their Social Security checks and government pensions, it will be even harder than it is now to use government to fix problems that should have been fixed long ago. Time is of the essence, for our own children and for our ability to leave a better functioning education system for the next generation of students. Simply put, the United States and its democracy can not afford to conduct education business as usual if it expects to remain strong in the emerging global economy—especially at a time when not only are our students consistently outperformed by their counterparts overseas, but our government is becoming increasingly preoccupied with paying the retirement and health costs of a graying society.

Drastic change is desperately needed, along with strong leaders who can stand up once and for all to choose the needs of children before the wants of school employees. Our political elders and mainstream media have engaged in what Matthew Miller, author of *The 2% Solution*, calls "a tyranny of charades"—that is, orchestrated hoaxes about how those in power plan to fix our modern education system by tinkering on the edges.[20] While reality demands a major revolution in the way we deliver education in this country, our politicians and press have lulled the public into a catatonic state that quietly accepts such "reforms" as calls for more money, school uniforms, block scheduling, and smaller classes—none of which offers the seismic shift in power that will finally put our kids first.

In Los Angeles alone, school leaders decentralized power by creating distinct regions overseen by superintendents in the 1970s. In the 1980s, they abolished the regions and centralized decision making, and in 2000 they reestablished the regions. As Frederick M. Hess notes in *Spinning Wheels: The Politics of Urban School Reform*, reform itself has become the status quo of modern education systems, often with disappointing results and always without a fundamental change in who has the power within the education system. Parents are seldom viewed as customers and their children continue to come last.

Elsewhere in this book, I will look at the specific role of the teachers unions in the operations both of school systems and the Democratic Party. I will also look closer at the bureaucracy, its internal tensions that create distractions from the core mission of educating students, and how that bureaucracy thwarts the efforts of teachers, administrators, and parents who really do want to make a difference. I will examine as well the role that philanthropists and business leaders play in the politics of education, and what each could do to help parents put their kids first.

Because these problems are political in nature, we will address in greater detail throughout this book the political solutions that might allow the public to take back its schools. As former Milwaukee public schools superintendent Howard Fuller told the Wisconsin Supreme Court in 1996: "Powerful forces conspire to protect careers, contracts, and current practices before tending to the interests of our children. . . . Although I strongly support public education, in the final analysis, it is not the bureaucracy that is important, it is the students. The question must be asked, what is in the best interest of the students, not what is in the best interest of the bureaucracy."[21]

It is a question that needs to preface every decision to be made regarding our children's education, whether it is asked by parents, voters, or policymakers. The answers to the question will in large part determine the future of public education and our nation as a whole.

The public has just about exhausted its patience with school reform efforts that never seem to bear fruit, while the adults who feed off of the system continue to make better lives for themselves along the way. Far more radical changes are needed to put real power in the hands of parent-consumers than most modern Democrats and Republicans have the guts to support. This disconnect between the political parties and parents, particularly low-income and minority parents who unlike many elected officials can't send their kids to private schools, is a political time bomb waiting to explode. Public education is either going to be about serving children or continuing to serve grownups. It is only a matter of time before frustrated parents start asking politicians and school leaders the question posed in the old labor song: Which side are you on?

# 2

# PUBLIC EDUCATION, AMERICAN STYLE

It was only the first day of school, and already Christyn Pope was in trouble. Pope, the principal at Chavez Elementary School in the Southcrest section of San Diego, gave a television news interview in which she happened to mention the fact that the school lawn had turned brown over the summer and that the weeds were out of control. But that wasn't what landed Pope in hot water. Schools all over San Diego in the fall of 2003 were reporting dead lawn and weed problems, the casualties of a hot summer and major cuts to school budgets up and down the California coast. In order to make sure that teaching positions weren't eliminated in San Diego, school offi-cials decided to look for savings just about everyplace else in the budget and eliminated 120 landscape caretakers and 90 gardener positions.

What got Pope in trouble that day was when she let slip the fact that some parents were interested in volunteering their time to pull the weeds and to fix broken sprinkler heads for the lawn. She had forgotten that the unionized landscapers had a right to do the work, and if they couldn't do it, no one was allowed to make sure the weeds were cut. "The union called me right away, and told me what I said was illegal," Pope told the *San Diego Union Tribune*, referring to the California Schools Employees Association, the union that represented the laid-off grounds keepers.

At nearby Marvin Elementary School, the weeds had grown to be five feet tall—taller than the students—and parents who volunteered to pull the weeds and haul away trash there also were informed by school officials that they were violating the labor contract of the grounds keepers who had lost their jobs. Union leader Eric Olson did what he needed to do if he wanted to keep his cushy leadership position: He fought hard for his members and made sure that people didn't get ideas about this kind of volunteering.

"What happens when the district gets in better financial shape—why rehire the landscape crews when the work is being done free?" Olson asked. "If people really want to help, they should be writing their elected officials about the budget."[1]

As Willy Surbrook, director of labor relations for the San Diego City Schools, explained to me several months later, union rules prohibit schools from outsourcing jobs or using volunteers for routine work once done by unionized employees, even if those jobs no longer exist due to budget cuts. "We have to limit that volunteer work to incidental work," said Surbrook, a former labor leader himself, who wasn't particularly pleased to have to operate under these types of restrictions. What he meant was that in order to be fair to the grownups who work in the system, school leaders must operate schools where the weeds sometimes grow taller than the kids. Surbrook noted that one of the reasons the grounds keeper jobs were cut in the first place is that in San Diego, like much of the United States, the health and welfare benefits for school employees are growing at a far greater pace than tax revenues,[2] a problem that is projected to get even worse as a wave of baby-boomer school employees starts hitting the retirement rolls with locked-in lifetime benefits.

Public education in America has become so consumed with meeting the frequent demands of employees and other adult constituencies that the needs of the customers—parents and children—often are an afterthought. The political nature of public education and the internal battles over how school resources are distributed apply various tensions to the school system; it is easy to understand why children aren't being better served. Those tensions often become the squeaky wheel that gets every ounce of grease school systems have to offer, assuring that students and their needs come last in the fight for the system's attention. In New York City, to cite just one example, many students attend schools where the clocks don't work, where bathroom toilets don't flush, and where a majority of students can't meet basic reading and math standards by the time they graduate. And yet the checks keep rolling for tens of thousands of employees, the politicians flap their gums about doing the right thing by kids, and the voters who stick around for the long haul are seemingly content to settle for schools in which the bar is set pathetically low by the very people who make their livelihoods from working within the system.

One answer to the San Diego weed problem, of course, is to simply find a way to spend more money on education so that it doesn't have to become an either/or choice between keeping teachers (who work directly with students) and keeping groundskeepers (who provide basic services that indirectly impact kids). Lawsuits all over the country have dealt with school funding levels and whether or not they are adequate or equitable within individual states, lawsuits that typically have been strongly supported by school employee unions who stand to benefit the most from an infusion of new revenue to school systems.[3] Additional funding may indeed be necessary, but it's hard to know because most school districts have been unable to solve the larger problem of how to shift the focus away from employee issues toward the needs of students. We honestly don't know how much it would cost to put children first because we have never tried. Simply adding more cash to the school system without structural reforms that put the focus on student learning first and foremost doesn't even come close to dealing with the long-term problem.

Apple Computer founder Steve Jobs learned this the hard way. Jobs used to give lots of computers to schools in the belief that technology would help improve conditions for learning. But like many people who work closely with school systems across the country, Jobs, too, came to the conclusion that the problem with public education is that the system isn't set up in a way that puts the needs of students, as customers, first. "No amount of technology will make a dent," Jobs told *Wired* magazine in 1996. Jobs cut loose on the problem as he saw it: "It's a political problem. The problems are sociopolitical. The problems are unions. You plot the growth of the NEA [National Education Association] and the dropping of SAT scores, and they're inversely proportional. The problems are unions in the schools. The problem is bureaucracy."[4]

Historically, public education in America has served a dual purpose. Yes, it has been about teaching children to read, write, and do math, but it has also served an important role in helping immigrants and low-skilled workers earn family-sustaining paychecks. While both are noble causes, the latter explains why we so easily lose sight of the former. Those dual purposes were able to coexist for generations, particularly when there was an abundance of middle-class factory jobs awaiting students who weren't successful academically. More recently they have collided with disastrous effects for children in an increasingly high-tech and global economy. San Diego school superintendent Alan Bersin put it this way:

> A fundamental issue here is whether large systems of public education are
> primarily sources of employment for adults rather than educational enter-
> prises of children. The answer, of course, is a synthesis properly framed of
> the two. Yet for most significant issues that are played out politically in

contemporary urban systems, there is a litmus test: Do we give adults what adults want for their jobs or give children what children need for their education? Traditionally, the answer has been the former because of the political alignments within public education and the ineffectiveness of coalitions trying to change it from the outside.[5]

We shouldn't be surprised that education may not exactly be the primary purpose of public schools. In practice, kids aren't even close to coming first. Former *New York Times* education columnist Richard Rothstein summed up the situation perfectly in a 2002 piece on a bus driver strike in Los Angeles. Rothstein argued that public schools have historically had a responsibility for helping create good jobs for those who would be unable to get them elsewhere. "The schools' essential function, of course, has been to educate," Rothstein wrote. "But for immigrant and minority workers, they have also been a source of better jobs, a first step to the middle class."[6]

Irish and German immigrants a century ago were able to pull themselves up by their bootstraps, in part because of high-paying school jobs they got through political patronage, Rothstein wrote. "There may be a point to insisting that immigrants, like Los Angeles's bus drivers, should now strive for upward mobility without taxpayers subsidizing their wage scales," Rothstein wrote. "But that is not how previous generations began to climb."[7] This entitlement mentality so deeply permeates school districts across America that employment conditions often trump student learning when decisions are made and policies are established for school systems.

Whether or not students' needs are best served—or even served at all—the highest organizational priority is placed on making sure contracts with adults are not violated. When five assistant principals in New York City were observed shopping at Lord & Taylor, Macy's, and Kmart during work hours in 2004, investigators discovered their assignment at the time involved sitting around doing absolutely nothing—literally—in a district office all day. After their positions had been eliminated in their schools, the assistant principals were assigned to the personnel office for the city's Region 9 in Manhattan. They couldn't do basic administrative tasks such as shuffling papers because it wasn't in their negotiated job descriptions as assistant principals. "It appears that the most significant responsibility assigned to each A.P. during the temporary reassignment was to show up on work days," special schools investigator Richard Condon wrote in a report to schools chancellor Joel Klein.[8]

Condon's investigators trailed the school-less assistant principals and found them doing all sorts of personal business and errands. The employees, who were allowed to turn down various tasks under the terms of their contracts, earned salaries from $65,000 to $106,000 per year. The entitlement mentality was so ingrained in the culture that five well-paid employees were allowed to come and go throughout the day without ever appearing on any higher-up's radar screen.

The culture that creates these kinds of entitlements for school employees grants very little power to parents and their children to help them compete with other special interests for the undivided attention of the school system. If a student isn't properly taught how to read, there is no grievance process established for the student or their parents to seek recourse. In fact, the complaining student or parents often are treated as if they are doing something wrong just by complaining. Yet if a teacher is asked to teach math, and she wants to teach reading instead and has been on the job for any length of time, she can file a formal grievance challenging management's authority to assign staff, and her formal complaint is considered business as usual by the bureaucrats who process the grievances. The teachers contract in New York City, for example, mandates that teacher bathrooms be cleaned and stocked regularly, but there is no such contract that guarantees the same for students. The school system is set up in a way that virtually guarantees that children will never be its prime focus.

Meanwhile, the people and groups that do have power within the system are actively promoting their self-interests. Sometimes this self-interest is harmless and advances genuine needs and fairness issues for hard-working school employees. This was particularly true during the period when teachers first organized and won the right to bargain collectively. Other times, however, this self-interest sucks the resources and energy out of school systems in the form of corruption, incompetence, or indifference to the educational needs of children. Structurally, the highly regulated nature of public education means that in order for people to get things done, they often must learn to work around the rules. Additionally, there are very few incentives in place for school employees and administrators to do a better job of serving parent-customers and their kids. A principal who runs a school that is wildly popular with parents is usually paid the same amount as the principal who runs a school that parents want to avoid like the plague. This is the obvious downside of a culture that doesn't know how to reward excellence: It often makes excellence itself irrelevant.

Not only is excellence not recognized, no one appears to be minding the store to make sure everyone is doing what they are supposed to be doing for children, or even for the people who are supposed to be teaching them. In 2003, after eight New York City school craftsmen and laborers were caught snoozing in city trucks, cruising the aisles at Home Depot, and bench-pressing at the local gym on what was supposed to be work time, Gail Baptiste, principal of Public School 308 in Brooklyn, put it in perspective: "I'm not surprised. We send in paperwork and requests and nothing ever gets fixed."[9]

## SCHOOL GOVERNANCE

House Speaker Thomas P. "Tip" O'Neill was famous for saying that all politics is local. Education politics is no exception. The locally elected school board, an institution once disparaged by writer Mark Twain as being one step above idiots,[10] is one of the few places where citizens can draw a clear link between their right to vote and local government. School boards influence property tax rates, determine curriculum, approve budgets and contracts, and hire superintendents. When your child's classroom doesn't have any books, and the teacher and principal shrug their shoulders at your complaints, it is the local school board to which you usually turn to raise some hell. School boards are elected by voters, and as such, are responsible to voters. If all voters were parents with children in the school system, this accountability arrangement would seem to work fine, as elected board members would be expected to place a high priority on meeting the needs of students and parents. Because many parents don't vote in school board elections, particularly in urban areas, their needs often are pushed aside by the wants of others who may have different agendas—whether they are retirees on fixed incomes who don't have children in schools and simply don't want to spend any more than necessary on schools, or organized employee groups within the system who stand to benefit through the election of a labor-friendly management team.

Increasingly, cities around the country are looking at alternative governance models like New York City's, in which the elected mayor is given near total control of the school system. The expectation is that mayors are more responsive to voters than school board members who are often elected in low-turnout elections dominated not by parents but by the special interests who earn their living off of the school system. New York City mayor Michael Bloomberg told a special court-appointed school finance panel in

2004 that aside from voting on election day, voters can hold him accountable for what he does with the schools by heckling him while he marches in parades.[11] Politics doesn't get much more localized than feedback in the form of cheers and jeers at the Three Kings Day Parade.

It's not always easy to know who to blame when things go wrong in schools, however. Regardless of whether it is a mayor or a school board that runs the show locally, it is state governments that are given the statutory responsibility for ensuring that every child in the state receives what that state considers an appropriate education. State governments have largely been responsible for the standards movement that took off in the 1990s, with state committees determining the standards for academic subjects such as math and reading, as well as how to test students to assess whether or not they have met those standards. It is also at the state level that any teacher and administrator licensing takes place. State governments typically provide some financial aid—usually from income tax, lotteries, or statewide sales tax—to local school districts to supplement local property taxes for education.

Further diffusing the authority over what happens in local schools, the federal government also plays a role, particularly in funding and regulating special education and Title I programs for low-income students. The No Child Left Behind law is an example of how the federal government attaches strings to the money it sends to local school districts and becomes another layer of bureaucracy.

So many people and forces are involved in delivering public education that it is far too easy for bureaucrats and politicians to point fingers of blame at one another when things go wrong. Classroom teachers blame their principals and "the system" when they don't have the tools they need to do their jobs. Principals blame the central administration. Central administrators and school board members point the finger at the state education department when things go wrong. Even more common is for the state and local districts to team up and blame the federal education department for what ails them. Since it is rare that anyone ever takes total responsibility for what ails our schools, it is often difficult for the public to know where to look for solutions (or which bums to throw out, as the case may be).

In schools, the end result of this triple-headed bureaucratic structure is a rules-based school culture that has become more obsessed with regulatory compliance than on whether or not good, sound instruction is being delivered to students. The legal group Common Good studied the New York City school system in 2004 and found more than 60 separate sources of laws and regulations, with thousands and thousands of discrete obligations. The sources included state, federal, and local laws, as well as legal cases used as precedents, labor contracts, and 720 pages of regulations issued by the state commissioner of education. The result is that school employees have been turned into "procedural automatons," dealing with paperwork and legal considerations all day long instead of concentrating on whether students are learning, said David Bloomfield, a former top lawyer for the city's old Board of Education. "They end up getting strangled by this red tape," said Bloomfield, a professor at Brooklyn College.[12]

The rules-based culture also stokes a sometimes-destructive sense of entitlement among employees who operate within the system. Experienced teachers often tell me they feel they have earned the right to pick their schools and their assignments within those schools based on a long-established practice that rewards staff people for waiting in line and putting in their time, rather than based on anything they have actually done or accomplished. Any time that sense of entitlement is threatened, employees need only file a grievance and take their case through a series of bureaucratic hearings in order to seek relief in the form of the status quo.

## SCHOOL CORRUPTION

Millions and millions of dollars that were theoretically earmarked for student learning have been wasted over the years on patronage, bribes, bid rigging and no-show jobs in American public education. New Orleans police superintendent Eddie Compass in 2004 likened fighting school corruption to "eating an elephant" but suggested cops in the Big Easy had taken the first bite when they arrested a school payroll clerk and seven school employees who stole $70,000.[13] The seven employees had worked as teachers, secretaries, and paraprofessionals in schools across the city and were paid for work they didn't do. The crooks would meet with the payroll clerk, Louis Serrano, in parking lots to kick back his share of the cash, an even 50 percent.

The arrests came just after another payroll clerk, Terri Smith Morant, was caught stealing $250,000 all by herself. In her case, she simply printed checks to herself under her maiden name and then cashed them.[14] "This is an example of the kind of looting that's been happening in the Orleans Parish school system and which the people around me are uncovering daily," U.S. attorney Jim Letten told the *New Orleans Times-Picayune*.

And while shakedowns and kickbacks have long been a part of doing political business in New Orleans, superintendent Tony Amato reminded the public that the stolen money had been entrusted to the school system to help children learn to read and do math. "What was taken away, more than $300,000 today and more to come, wasn't taken from a nameless, faceless system," said Amato, who urged school crooks to look into the eyes of the neediest kindergarteners in the city. "They were stealing from our kids."[15] For several years, the payroll function in New Orleans apparently was turned into a piggy bank for crooked school employees. A state audit in 2004 found that employees in the Big Easy had cashed as much as $3 million in paychecks that were either errors or deliberate attempts to steal money that was supposed to go toward teaching kids.

New York City's school history is filled with legal cases involving employees and vendors who wore wires to help investigators uncover fraud, administrators and contractors with ties to organized crime, and cases so severe that the actors involved were murdered, permanently disappeared, or committed suicide (see chapter 5).

The end result of all of this corruption over the years is that, once again, the needs of students come last. Every dollar that is spent lining some adult's pocket is a dollar that could be spent teaching a child how to read or do math. At one point in the late 1980s, corruption probes were underway involving 11 of New York City's 32 elected community school boards. An assistant principal in the Bronx claimed she was demoted after she refused to make a $5,000 payoff to an elected board member. Another said she was punished after she rebuffed a board member's sexual advances. One official was accused of demanding kickbacks from a textbook publisher; another was accused of stealing a $10,000 piano from a school.[16] Allegations of bribery were widespread.

Lydia Segal, a former investigator and attorney in the office of New York City's special schools investigator Ed Stancik, in her 2004 book *Battling Corruption in America's Public Schools* notes that words like "children" and "learning" seldom crept into high-level discussions among the community school board members. "These boards carved their districts into fiefdoms where jobs were doled out to loyal campaign workers, lovers, and family members or sold for cash. The way for a teacher or assistant principal to get ahead was not to create excellent lesson plans or find better ways to teach math but to work on campaigns and run errands for board members. As one board member from Brooklyn's District 27 put it in a secretly recorded conversation for investigators, 'I'm a political leader, that's why I'm here . . . I make sure my people get f—ing jobs.'"[17]

Because the community school board elections in New York didn't coincide with elections for other city positions, local political machines were able to dominate the low-turnout voting and the city schools naturally became a part of that machinery, particularly since there were always jobs in schools that could be given to loyal campaigners. Additionally, since the boards could fire most nonteachers, or at least make their lives difficult, they were in a perfect position to exploit them for cash or sex. It was hardly surprising then that children came last in the city schools. By 1996, there had been so many scandals and indictments that the state legislature stripped the elected community school boards of much of their power, including the ability to hire the local superintendent, and gave it to the schools chancellor.

## NEPOTISM AND SCHOOLS

Nepotism has its own rich history in the city schools. In 1978, a New York City Board of Education rule was imposed banning school custodians from hiring family members after it was discovered that a custodian had hired his wife and didn't require her to actually do any work. It didn't take the custodians much time to find a way around the rule, however, as they soon began putting each other's relatives on the payroll in an informal form of mutual back scratching. Nearly a decade after the antinepotism rule was put into effect for custodians, New York State comptroller Edward V. Regan found that there was no indication that the problem had been addressed. Said Charles Haughey, president of the custodians union in 1987: "Nepotism exists throughout the board (of education) and in every city agency."[18]

Sometimes patronage and nepotism intersected—with tragic results. A high-profile 1998 case in Brooklyn in which a falling brick from a school roof hit and killed a passerby also ended up exposing the political underbelly of the school system. An investigation at the time by the *Village Voice* discovered that the School Construction Authority's project manager at the site had been hired for the job—"despite a long arrest record and dubious qualifications"—because of his political connections to Governor George Pataki. Investigative journalist Wayne Barrett discovered that the manager was married to the $68,346 per year special assistant to Paul Atanasio, the School Construction Authority (SCA) trustee who was appointed by Pataki. The same woman happened to serve as the Bay Ridge (Brooklyn) Conservative Party district leader and was a member of the state Conservative Party's executive committee, which had been instrumental in electing Pataki to office.[19] Not only did this SCA manager appear to get his job through political and familial channels, but because he did so, he was considered untouchable by the SCA, even after complaints from the school principal that he was drunk at the work site—when he even showed up at all. The manager resigned from his position shortly after the passerby's death and Pataki went on to win reelection and even to have his name frequently bandied about for national office or a Republican cabinet-level position.

This was the culture of corruption that Mayor Bloomberg inherited and set out to reinvent in 2002 when he was given control of the city's schools. He and Klein termed their reforms Children First and claimed they were setting out to remove all politics from their governance of the system. But as we've noted, a school system with $15 billion at its disposal each year that also happens to be run by a mayor who must get reelected in order to keep the reforms alive will never be able to totally remove politics from the equation. Because of that, corruption issues continued to pop up even after Bloomberg won control of the system. In one case, Bloomberg dumped his deputy chancellor, Diana Lam, for old fashioned nepotism after she was caught trying to get a $100,000-per-year administrative job for her husband.[20] The system's top lawyer also had to resign over his role in the scandal. (He had issued a statement to the press insisting that Lam's husband was looking to *volunteer* for the six-figure job, thus suggesting it wasn't technically nepotism. An investigator later found that the man had every expectation of being paid for his work and that the lawyer's response was little more than spin designed to sweep the problem under the rug in the press.) At a time when the New York City schools' top educator and top lawyer should have been tending to the needs of a school system in which only one in ten black or Hispanic high school students graduated with a Regents diploma after four years, they were distracted by issues involving the employment of adults.

## SCHOOL CONSTRUCTION RIP-OFFS

While classrooms in parts of the city were bursting at the seams with overcrowding, the city's Independent Budget Office estimated in early 2002 that one reason billions of dollars worth of school construction wasn't making a dent in the crowding issue was that it cost 400 percent more to build new schools in New York City than in other parts of the state and across the Hudson River in New Jersey.[21] The result was that New Yorkers for many years were paying construction costs for four schools but getting only one in return.

"These schools are costing far more than they should," said Peter Lehrer, chairman of a school commission appointed by former chancellor Harold Levy in 2001 and cofounder of the construction management company Lehrer McGovern.[22] Lehrer's commission in 2002 found that it cost $425 to $450 per square foot to build a new school—far more than the $300 to $325 per square foot it took to put up office towers, luxury condos, and hospitals in the same city. The commission noted that one reason the costs weren't lower was that no one at the School Construction Authority seemed to even care how much things cost. Essentially, there was no customer to complain if things came in over budget. With no one keeping an eye on costs, it almost assured that more would be spent than necessary and that efficiency was never an issue.

Additionally, the fact that the people at the School Construction Authority seemed to go out of their way to be as unpleasant to work with as humanly possible ended up costing taxpayers millions of additional dollars. New York State's Moreland Commission in 2002 blamed the constant infighting between the School Construction Authority and the Board of Education about their overlapping work responsibilities for the city's amazing ability to spend billions of dollars to build only a handful of new schools. "This dysfunctional system is a fundamental cause of New York City's current school construction crisis," the report said.[23]

The same report found that contractors routinely jacked up their prices by 20 percent as a sort of payment for the frustration. They even had a name for it: the "aggravation tax." [24]

To his credit, Mayor Bloomberg made slashing the mind-numbing cost of building new schools a priority once he got control of the city schools and the School Construction Authority. Former chancellor Harold Levy, at the end of his term in 2002, got his bureaucrats to design more complete plans before projects were put out for bids, in theory reducing the number of costly change-orders once work began. Bloomberg continued the practice and also courted the biggest builders in the city, who had refused to work with the schools because of all the headaches involved—namely the enormous difficulty they had getting paid and closing out projects. Bloomberg promised these builders they would be paid promptly and work in a more professional environment. As 2005 began, the agency appeared poised to see some turnaround in the school-building process. The result of Bloomberg's raising the bar was that school officials were able to pare down the opening bids for new school construction from $433 to $300 per square foot. During a press conference at the groundbreaking ceremony for the High School for Architecture and Urban Planning in Queens, Bloomberg called the new bidding process "more rational and accountable."[25]

It is worth noting, however, that in the spring of 2004, the Bronx Prep Charter School managed to complete its own state-of-the-art new building for $250 per square foot—well below even the "reformed" School Construction Authority's costs. Architect Peter Gluck, who designed the new Bronx Prep building, said the School Construction Authority's rules and requirements for construction, which involved building schools that could practically withstand nuclear attack, were so stifling that they invariably ended up inflating the final building price. The requirements, for example, included guidelines on construction materials and how space is to be divided between offices and classrooms. They encourage indifference on the part of school designers and builders by removing all of the thinking that goes into finding better and cheaper ways to do things, providing instead a general script for the actors to continuously follow. "It's hard to find the most efficient way to do things if you are constantly told what you can't do—why you can't do this and why you can't do that," Gluck said.[26]

Even a bunch of students showed in 2004 that they could build schools cheaper than the city's School Construction Authority. Urban planning graduate students from Manhattan's Hunter College designed a 300-student, six-story middle school with an estimated building cost of $250 per square foot. "One of the things that gave us flexibility is we were working with a charter school," said James Rubin, 32, a member of the design team.[27] Additionally, in 2004 the Bronx Charter School for the Arts, in Hunt's Point, completed its new building renovations on time and under its amazingly low $138 per square foot budget.

## A NEW KIND OF POLITICS

It is not a coincidence that all three projects just described are charter schools. Charter schools are public schools that are allowed to operate independently of the traditional public school system. They are not normally part of "the system" but are treated instead by the state that grants the charter as if they were their own system. By their definition, they have an easier time making the most efficient use of their per-pupil funding allocations because there are fewer hands in the cookie jar. This is one of the reasons charter schools have been so popular with both fiscal conservatives and social liberals. Charter schools have emerged all over the country as one way to shift the focus of education back to students. Charter schools recognize parents and their children as consumers purchasing an important service. They build their budgets and programs around the needs of students or they don't stay in business for very long.

Because charter schools tend to be small and don't normally have to support a bloated bureaucracy, the money they get to educate kids tends to actually get spent on things that are more than remotely related to instruction. And even more importantly, when children leave the school, their money leaves with them. Parents are treated as customers with power, which is exactly the way it should be. This is an important difference between charter schools and traditional public schools: The former have an incentive to put kids first, so much so that they will cease to operate if parents don't choose to enroll their children there. Public schools, in contrast, have a reverse incentive. The worse schools get at serving their students, the more money we give them. It's no wonder children come last.

While politics, rather than education, drives much of what happens in school systems, the right kind of democratic politics—in which parents can let schools know what they think of them by bolting and taking their tax money with them if they are not satisfied—can at least give children a chance to emerge as the people who come first in public education.

Parents historically have been too nice for their children's own good. Many of the political battles that take place within public education are anything but nice, and parents must understand that they themselves must sometimes engage in the kinds of hardball politics employed by the people who run the show if they want anything to change. Former United Federation of Teachers president Al Shanker once described the rationale behind employing cutthroat tactics: "I asked [Mayor Robert] Wagner why it was that during a previous negotiation he had said that there was not a penny more yet, when a hurricane came, [he] found millions of dollars. He said that was a disaster. I said, 'In other words, if we become a disaster you would find more for us, too.' We both laughed. But from that day we decided to become a disaster."[28]

Later in this book, I will explore ways that parents themselves can "become a disaster" that will push the needs of their kids to the top of the public education priority list. Parents never seem willing to step into the same ring as the people who have the real power. The sad reality is that if parents don't roll up their sleeves to fight for their kids, no one else will. As Hudson (Ohio) Education Association president David Spohn said in 2003: "We expect parents to work in the best interest of the kids. We're working in the best interest of the teachers."[29] Union leaders like Spohn should be expected to fight for the interests of their members. It is their legal responsibility to do so and it is what they are paid to do. But parents also should be expected to fight for their kids when it becomes necessary. It is their moral responsibility.

Nice parents usually play by a more genteel set of rules than the special interest groups inside the system, and their children pay the price. When is the last time you read about parents going on strike, boycotting parent-teacher conferences, or holding a rally, march, or vigil that disrupts rush hour traffic to demand better schools for their children? Too many parents either pick up and move someplace better without fighting or quietly settle for far less quality (and put up with far more grief) than consumer-minded parents who pay tuition at private schools would ever dream of allowing. The differences here between public-school and private-school parents are noteworthy, as is the difference between the way public and private schools view parents. In most public school systems parents are by and large a captive audience. When the going gets tough, those who can afford it get going either to another community or to a private school. Often, these students are simply replaced by others and there is no consequence to the public school for losing the students in the first place. In this sense, if there is any "customer" at all within the public school system, it is hard to argue that it is the parent or child. Furthermore, those families that don't have the means to pack up and leave for greener pastures are pretty much forced to take what they are given, as there is no customer-driven pressure for the school system to really do anything differently.

In contrast, every parent who elects to send a child to a private school makes a conscientious decision to do so based on whatever criteria they deem important. They exercise a form of school choice. They are customers of the school. As long as they are satisfied with what the school is providing, they will presumably continue to send their children to the school and the school will continue to receive tuition, allowing it to remain in business.

For parents and reformers who want the best for their kids, the answer comes down to the need to create a climate in which misguided and corrupt systems face extinction unless they take radical, child-centered steps to survive. The bar must be set high for school leaders. Competence must be demanded, corruption must not be tolerated, and parents who want what is best for their kids should become the most powerful special interest in the school system.

# 3

# THE PUBLIC EDUCATION CARTEL

There was an old joke at the New York City Board of Education's former headquarters at 110 Livingston Street in downtown Brooklyn. Constructed in 1925, both the 12-story, 361,000-square-foot building and the phrase "110 Livingston Street" eventually became synonymous with an educational bureaucracy that served grownups before kids—and even that service came slowly and expensively. The most efficient department in the building, the joke went, was the one responsible for scratching each departing chancellor's name off the door and quickly replacing it with the name of the latest chump who was brought in to attempt the impossible taming of the nation's largest school system. By the time the task was completed, the story went, departing chancellors, a regular sight in the building, would still be saying their goodbyes to colleagues down on the first floor.

School leaders come and go. New York City changed chancellors 17 times between 1964 and 2004. But the bureaucratic creatures who seem to permanently inhabit American school systems are survivors who often appear to be able to withstand political, if not nuclear, attack. While there are many well-intentioned people who slave away pushing paper in central offices, many high-paid educrats spend enormous sums of money on things that have nothing to do with classrooms, such as training sessions at spas and consultant reports that sit on shelves and gather dust. Nationally, approximately 40 cents of every education dollar goes toward something other than instruction—a striking figure if you believe that instruction is supposed to be the name of the game.

In Washington, D.C., the public school system has 1,500 employees in the central bureaucracy, which oversees 146 schools. In contrast, the education office of the Washington Metropolitan Archdiocese has a mere 11 bureaucrats overseeing 110 Catholic schools.[1] The New York City Schools, with 1.1 million students, has a regional and central office staff of 6,000. The Archdiocese of New York, with 200,000 students in its Catholic schools, has about 35 central office workers.[2] The difference, in large part, comes down to culture. The Catholic schools are focused primarily on education, while the focus of public school instruction is clouded by a culture of rules-based compliance, paperwork, and meetings.

When former Long Beach, California, superintendent Carl Cohn was considering taking on the job of running Washington, D.C.'s public schools in 2004, he suggested that an outside firm be brought in immediately to clean house and put the focus back on educating kids. By "cleaning house" Cohn meant tearing apart the bureaucracy and starting all over with a framework that supported schools. An outside firm was needed, he suggested, because the political nature of the schools was so tangled with the bureaucracy itself that it would be against special interests to change anything. An outsider, he surmised, might have an easier time upsetting the applecart. This idea, he later said he was warned, was a nonstarter because "people said that won't work in Washington because the system has so many patronage jobs and the city's workforce depends on having all those jobs."[3]

Not only was Cohn astonished by the cavalier attitude with which Washingtonians so willingly talked about the importance of school jobs rather than classroom education, he had trouble understanding where all the money was going. In Long Beach, for example, he had been spending $16 million for transportation for the entire school system. In the nation's capital, which is a smaller school system than Long Beach, they were spending $75 million on special education transportation alone. Washington's school system, he realized, was out of control.

Former Washington city councilman Kevin P. Chavous called the central bureaucracy a "quagmire" that prevented school money from making its way to classrooms where students could benefit. "The existing school infrastructure works hard to maintain itself and the status quo—that is, the salaries of the assistant to the assistant and the contracts for the brother and sister-in-law of the assistant," Chavous notes.[4]

The problem with school bureaucracies, aside from the fact that they aren't focused on helping children learn to read and write, is that they value means over ends—inputs rather than outputs. They get bogged down in process, compliance forms, and meetings. In the conference rooms of New York City's Tweed Courthouse school headquarters, one seldom observes meetings in which fewer than six participants are present. It's almost as if they sit in one meeting or another the entire day, spending more time talking about what they plan to do rather than actually doing it. The one sure thing that will be accomplished is the setting of a date for future meetings to follow up on what was discussed at previous meetings.

The resources we hope will turn around failing school districts typically are used to prime the pump of the monopoly that holds kids hostage to a substandard education. The end result is a system that doesn't work for our neediest kids and is extremely difficult to ever reform, because there are so many grownups who are served quite well by the failing system.

University of Wisconsin–Milwaukee professor Martin Haberman contends that the pattern of failure in urban school systems is a "predictable, explainable phenomenon, not a series of accidental, unfortunate, chance events."[5] We recognize that the needs of school children aren't being addressed, but our society does nothing to put its foot down to change it. "The extensive resources funneled into these systems are used for the purpose of increasing the district bureaucracies themselves rather than improving the schools or the education of the children," Haberman notes. "This massive, persisting failure has generated neither the effort nor the urgency which the stated values of American society would lead us to expect."[6]

## THE CARTEL

One of the best descriptions of the way the American education bureaucracy operates comes from Wellesley College political science professor Wilbur Rich, who refers to the internal power structure of school systems as "school cartels," which are interested primarily in self-perpetuation rather than teaching and learning in the classroom. In the world of commerce, cartels are agreements between most or all of the producers of a product to either limit their production or fix prices. Rich claims in his book *Black Mayors and School Politics* that while the actions of the education cartels profoundly influence the culture of school systems, pretty much none of what happens within the cartel has any direct influence on the academic lives of children. One of the things that keeps the cartel running smoothly is its power over vast sums of other people's cash: "This economic significance of school politics has produced a cartel-like governing entity. . . . A coalition of professional school administrators, school activists, and union leaders maintains control of school policy to promote the interests of its members. Membership in the cartel confers income, status, and perks. Members agree to follow cartel norms and rules. Violation of these rules can result in sanctions by the cartel."[7] Cartel members tend to honor each other's labor contracts, for example, even when they conflict with one another. The principals union doesn't criticize the teachers union contract, and vice versa, even though much of what is contained in each contract affects the working conditions of the other. Cartel members also declare war together on any plans that weaken any individual member's power within the school system, often declaring such threats "attacks on public education." In that sense, the distinct members of the cartel are united by virtue of the fact that they have a common enemy.

When it comes down to preserving their own power within the bureaucracy, Haberman notes, the cartel members "demonstrate political acumen that would rival Machiavelli when faced with protecting their sinecures."[8]

Members of the cartel get their power in a number of ways, primarily through the fact that they get to implement nearly everything that happens in school systems. In 1998, the elected School Board in Milwaukee voted to "radically redesign" the way the school system handled budgeting. The board approved a plan to shift more resources to schools and allow them to "buy back" whatever services the principals deemed necessary from the central office. They also approved a plan to base payments to schools on the average daily attendance of students, rather than just the attendance on one day in September—the method used by the state to fund the school system. Both measures, which became the official policy after they were approved by the board, were designed to create incentives in a system that wasn't used to them. Board members hoped, for example, that by making schools "pay" for the central office services they received, they might force some nonessential functions of the bureaucracy into extinction. They also hoped that by basing payments to schools on students' average daily attendance, they would create incentives for schools to keep students enrolled beyond the first month of school. Before the policy, principals had an incentive to enroll kids in September to help pad their budgets, and then force them out of school after September, before they could take any standardized tests that would make the school look bad.

But the unelected forces within the bureaucracy didn't like either plan, because the major change to existing practices represented a significant weakening of their power. The plan to have schools buy back central office services was sent to a committee of bureaucrats, never to be heard from again. The attendance policy, after being officially approved by the board, was sent to another committee of administrators who officially decided to blow it off. "While some schools would benefit greatly, there are others that would be severely punished by the process," Rogers Onick, principal of

Samuel Morse Middle School, explained to the board (technically, his employer) a year later, regarding why the schools wouldn't follow the policy.[9] The committee felt that it would be unfair to reward schools with good attendance and punish schools with bad attendance—even though that was specifically the point of the elected board's policy.

The attendance committee, in rejecting the orders of the school board, offered its own set of lame recommendations to improve education without disturbing the incentives built into the system: "Conduct an all-out promotional campaign about the importance of being in school throughout the school year," and "Gauge parental involvement by having teachers grade parents on attendance, completion of homework and support of respectful classroom behavior." Milwaukee school board members were furious with the inaction of the administrators as they realized that the bureaucrats really held the decision-making power of the system in their hands. Board member Leon Todd said, "It appears there is a growing gap between what the board deems as a necessary policy to run the district and what the administration chooses to implement."[10]

In addition to having power through implementation, members of the school cartel often are the holders of institutional memory within the system. They remember how things got the way they are and they keep excellent files. In San Diego, when the management team of schools superintendent Alan Bersin (whom the members of the cartel considered an interloper because he was a nontraditional school leader from the outside who didn't follow the cartel's established rules and norms) had a dispute with the teachers union over the intent of original contract language that granted a 30-minute "duty-free" lunch, the union produced a 1993 memo from its files that spelled out the agreement and ultimately worked against management's case. "We didn't even know that memo existed," Bersin's labor relations director Willy Surbrook told me.

Institutional memory often is valued more by the members of the cartel than by the elected and appointed people running the system. In New York City, the United Federation of Teachers hired away some of the most knowledgeable insiders from the Board of Education after mayor Michael Bloomberg was given control of the school system.

Sometimes the various factions or cliques that exist within the cartel have unofficial names, a nomenclature very similar to the jocks and geeks of high schools. When I worked in Milwaukee in the 1990s, several groups held power within the administrative structure of the school system. Whenever someone was promoted, there was speculation as to the role higher-ups within that clique played in making it happen. Close attention was paid to the promotions at the very top of the system, because it indicated which clique was in favor with the superintendent.

One of the main Milwaukee cliques was referred to as the Deltas. Named after a college sorority, the clique tended to include the most powerful black women in the system. Another group was the "good old boys club" and tended to include older white guys. A third clique was known within the system as "the boys and girls club" and included gay and lesbian educators and administrators. Within these cliques, members often tended to look out for their own when it came to internal politics. Few in the outside world, however, paid much attention to the power struggles that existed among these groups or to the distractions they caused for school leaders trying to focus primarily on student achievement and learning.

The people inside the education cartel speak an entirely different language than parents and the rest of the public. Developing insider language or jargon is typical of groups seeking to exclude others and to protect their own power, and adds to the disenfranchisement and alienation of parents and the public. For her graduation ceremony from the New York City Leadership Academy's aspiring principals program in the summer of 2004, Rebekah Marler wrote a sardonic essay in which she described being caught in a nightmare of school-based acronyms. "I've been kind of busy with the *ISS* and the *RIS*, and the *AUSSIE* preparing for the *ELA*," Marler wrote. "I must confess it was quite an experience with all the *504s*, *LEPS*, *ELLs*, and *IEPs*. Hopefully, all of the *AIS* will help us make the *AYP*. *CSRD* programs were actually quite helpful in preparing for the *ELA* and the *CTB*."[11]

All told, Marler's humorous essay referenced 100 different widely used (but seldom understood) acronyms that she was forced to learn and employ in her regular vocabulary in order to run a school. (Experienced principals in New York say there are even more.) But to many parents who simply want their kids to get a good education, such talk illustrates the vast difference between their world and the cartel's world.

On her first day as principal of Public School 50 in East Harlem in September 2004, Marler was still talking about all the acronyms and how much they bothered her. "I was floored by the edu-babble," she told me. "A lot of times we speak to each other in code that other people don't understand and we need to watch ourselves."[12]

One of the most bizarre aspects of the education cartel's playbook is the way the members try to hold back people within the system who show too much initiative. They become expert in throwing up roadblocks to make life difficult for these dissidents. As principal of the first year-round public elementary school in Milwaukee in the mid-1990s, Mary Beth Minkley got used to hearing from unsupportive bureaucrats all the reasons she couldn't do things at Congress Elementary School. A soft-spoken woman with white hair and glasses, Minkley heard every excuse for why she couldn't get her building air conditioned in the hot summer months. The bureaucrats weren't happy that Minkley was creating extra work for them, particularly in the summer. Their reluctance to support Minkley's unique year-round program eventually spilled over into resistance to her attempts to enlarge the Congress Elementary. She was warned that she had no business creating an early childhood education annex, much less housing it in the vacant St. Stephen Martyr Catholic School building in the neighborhood.

Essentially, bureaucrats within the Milwaukee Public Schools worked against Minkley at every turn, trying to block her ambitious plans to expand the school calendar and the size of the school. Those unfamiliar with how school systems really work might be foolish enough to believe that school administrators—the educrats—exist to help crackerjacks like Minkley do the best job they can for their students. The reality is that the internal politics of the cartel usually rule the day. Some principals get what they want because they are part of the right clique and play by the established rules: They attend the right church or synagogue, work on the right political campaigns, are members of the right sorority or fraternity, et cetera. Principals and parents who aren't part of the cartel encounter barriers that often prevent their students from getting what they need.

Minkley, who referred endearingly to her youngest students as her "babies," was nonetheless tougher and more resilient than school officials would have preferred. At a 1999 breakfast on year-round schooling sponsored by the University of Wisconsin–Milwaukee, Minkley told the crowd: "I know there are people from the central office in the audience, but you made things extremely difficult for us when we were trying to make this happen."[13] They did so by throwing up hoop after hoop for Minkley to jump through because they didn't particularly care to see any school convert to a year-round schedule, which would ruin their own well-established bureaucratic routines.

Meanwhile, Minkley was so successful in giving parents in Congress' north side neighborhood what they wanted that she had people pounding on the doors to get their kids enrolled. What the private sector would call increasing market share with a quality product that consumers desperately crave, the public education system considers rocking the boat. Minkley eventually turned Congress Elementary School into a mini-empire on

Milwaukee's north side, yet she wasn't paid a penny more than other principals who were content to follow the traditional rules and wishes of the club that controlled the schools.

## KEEPING PARENTS IN THE DARK

Part of the cartel's power (and its ability to successfully alienate outsiders such as parents) comes from its tight grip on data and information. Because the education cartel controls the flow of information to the outside of the system, parents and the general public often rely on dubious forms of transparency in their attempts to make heads or tails of their child's education. A 2004 report by the New York City Council's Education Committee, which provides legislative oversight for the city schools, studied a random sample of school report cards for 30 New York schools and found that the city's public school report cards often omitted crucial information for parents, such as class size, and often provided glowing reviews for schools that were terrible. It becomes problematic when schools and school systems are allowed to evaluate themselves, forcing the parent and student consumers to accept the producer's word for the quality of the product.

For example, one of the schools in the city council's sampling, Brooklyn's South Shore High School, described itself in its official school report card as having been "recognized three times by the New York State Education Department as a School of Excellence and by *Redbook* magazine as one of America's best schools." It further boasted that it has a special math and science institute at the school. It sounds wonderful, except that recent statistics present a different reality: the crime rate per thousand students was listed as 32.3, making it one of the more dangerous schools in the city; SAT scores, at 395 for verbal and 410 for math, were far below the citywide average, and its graduation rate of only 57.5 percent made you wonder in what decade that *Redbook* accolade had been awarded.[14]

The Powell Middle School for Law and Social Justice in Manhattan wrote in that same report that it strives "to provide our students with the tools needed for success through a rigorous academic course of study that will enable them to achieve at the next education level." Yet its test scores showed that only 7.6 percent of its students passed the state's reading test, and only 3.6 percent passed the state's math test. By trying to pull a fast one on parents and students, the education cartel seeks to avoid bringing any attention to problems if the possible solutions would discomfort the cartel's status quo.[15]

The *Detroit News* in 2004 analyzed all of the school report cards in Michigan and found that 83 percent of elementary and middle schools that were considered failing for at least four years had given themselves As on self-evaluations worth a third of their overall grades. In Detroit, for example, where schools are allowed to grade themselves on issues ranging from their test scores to teacher quality, George Ford Elementary School in 2003–04 gave itself a perfect score for the condition of its facilities despite the fact that it was closed in October 2003 because it started sinking into the ground.[16] "Maybe the community or parents should grade the schools," parent Trina Parker told the *Detroit News*. True transparency would go much further to remove the foxes who are guarding the education henhouse. Being a public school parent is often like being stuck at an airport due to a delayed flight that no one from the airline seems able or even willing to explain.

## WHO IS STEERING THE SHIP?

Many times, well-meaning superintendents and chancellors take on the job of trying to turn around top-heavy school systems only to discover that they are not actually the ones who are in charge. This became particularly noticeable in the 1990s when districts around the country began seeking out nontraditional superintendents and chancellors who did not come up through the ranks of the school system. Noneducators, like San Diego's Alan Bersin, Los Angeles's Roy Romer, and New York City's Harold Levy, and, later, Joel Klein, were specifically sought after because there was a belief that these types of highly effective people could come to the system with a blank slate to re-create the culture so that it would be focused more on students. Each of these school leaders, tapped by supporters who believed the Great Man Theory of History, quickly came to realize that the cartel won't allow anyone—no matter how clever, intelligent, or pedigreed they may be—to slash at their internal power system without a drawn-out fight. In public education, there is no such thing as a clean slate for school leaders because when they inherit the job they find the true power within the system rests in labor contracts and rules and regulations that help solidify the power of the various internal players within the education cartel. Furthermore, running large school systems, some of these nontraditional school leaders learned, is nothing like running a major corporation, because what you say and do at the top of school systems doesn't necessarily trickle down past the bureaucrats to classrooms where the rubber hits the road. While the superintendent or chancellor appears to have power in the official top-down administrative structure, the real power over the day-to-day operations of school systems is in the hands of the entrenched members of the cartel, most of whom will still be there long after the Great Man is a distant memory.

School governance expert Paul T. Hill, of the University of Washington, notes that the bureaucrats have established political and economic bases. They know where their money comes from and they know how to exert power to keep it coming. They have longstanding "I scratch your back, you scratch mine" relationships with elected officials, teachers unions, and parent groups. Those same constituencies can quickly be (and often are) called upon to create resistance whenever a superintendent or legislature threatens to put an end to their pet projects or causes. When programs like prekindergarten are in danger of being cut during lean budget times, for example, the employees who work in these areas usually are able to tap into established coalitions of early childhood education providers and private foundations interested in the issue to organize parents to fight it. Smaller-class-size programs, special education, arts education, and gifted and talented programs also have these built-in constituencies that can turn out large groups of parents to board meetings and budget hearings if their programs are in danger of reduction or elimination.

The end result is that it becomes almost impossible, politically, for hard-charging superintendents to swoop into town and set new priorities if things aren't working. The priorities are already set, and they are set in a way that no one ever has to take the blame for problems, other than the top people who are powerless to do anything about them. "The business of such bureaucracies is not to promote school quality, but to isolate problems and diffuse responsibility," Hill notes. "The hero-superintendent is an ideal seldom realized. The whole governance structure is tilted against strong executive leadership."[17]

New York City's chancellor, Joel Klein, learned quickly that even though his name was on the stationery for official school system business, he wasn't really in charge of what happens in schools. Klein and then–deputy chancellor Diana Lam attempted to beef up math and literacy instruction in the city's long-troubled middle schools by requiring double periods of each subject (90 minutes) daily, starting in the fall of 2003. Lam justified the move by saying it was designed to improve student performance. But the United Federation of Teachers managed to poke significant holes in that particular reform effort, complaining that their contract forbids teachers from having to work more than three straight 45-minute classes, a work rule that had been given away by the city years ago in lieu of more significant pay raises. These longer blocks of class time scheduled into a relatively short school day often required middle school teachers in these subject areas to work back-to-back 90-minute blocks, representing clear violations of the contract. The union threatened to take the change to arbitration. Klein's top administrators were forced to inform principals that back-to-back teaching blocks were no longer allowed after management realized it could not win in arbitration with the union.[18] Klein's staff included the issue on its long list of things it wanted changed in future teacher contracts.

An even more pathetic display of the impotence of the job of chancellor in New York City involved "reading rugs" in the first school year (2003–04) that Klein's Children First reforms were in place. The reforms included a citywide "balanced literacy" program that gave students access to a wide range of books, which they tended to read individually. Rugs for students and rocking chairs for teachers were intended to make reading periods more homey and comfortable, and thus more effective. Many teachers, who were used to doing things differently, and other critics considered it unnecessary and micromanaging.[19]

But the real problem, and defeat of Klein's good intentions, came when the question of cleaning the rugs arose. "Custodians are making issues that vacuuming is not their job," an anonymous principal testified before the City Council's oversight committee on education via audiotape in November 2003, weeks after the rugs became mandatory in classrooms citywide. "They cite their contract, that they don't have to do it."[20] Because the school custodians' contract in New York City didn't specifically require them to vacuum carpets more than once a week, some initially refused to do so, and after several months many of the rugs began to stink and cause allergic reactions in students and teachers. In February 2004, the United Federation of Teachers (UFT) took samples from rugs at nine public schools in the city and had them tested by Olmstead Environmental Services in Garrison, New York. The results were absolutely disgusting: Detected in the rugs were particles of skin flakes, insect parts, rodent droppings, and molds. One carpet, from Public School 89 in Queens, had 15 percent fibrous glass or dust that can cause skin, eye, and throat irritation.[21] The rug was removed after children complained of rashes.

"These rugs that were supposedly for comfort have become a contamination zone," teachers union president Randi Weingarten told reporters.[22] The environmental testing was disclosed after an unrelated bargaining session between the union and the city over a new labor contract. The teachers were not in agreement with the custodians who felt that cleaning rugs wasn't their job, and essentially used the issue to divert attention from the negotiations that were under way with the city, which at the time had proposed tossing the 200-plus-page teacher contract and replacing it with an 8-page "thin contract" that didn't include so many work rules that management found stifling for reform.

What happened next tells you just about everything you need to know about how things really work or don't work in the New York City schools. Neither the mayor's office nor the chancellor disputed the serious need to get the reading rugs cleaned. In fact, deputy mayor Dennis Walcott responded to the UFT rug tests by assuring the city that the rugs would be thoroughly cleaned over the February break. The break came and went, and many teachers found that their rugs went untouched. Two months later, after both the February break and the spring break, many of the rugs still had not been cleaned.

Top school officials claimed they had issued instructions to the city's ten regions to make sure the rugs were cleaned and that central administrators were "not aware of any problems."[23] But there were big problems, including the fact that the people ultimately in charge of the school system had no idea whether their orders were being carried out. Further, even if top officials had known that the cleaning had not been done, there was nothing they could do—in the form of sanctions for nonperformance or rewards for performance.

The rug case illustrated a more fundamental problem with the way the city school system operated: What should have been a problem solved by a little common sense became an issue that had to be negotiated between labor and management. Four months later, Chancellor Klein (who gave numerous speeches about the need to reduce the bureaucracy and replace it with a culture of trust and common sense) in June 2004 unveiled a new two-page policy titled "Guidelines for Area Rugs in Classrooms." The negotiated policy, worked out with the teachers union, required that all reading rugs be vacuumed at least once a week and steam cleaned twice a year. The assumption was that custodians would do this work, even though some still complained it wasn't their job. The rules were reasonable, but remarkable since they were coming from a chancellor who was pushing for fewer rather than more rules. The fact that they had to legislate what many people considered common sense showed that the rules-based culture was starting to get even the best of reformers like Klein. In classic educratic form, the new policy bypassed allowing school employees to exercise common sense and legislated exactly what kinds of rugs were required: Shag rugs were a no-no, as were wool rugs and wall-to-wall rugs. The classroom rugs also were required to have either rubberized backing or a mat beneath the rug to prevent tripping and slipping. "Rug placement should avoid, to the extent practicable, high traffic areas such as the entrance of the classroom, or in front of bathroom doors of classrooms with bathrooms," the new policy stated.

In case it wasn't obvious to the people in charge of the lives of students while they are at school, the policy stated that any student or teacher who believed the rugs were exacerbating respiratory symptoms like asthma or severe allergies should contact their physician. It then outlined the steps necessary to request the removal of a sick rug: start with a letter from the personal physician to the Office of School Health, who will consult with the physician and make a determination as to whether the rug is the culprit for medical problems. If the rug is the problem, the OSH will begin the process of having the rug removed. Lost in the process was that teachers are adults who should, or at least might, be entrusted with independent judgment. But independence was in the interest of neither the unions nor the administration: Rules and regulations are more about protecting interests, exerting power, and not least, preventing liability or even pushing it off on other parties, and less about enabling people to teach and students to learn.

If the New York City Department of Education was truly able to put Children First it wouldn't have a need for such a policy. Competent school principals and their teachers would simply be allowed to decide on their own—like actual professionals—if a rug was a problem. If they felt it needed to be removed, they'd simply ask the custodian to haul it off to the trash. Adding a new layer of bureaucracy clipped the wings of the people we need to hold responsible for keeping our students and teachers safe. Just think about it: This system is so bogged down by the need to collaborate on everything, which necessitates continual additions to the heaps of regulations governing the schools, that the man ultimately in charge of the city's 1,300 schools has little power on his own to make sure the rugs are cleaned.

## GIVING PARENTS THE RUN-AROUND

One of the golden rules of membership within the education cartel is you have to work as hard as humanly possible to make the system so difficult for parents to navigate that they give up and cede all control of what happens to their children to cartel members themselves. On the first day of school in New York City in the 2004–05 school year, thousands of parents waited in long lines outside regional enrollment centers in a futile attempt to get their kids out of lousy high schools. It is worth comparing and contrasting the first day of school for Chancellor Klein with that of one of the frustrated parents, Felicia Windham, who waited in one line for eight hours in an attempt to find a school for her 14-year-old son, Trevone. The comparison is offered here not as a commentary on how easy Klein's day was, but to illustrate how difficult it is for parents to do basic tasks in school systems, such as enrolling their children in schools.

Trevone had been discharged from his old school, Benjamin Banneker Academy, at the end of the last school year because the school was not equipped to assist him with a specific learning disability. When classes began, he had no school assignment because enrollment workers had been swamped throughout the summer with more than 15,000 new students, referred to by administrators as "over-the-counters." Many of the city's high schools were already jam-packed with students. The first day of school for Klein and Windham couldn't have been more different.

At 7:30 A.M., Klein, dressed like an attorney heading to argue a big case before the U.S. Supreme Court (which he used to do in his previous professional life as a litigator), visits Thomas Jefferson High School in Brooklyn, one of many large high schools that was being converted to smaller "schools within a school." He joins Mayor Bloomberg and police commissioner Ray Kelly in announcing a $6.25 million federal grant to hire 50 more cops to restore order in crime-ridden middle and high schools. "I believe this city's public education system will become the envy of this nation," Klein says in his optimistic remarks.

Windham, meanwhile, who has taken the day off from her job as a cleaner for the Metropolitan Transit Authority just to try to enroll her son in high school, makes oatmeal and toast for her two children. She takes her younger son, Lee Price Jr., to third grade at Public School 256 in Bedford Stuyvesant. It's a predominantly black school of 750 students, 84 percent of whom are poor enough to qualify for a free lunch, and only a quarter of whom are reading and doing math on grade level, according to state and city exams.

At 9:30 A.M., Klein visits Public School 22 in the Graniteville section of Staten Island. It's considerably better off than the Bedford Stuyvesant school where Windham has dropped off her son but is still a struggling school. Predominantly Hispanic, the school enrolls significantly fewer low-income students (only 56 percent qualify for a free lunch) and the percentage of students passing their exams (50 percent) is twice as good. Klein reads the children's book *Miss Nelson Is Back* to the students of third grade teacher Elissa Cucchia. "This year I slept like a baby," Klein tells reporters at his second news conference of the day, describing how this start of school was less stressful for him than the previous year, when he and his administrative team were rolling out their new citywide curriculum under his new administrative structure. Klein is all smiles and optimism.

At the same time, Windham and Trevone take the B38 bus for the half-hour trip to the old Board of Education headquarters at 110 Livingston Street in Brooklyn, which has been temporarily reopened as a center to help deal with the thousands of students who still need to be enrolled in schools. By the time they arrive, they find that hundreds of other parents and students have camped out ahead of them and are lined up around the block. "If it was running smoothly, they wouldn't have so many parents here," Windham says in a tone much less optimistic than the chancellor's.

By 10:45 A.M., Klein has been shuttled by his chauffeured town car to P.S. 50 in East Harlem, a low-performing school packed with students from the nearby Metro North public housing complex. There, Klein joins students doing a "welcome dance" to hip-hop music in dance class. Klein, still smiling several hours into the school year, heaps praise on new principal Rebekah Marler, noting that he helped convince her to attend the city's Leadership Academy for teachers who wish to be trained to become principals. "I want credit as the best principal-picker in the city," Klein says.

While Klein dances to hip-hop music, Windham and her son are still waiting in line in the September sun at the enrollment center, where tempers are starting to run hot.

Klein visits several more schools, finishing the first day of classes at Flushing International High School, a new school housed in Junior High School 189 in Flushing, Queens. The school was designed to educate students who recently immigrated to America and who don't speak any English. Klein attempts to speak with some of these students, but the language barrier is a problem. At the end of his visit, he pops into the gym and perfectly nails an 18-foot jump shot on his first try while reporters and administrators cheer him on. He raises his hands in victory, hugs administrators nearby, and darts off to the hallway with his biggest smile of the day. "It's going to be a great year," Klein declares. "Nothing but net!"

At almost precisely the same time the ball sails through the hoop, Windham and her son finally make it to the lobby of 110 Livingston Street. They are given a number (#208) by intake workers and told to wait until it is called. They are currently serving number 165.

At 3 P.M., while Klein heads back to his office in Manhattan's Tweed Courthouse, to tend to other back-to-school issues, Windham's number is finally called. But the number she has been given only gets her to a person who gives her an intake form to fill out to explain exactly what her child's enrollment needs are. A low-level bureaucrat gives her both the intake form and a new number (#2930). About 15 minutes later, Windham's new number is called. An intake counselor verifies her address and her son's birth certificate. She is told to return to the lobby until number 2930 is called again.

Windham's number is called again at 3:45 P.M. She is told to go upstairs where she is given yet another number (#304). They are currently serving number 220 and it begins to feel hopeless, as the first day of school for students is now long over. "This is sad that people have to come down here and spend hours in line just to get our kids into a good school," Windham says. By 5:30 P.M., ten hours after her day began, she leaves the enrollment center with a transfer to Boys and Girls High School, near her home in Bedford Stuyvesant. But the enrollment nightmare isn't over. She is told to go to the school and attempt to register him there the following day. "What if I get there and there are no seats left," Windham says. Trevone eventually enrolled in the school, but the anecdote serves as an important reminder of how the system treats customers differently than its top employees. Klein's day was designed by his handlers to be as smooth as possible. At no point was he required to take a number for basic service. Parent customers should be so lucky.

## BREAKING UP THE CARTEL

In St. Louis, Missouri, the school system's finances were so screwed up in 2003 that the poor academic performance of its students was the least of their problems. Taxpayers were forced to turn over their system to a bankruptcy firm from New York City for some tough love for a year. The time period was basically designed to establish a clean exit strategy for the firm. The consultants could make the kinds of hard choices that are normally politically impossible, then, on the specified date, they could ride into the sunset to get away from the controversy they caused.

The firm, Alvarez and Marsal, which usually did consulting work for businesses and corporations, quickly learned two important lessons. First, the school district's financial books were a disaster. Second, that schools must operate in a realm of local, state, and national politics that most corporate executives couldn't possibly imagine. Alvarez and Marsal sent their vice president, Bill Roberti, to St. Louis as the acting superintendent for a year, with the understanding that he would take the year to save the system before turning it over to someone with education credentials to work on the academics.

Trying to reconcile a deficit of between $35 and $90 million, Roberti closed 16 schools, sold 40 properties, slashed the number of unfilled school buses in a way that reduced costs and increased efficiency, and brought in private companies to more effectively and cheaply take care of tasks like maintenance and food service. Previously unused textbooks had collected dust in warehouses; the consultants instituted a modern inventory system, consolidated underused warehouses, and sold back unnecessary books to their publishers.

A politically untouchable Roberti slashed the number of employees from 7,000 to 5,000 without cutting a single teaching job, and along the way trimmed $79 million from the annual operating budget. You can file that $79 million under "money the system was spending that had no or little benefit for children." "This is not a jobs program," Roberti said, defending the drastic cuts to the number of people on the payroll for the district. "This is a school system that is supposed to teach kids, not to provide jobs to the community."[24]

The St. Louis experience shows that these severely broken systems can be fixed, but it also demonstrates how difficult it can be and how reforming schools is a very different ball of wax than turning around sluggish businesses. As Roberti told journalist John Merrow in 2004: "St. Louis brought in a firm from outside to do this difficult work because no one inside the city of St. Louis could get away with some of the things that have to be done and live here without suffering the consequences."[25]

The *St. Louis Post-Dispatch* has noted that Roberti and his firm learned some interesting lessons in their work there. "A school district is not as simple as running a business," reporter Jake Wagman wrote. "The reality is that patronage and politics have been institutionalized in St. Louis and many other urban school districts."[26]

Even Roberti was forced to acknowledge that his team had to play some politics, hiring consultants with political ties to the school board for certain tasks, and hiring early vocal critics of the management team to gain their support or at least their silence. "That's part of the cost of business," Roberti said. "There isn't a city in the United States of America that doesn't have some sort of patronage. Name one—can you?"[27]

I can't. That's one of many reasons why our children always seem to come last in our schools. In the meantime, while places like St. Louis get their school houses in order, parents of the children enrolled there are left with few options other than a depressing cocktail of patience and a substandard education.

St. Louis took the unprecedented step of bringing in someone from outside the community in order to upset the political applecart within the school system. But it doesn't have to be this way. Later, we will see what can happen when parents decide that their children are more important than the sacred cows of the education cartel. Public education can be saved, but only if parents are ready for a knock-down, drag-out fight with the people who hold the power in public education.

# 4

## THE PLIGHT OF TEACHERS

New York City teacher Zelman Bokser fought two battles that are noteworthy for our purposes here: one against a bureaucracy that was reluctant to
hire him and a second against an administrator who told him he'd never be
able to teach a bunch of inner-city kids how to play the violin. Bokser had
the kind of credentials parents would kill to have in a teacher for their child.
A Fulbright Scholar with a Ph.D. in music, Bokser had nonetheless been
turned away from teaching. "They told me I wasn't qualified, because I did-
n't have student teaching or enough education courses," said Bokser.[1] His
work experience as an orchestra conductor and his teaching experience at
the university level didn't qualify him as a teacher, and the human resources
people at the city's Board of Education wouldn't give him the time of day.

A New York City program designed by former chancellor Harold Levy
to attract career-changers to the school system as teachers gave Bokser an
opening and a chance to prove that he could make a difference. The program granted temporary license waivers to promising teachers who agreed
to take graduate education courses (at the public's expense) and become cer-
tified. Levy was very proud of the program, although some people within
the school system who had taken the traditional route treated the teaching
fellows as "outsiders" long after they began teaching in the classroom. This
outsider status, typical within the education cartel, meant these new teachers often were left to fend for themselves. With little support from more
seasoned educators, they sometimes even saw their efforts sabotaged by
their colleagues. The end result was that while many excellent teachers like
Bokser were attracted to the classroom, because they weren't given much assistance in their schools, most didn't stick around for very long after the
public had paid for their master's degrees.

In 2000, Bokser landed a teaching job at Brooklyn's Public School 75, but he immediately encountered resistance when he came up with a plan to teach violin to his struggling students. It would be "too difficult" and a waste of time for the kids to learn to play the instrument, he was told by higher-ups at his school when they learned of the plan. One administrator encouraged him to drop the idea rather than face certain disappointment, a reminder of how low many individuals within the system set the bar not only for students but for the staff as well.

Bokser ignored the advice and pushed forward. Two years later, as his students tuned their violins inside Manhattan's Hammerstein Ballroom for a performance welcoming the new crop of teaching fellows, Bokser told his new colleagues about the resistance he encountered from the people running his school. He let his excited students tell the end of the story with their instruments.

The story incensed deputy mayor Dennis Walcott, who was present for the performance and whose boss, Mayor Michael Bloomberg, had gotten control of the city's 1,200 public schools just days earlier. Waiting offstage as the dozen grade school musicians packed up their instruments, Walcott was beside himself with anger. He used the opportunity to deviate from his prepared speech to the teaching fellows. "Who was that individual who said that these kids couldn't do this?" he asked Bokser, who politely refused to give up the nay-sayer. Walcott called the administrator's attitude "totally unacceptable," and later told the crowd: "I'm going to try to find out who that was, because that person shouldn't be part of the system."[2]

The school bureaucracy in New York and in school systems across America is filled with nay-sayers like the one who was convinced the idea of teaching a bunch of low-income students to play a musical instrument was a waste of time. Rather than promoting the idea of risk-taking and the otherwise unconventional, the bureaucratic mindset has everyone moving at the same pace, complying with the same regulations, and getting the same less-than-stellar results. I haven't met anyone who hates the school bureaucracy more than the teachers who have to work alongside it everyday. Unlike teachers unions, whose interests rest primarily with protecting jobs and benefits for their members, it is individual classroom teachers who have the best chance of putting the needs of students at the top of their agenda. Successful schools often are able to protect teachers from bureaucratic distractions (such as specifying bulletin board or classroom seating arrangements to comply with established rules and regulations) so that they can act as true professionals and focus on their specific students. When the bureaucracy does little more than create constant roadblocks for teachers, it ultimately impacts their ability to do their best teaching.

Teachers in New York City complain often about having to take off time to get their human resources paperwork processed, careful to get receipts to prove that they have submitted various forms so that they know who to blame when their paychecks get messed up or, worse, when their paychecks don't arrive at all. Paul Egan, a teacher in the Bronx and a chapter representative for the United Federation of Teachers (UFT), in testimony before the City Council Education Committee in 2002, described the out-of-control paperwork process that drives teachers in the system nuts: "You come in, you still have to give your bachelor's degree transcript to get your teaching license, then you have to give it again when you put in for your first [pay] differential, then you've got to give them the same transcript again for the intermediate [differential] the same again for the second differential; you're doing the process over and over and over again. . . . There is no reason, as far as I can see, why when a person comes into the Board of Ed, that all this paperwork can't be done in one shot, and people get paid immediately rather than months down the line."[3]

At the same hearing, another city teacher joked: "I mean there's, I think, 12 floors in the [administration] building, and, you know, I would say my transcripts are probably on every floor." Seasoned teachers said they learned over time that if you had an educrat on the phone who seemed clueless when you called with a problem, all you had to do was hang up, call back, and hope that someone different answered the phone.[4] Ron Cook, a history teacher at Intermediate School 125 in Queens, claimed that he once received a check in the mail from the Board of Education for one cent—sent to him in an envelope with 37 cents' worth of postage. "To stay in teaching, you need to have a tremendous sense of humor," he said.[5]

In addition to the stifling bureaucracy, many urban teachers complain that they are left to fend for themselves in often violent situations. "I actually have a tear in my stocking due to a fight in my classroom today," Sandy Bravo Boyd, a fifth grade teacher in East Harlem, told the council committee. "And you know, ten-year-old boys who are fighting, but literally the fact that they're allowed to fight and to physically hit each other in the head, and that this goes on in a school is one of the main reasons that teachers want to leave the system."[6]

## RESOURCES DON'T REACH THE CLASSROOM

One Friday afternoon in April 2004, the Internet site "Craig's List," which had a section for teachers seeking donated supplies for schools, listed more than 140 New York City teachers asking for classroom charity. The Web site matches donors, teachers, and a participating supplier in San Francisco. These teachers weren't looking for anything out of the ordinary, which itself is utterly depressing. The most common plea: cleaning supplies and essentials such as paper towels, soap, and vacuums. "Almost all the students in my class suffer from asthma, and it is important to keep the rooms clean," wrote Jena Mittelman, a teacher at William Floyd Elementary School in Brooklyn. Kindergarten teacher Heather Klinkhamer, of Public School 59 in Brooklyn, asked donors for Lysol, rug cleaner, a mop, and paper plates. Rachel Pinson, of Middle School 54 in Manhattan, desperately needed glass cleaner.[7]

There is lots of money kicking around the system, the question is whether or not it makes its way to kids. "If teachers and parents have to pay for basic school supplies, it's a pretty good indicator that the principal isn't doing a great job of managing the building," Ginger Hovenic, president of the Business Roundtable for Education in San Diego and herself a former school principal told me. Hovenic joins the growing list of observers who confirm a budding "paper towel–school leadership" theory—that is, you can tell when there is a good principal in a school building when they have made sure that basic issues such as cleaning supplies are somehow taken care of.

Teachers cite a lack of basic supplies as one of their top frustrations working in the system. Sandy Bravo Boyd told the City Council in 2002 as it investigated problems teachers face in schools: "I have a sink in my room and I have fifth graders, and I had asked the custodial staff for paper towels; and I was told that they're not allowed to give paper towels to the regular ed class. They're only supposed to give them to the special ed classes. So, instead of fighting that fight, because there's many others, and I don't have that much time to go chase after somebody else, I buy my Bounty paper towels and bring them because I have to wash my hands and my children have to wash their hands."[8]

When teachers complain that they don't receive support in their jobs, this is the kind of thing they are talking about. It's not a sanitation problem as much as it is a people problem—those who run schools too often don't exercise enough common sense. School administrations need to provide these necessary resources to classrooms so that teachers can actually teach.

## IMPROVING TEACHER QUALITY

The best teachers will often be the first to tell you that a major problem in public education today is there are too many ineffective teachers occupying classrooms. The third grade teachers know who the weakest second grade teachers are in their building, because they can see it in the preparedness of the children they inherit the following year. The problem directly impacts students who waste school years in their classes, but it also impacts teachers. Effective teachers often have to play catch-up with students who have not been properly taught in earlier grades. In the broader world, the image of the teaching profession as a whole suffers from the insufficient work of those who aren't cut out for the job. As Florida's Dunedin High School principal Mildred Reed told the *St. Petersburg Times* in 2002, not everyone was born to be a teacher. "It takes a special person to be a teacher," Reed said. "Everyone can't walk in off the street and teach a class."[9]

Perhaps because of the better-paying options in other fields, college students in education schools tend to be among the weakest students on their campuses. A 1999 study by the Princeton-based Education Testing Service analyzed the SAT scores of 140,000 college students who passed the PRAXIS II exam for teaching licensure used in 30 states and documented the dismal results. The prospective teachers had average scores of 507 on math and 522 on verbal, compared with 542 and 543 respectively for average college graduates. For elementary education majors, the scores were even lower: 486 in math and 498 in verbal.[10]

As former AFT President Sandra Feldman conceded to author Matthew Miller: "We've been saying for years now that we're attracting from the bottom third. This is a tough thing for us to say because we represent all these people."[11] The issue of teacher quality is one of the most important issues our modern schools face and one that directly impacts the quality of education children receive, but the politics surrounding such a touchy subject seldom lead to any real efforts to fix the problem. Massachusetts set off a political atom bomb in 1998 when it required prospective teachers to take a mandatory basic skills exam. Of the nearly 1,800 teacher hopefuls who took the test, more than half (59 percent) flunked. Thomas M. Finneran, speaker of the state's House of Representatives, added gasoline to the flames by calling the flunkees "idiots" while educators reflexively trashed the quality of the test.

There was significant debate in Massachusetts and across the nation that summer on the overall poor quality of the nation's teachers colleges, but the discourse rarely extended back even further to the dismal state of K through12 education in general. "The problem is much more widespread," lamented Arthur Wise, president of the National Council for Accreditation of Teacher Education in Washington, D.C. Much of the material on the controversial test, Wise noted, should have been mastered by the teachers before they graduated from high school.[12]

The teacher quality problem is typical of most of the problems facing education in that there are plenty of culprits to share the blame. It also reminds the public that the problems themselves create cycles that need to be stopped before they bring down the system once and for all. That so many teachers themselves were so poorly educated in middle and high school obviously has an ominous effect on the kind of education their students receive from them today. Just as important is the mismatch between what these teachers are learning in education colleges and the reality they must face on the job once they graduate. In 2004, New York City chancellor Joel Klein dared local education colleges to take on the job of running some of the worst schools in the city, in part so that they would better understand the issues the system was up against. "The simple truth is that . . . the training in our ed schools is not aligned with the needs of teachers who will become responsible for the challenges of urban education," Klein wrote in an e-mail to the city's 1,300 principals.[13] Klein's team felt that too many of the people teaching young men and women to become teachers had no idea, themselves, what it was like to do the job.

The issue of improving the quality of the people paid to make sure our kids are learning is a hot potato for politicians, who face enormous pressure from unions and education schools not to rock the boat or otherwise engage in any new policies that might prove too embarrassing. When he was governor of Arkansas, Bill Clinton learned the hard way that it was best not to mess with the idea of testing teachers to make sure they understood content. In 1985, some 37,000 Arkansas teachers took a mandatory skills test, and while only 3.6 percent flunked this one, it created such a maelstrom in the state capital that the test was scrapped entirely.[14]

It is not impossible to recruit and retain high quality teachers and principals to work in schools. Increasing pay to compete with other school systems and careers would help, but it doesn't stop there. Since great teachers and principals are crucial ingredients in creating great schools, the public should support measures that reward and retain the best while making it easier to steer those who aren't cut out for the classroom toward serious remediation or other careers entirely.

This is an area where transparency—and brutal honesty—is crucial. The public must understand the sum total of pay and benefit packages for teachers in order to make fair comparisons with competing private sector jobs. It also should be noted that the existing pay structures offer few incentives for good teachers to stick around because they get paid the same as the klunkers with the same amount of experience.

It isn't antiteacher for a school to want to hire the best educators possible, rather than settling for the most senior teachers for openings, as is commonly practiced around the country. In Dade County, Florida, union officials allowed one of its vocational-technical high schools, Turner Tech, to have 100-percent control over who teaches there. Because there is a strong emphasis on math at the school, for example, school officials explained to me, they prefer to hire math majors to teach that subject, rather than education majors. "If we want to survive as a successful school, we need to hire the best possible people for the job, not who the district wants to place in a job," assistant principal Al Carvalho told me during a 1998 visit to the school.[15]

## THE HOLE WE'VE DUG

The way we as a society treat teachers figures into all the discussions involving the teachers contract and its impact on schools. One reason many teachers contracts have work rules—like rules limiting the amount of time they are required to work, rules allowing teachers to determine which grades and classes they will be teaching, and rules clearly stating what principals may and may not ask teachers to do—is that they were often negotiated into contracts in lieu of pay raises during tough fiscal years. Giving away management's right to actually manage schools has been disastrous in terms of our ability to empower anyone to come in and turn around failing schools.

In Los Angeles in 1990, to give just one example of what has played out nationwide over the last generation, a recession prompted school officials to offer a 10-percent pay cut for teachers in exchange for giving teachers more power to determine their assignments. School principals and superintendents, the people we normally think are managing the schools and making those kinds of personnel decisions, lost some of their ability to impact how things work in their own schools. This is not treating teachers as professionals: Most professionals still have to work for a manager who is able to make decisions and who is held accountable for those decisions.

Here the distinction between the unions and the teachers becomes important. Treating teachers as professionals and providing them with the support they need sometimes works against the desires of the union's elected power structure. When the Milwaukee Teachers Education Association agreed in 1999 to ease some of the seniority-based hiring rules in the contract (against the desires of union staffers who argued a more hard-line stance), president Paulette Copeland, a reading teacher at Samuel Clemens

Elementary School, remarked: "This takes away some of the power of the union and gives it to our members, and that's the way it should be."[16]

San Diego superintendent Alan Bersin has based his entire legacy as a school leader on the notion that the support given directly to teachers—specifically in the form of intensive staff development training—is more important than whether the union leaders are happy with him as a leader. He has enjoyed very little support from the union (leaders held signs comparing him to Hitler during one of his performance evaluations with the school board), but he has managed to survive longer than any other current school leader at the time of this writing. He spent millions of dollars on professional development for his teachers, and during several rounds of major budget cuts due to California's struggling economy he protected teachers from the budget ax.

Bersin is an example of how a school leader can attempt to bolster the professionalism of classroom teachers; his case also shows the limitations of any major reforms that don't involve radical changes to the labor contracts. Bersin couldn't, for example, assign his best teachers to his lowest performing schools because of a burdensome post-and-bid process that fills assignments by teacher seniority. Under the contract, all teaching vacancies known at schools for the following school year must be posted by specific dates (February 10, May 10, and July 10) so that existing teachers within the district can bid on filling those slots. Administrators must fill those slots by selecting from the five bidders with the highest seniority—regardless of whether they are a right fit for the school or whether uprooting them from their current assignments would have a negative impact on their current students. The post-and-bid process for the 2003–04 school year had nearly 60,000 bids, according to estimates made by the San Diego Education Association.[17] Human resources officials in San Diego said they spend a good chunk of their work year managing this complicated bidding process, taking time and energy away from their efforts to recruit and retain the best teachers in the region.

Bersin and other critics complained that the process—combined with lock-step pay scales contained in the contract, which prevented offering pay incentives to get the best teachers to work in the worst schools—had the practical effect of enticing the most experienced teachers to flock to the best schools, most of which happened to be in the northern (and most well-off) part of the city, leaving schools with low-income students in the southern half of the city filled with the least experienced teachers year after year.

The core of Bersin's reforms, interestingly, revolved around his attempts to professionalize the teaching force through heavy investments in teacher training and coaching programs. Yet they were not warmly embraced by union leaders in San Diego. The complaint most commonly raised was that Bersin's reforms were too "top-down," a complaint that loses some luster when you understand that Bersin was brought in to try to tame the bureaucracy from the top. As an outsider, or an interloper, to the education cartel as it existed in San Diego, his attempts to upset the applecart were perceived as too harsh by union leaders, who worked against Bersin for his entire tenure. "The infrastructure that is set up here is very teacher-friendly, but it has not been perceived as teacher-friendly," said Stanford University professor Larry Cuban, who has studied the San Diego schools extensively. "It has been perceived as disrespectful and this is part of the tragic story of this district."[18]

Most professionals have a boss, and top-down management exists in most sectors—one of the reasons top executives are highly sought after and highly compensated. In order for failing school districts to be turned around, school leaders must be allowed to manage—a task that becomes difficult when management prerogatives have been given away over the years in collective bargaining with school employee unions. Hardly a day goes by that urban school leaders don't bump up against restrictive language in the labor contracts that govern schools. An engaged public that treats teachers as true professionals will come to understand that even the best teachers in the system are often hurt by the inflexibility in their own collective bargaining agreements.

In January 2005, two months after a change in the makeup of the San Diego school board gave power to his teachers union-backed critics, Bersin agreed to step down by June 30 of the same year. His final day on the job would be exactly a year before his contract was set to expire and seven years after he was brought in from the outside to shake up the school system. The new school board, upon announcement of Bersin's lame-duck status, immediately began dismantling many of the reforms the superintendent had put in place. In April of the same year, California governor Arnold Schwarzenegger, a Republican, named Bersin, a Democrat, to serve as his secretary of education, starting July 1.

In 1990, Cathy Nelson, a 13-year veteran at Fridley High School in suburban Minneapolis, was named Minnesota Teacher of the Year. The highly regarded teacher came from a long line of educators, but she had the least seniority among the social studies teachers at her school and was let go that same year in a cost-cutting move. "What happened is obvious," explained principal Donald A. Meyers. "Last hired is the first fired."[19]

The same thing happened in 1998 after Sarah Gustafson was inducted into the Florida Educator Hall of Fame. Gustafson, who had been Florida's

Teacher of the Year in 1991, was fired because she also didn't have enough seniority to survive budget cuts at the time.[20] In 2003, two of Wal-Mart's national Teachers of the Year—Marci Richmond, a teacher in Chino, California, and Lauri Cerasani, of Elgin, Illinois—were let go for the same reason. "It's kind of a bittersweet thing," explained Cerasani, whose school got to keep the $1,000 gift from Wal-Mart while she got to take home a certificate and a blue vest from the retail giant.[21]

Some people would look at the Teacher of the Year anecdotes I've described and see them primarily as budget problems. But the reality is that the inability of school leaders to make personnel decisions with an eye toward keeping the best and brightest teachers in the classroom whenever a financial crunch hits (or any other time for that matter) is a permanent structural problem, one that is far worse than shrinking school budgets. Although many schools can continue to operate effectively with fewer discretionary dollars, if you force your best teachers out the door, the impact is immediate and profound. Politicians, voters, and parents must insist that common sense be allowed to prevail in management decisions, so that the needs of students (who deserve the best teachers we can give them) are given top priority.

Not only do portions of teacher contracts work against the interests of children; often, like in the cases of the Teachers of the Year, they work against the teachers themselves. Asked by the *New York Times* in 2005 whether lifetime tenure, seniority, and the traditional pay schedule found in most teacher contracts work in everyone's best interest, National Education Association president Reg Weaver replied: "Of course not. But I can't say that. Our enemies will take that and use it against us."[22]

## WHY UNIONS EXIST

Later in this book, I will look at the amazing role powerful teachers unions play in influencing school policies, legislation, and party politics in ways that often rank the needs of students behind the wants of employees. It is important to note up front why teachers unions exist in the first place. For years, teaching was considered a job for women, many of whom were either single and living with their parents or married to a man who had a better-salaried job to help pay the bills. School leaders didn't view salary as much of an issue when it came to recruiting teachers: These women tended to live and work in their communities. To make it worth their while, school leaders offered nonsalary sweeteners such as pensions and other benefits (which would be paid for overtime), but salaries remained low. The teachers organizations at this time, particularly the National Education Association, were widely regarded as "tea and crumpets" groups.[23]

In the 1960s, the scenario began to change because of two main forces: the beginning of collective bargaining for teachers and other public sector employees, and an influx of men into the teaching profession during the Vietnam War.[24] This transformation of the teaching force coincided with the transformation of the teachers unions from a professional association to a more traditional labor union, employing tactics like work slowdowns and even strikes over wage disputes.

One of the arguments that was often made at the time was that a better contract for teachers would result in a more satisfied workforce (in terms of both pay and job satisfaction) and thus, by extension, better-educated students. Ironically, a generation later and despite all of the power the unions have amassed through successive labor contracts, teacher morale and pay remain low, student achievement is poor, and relations between teachers and school leaders are often so acrimonious that it keeps reporters like me writing silly labor-management dispute stories on a regular basis.[25] The notion that collective bargaining for teachers would benefit students over the long-run simply hasn't borne fruit.

I mention all of this before I launch into a discussion about the ways the unions themselves can interfere with the schools' ability to meet the needs of children because I think hidden in the teachers' overall frustrations lie the obvious answers to overcoming the unions' grip. As one New York charter school operator told me in 2002: "How do I keep the unions out of my school? I make sure I'm always treating my teachers one step better than the union could ever produce in a contract. If my teachers are happy, they won't have any interest in organizing."[26] The charter school offers competitive pay, a good work environment, and professional support to help the teachers do their work with students to the best of their abilities.

Even if teachers unions fight it, the public must do a better job treating teachers as professionals. One way to do that is by setting the bar high for administrators and demanding that they act competently toward their teaching force. Schools should be run so well from the top that teachers don't feel a need to join an industrial-style union or to be beholden to wacky work rules negotiated in their labor contracts. For starters, this means significantly improving payroll and other human resources systems that provide services for teachers. Many New York City teachers in the fall of 2003 didn't get paid until Thanksgiving due to human resources glitches; others didn't have health insurance until January. Another example of the message sent to teachers by the New York City schools: When new teachers are hired, their first paychecks in their new jobs are $115 lighter than they should be because the school system makes deductions for paperwork processing and criminal background checks.[27] In contrast, I have friends who as new lawyers were given clothing allowances by their firms before they even began work. The messages sent to teachers are clear: We say we think you're an important part of the quest for better schools, but we'll do everything possible to make you wonder why you even bother.

School management can complain about the teachers union all it wants (and many parts of this book will back them) but it's hard to ultimately take school leaders seriously when they treat school employees so poorly.

Willy Surbrook, the director of labor relations for the San Diego City schools, explained to me that when school principals and administrators make the kinds of mistakes that result in legitimate labor grievances being filed, it hurts management's ability to make a strong case with teachers that managers need more contractual control over what happens in schools. It particularly hurts if school leaders are trying to move toward a culture of professional trust in the schools and happen to be asking the union to buy in. "They say, 'Why would we negotiate something that requires trust when you aren't showing you can be trusted,'" Surbrook quoted the union leaders as saying.[28]

## THE PLIGHT OF UNION LEADERS

The historically low salaries of school teachers and the bizarre inability of school systems to adequately handle basic human resources functions, such as cutting paychecks, are reasons the teachers unions exist in schools in the first place. Before I jump into the role of teachers unions as the sun around which school systems orbit, I need to briefly touch on the precarious situation in which teachers union leaders often find themselves. Understanding their own political situation is important when contemplating how to fix our school systems.

The unions that represent teachers, both the National Education Association (NEA) and the American Federation of Teachers (AFT), operate under ostensibly democratic principles. Simply put, union presidents have a tremendous degree of power on the local and national political stage because they have the weight of their members behind them; they also cannot act in ways with which their membership disagrees. Randi Weingarten, president of New York City's United Federation of Teachers, for example, took heat from her members in the fall of 2004 after she was spotted on television sitting with Mayor Bloomberg in his box during a Yankees playoff game. Union presidents are essentially politicians whose power comes from their ability to get reelected. Even when union leaders know, for example, that the union contract can be destructive to kids, they aren't in much of a position to do anything about it if it will be perceived by the rank and file as caving in. "[UFT president Al] Shanker used to say 'Listen, I agree, but there's no way I could give that,'" said Bert Pogrebin, a labor lawyer who used to negotiate with the union.[29]

To make things even more complicated, the unions themselves are run by their own bureaucracy of sorts, including union employees who themselves are unionized and must negotiate their contracts with the union (which in these cases is actually "management"). Like the school system itself, the union's own bureaucracy is based on which factions within the union have amassed power. Also like the school system, the union's bureaucrats understand well how to preserve and extend their power. Union presidents may come and go, but the staffers seem to stay on forever.

Paulette Copeland, the former president of the Milwaukee Teachers Education Association (MTEA) was, without question, one of the kindest individuals I've met in the education world. She was passionate about teaching as an art, compassionate about the importance of meeting the needs of students who lived in the inner city, and determined to move her union in a direction that favored craft unionism over the industrial union tone that had dominated the MTEA since the 1960s. While the people who ran the union as staffers tended to be white men who lived in the suburbs, Copeland was a black woman who lived in the city and who was a regular part of many of the cultural and civic activities of Milwaukee. She even campaigned for union office without trashing the city's residency requirement for teachers—a rule that many of the old-guard white teachers opposed.

Copeland, in fact, once crossed the union's own picket line in 1977 (long before she was president) because of what she considered the racial overtones of the strike, which came while Milwaukee was settling a contentious school desegregation lawsuit. Her opponent in the race for union president 20 years later said her role as a "scab" back then was an issue for members. But it was obviously not enough of one to keep her out of office. In a newspaper interview after she was elected, she said she crossed the picket line because no one could explain to her at the time why the union was on strike, other than that some white teachers didn't seem to want black teachers working in their schools. "After the strike, a lot of black teachers were leery of the union," said Copeland, who set out as president to repair relations between the union and inner city neighborhood groups. "At some schools they were really treated terribly."[30]

When she was elected to office in the spring of 1997, however, there were many signs that indicated the union staff itself wasn't wedded to the idea of letting Copeland take control of the union she had been elected to lead. Bruce Murphy, then a writer for *Milwaukee Magazine*, noted that the staff of the union for months wouldn't even give her the keys to the union headquarters.[31] Yet, at the same time, many others considered her to be a breath of fresh air, as the union's 23-member executive board was still dominated by what many of Copeland's supporters called the old guard of the union. Union leaders can only do so much.

The fact that democracy is at play within the union often means that union leaders who wish to move the union in a direction that better fits with what the public wants and expects from teachers have no real ability to do so. Former NEA president Bob Chase tried desperately to move the national union in a direction that would at least leave the door open to the idea of merit-based pay for teachers. Armed with internal reports from consultants indicating that the public was tired of watching the teachers union oppose every school reform that came down the pike, Chase used the union's internal apparatus to push for the approval of a merit-pay resolution at the union's annual Representative Assembly in Chicago in 2000.

The Representative Assembly is one of the most amazing displays of democracy I've ever had a chance to witness. For days leading up to major votes, caucuses within the union make their pitches in the hallways of the convention center during the day and from bar stools of local taverns at night. Debate on the 1998 proposal to merge the National Education Association with the American Federation of Teachers spilled out onto Bourbon Street at night as teachers openly argued the pros and cons; the vote failed. Teachers spend hours on the official convention floor discussing the issues and various factions make deals behind the scenes for endorsements from state unions. New Jersey, for example, might offer up all of its delegates to support something that Oregon wants, in exchange for Oregon returning the favor on something New Jersey wants.

So it was rather dramatic in 2000 to watch Chase, one of the most powerful men in America by virtue of his position, use every weapon he had at his disposal to push a merit pay plan that was eventually shot down by his members. Not only did the membership oppose Chase's resolution seeking to open the door to considering additional pay for teachers who meet certain goals, it voted instead to approve a resolution that shut that door firmly regarding any future discussion of the merit pay issue.

So as we prepare to look at some of the ways the unions influence education and politics, it is important to understand the reality that confronts us: Even powerful union leaders who understand full well that their unions are steering public education toward certain disaster may not be in a position to do much of anything about it.

# 5

## NO VENDOR LEFT BEHIND

This is a tale of two school leaders from the suburbs of Washington, D.C., and one vendor trying to get a foot in the door to peddle its $60,000-per-school algebra software. It is a clear reminder that the needs of students often must compete with outside interests whose livelihood depends on getting lucrative contracts from school administrators and politicians, regardless of whether their products are best for children.

The vendor, Minnesota-based Plato Learning, heavily subsidized a free International Educational Seminar in the summer of 2003 that was organized by the National Alliance of Black School Educators. Three dozen top administrators around the country got to take a ten-day junket to South Africa paid in part on the software company's dime. The event was billed as a "public-private partnership." Even though executives and other employees from Plato joined the administrators on the trip, the company insisted to the *Baltimore Sun* newspaper in 2004 that they were careful not to discuss business at any point.

"There are no sales presentations associated with these trips and participants and our staff and business partners share the powerful experience of visiting with local schools, colleges, policymakers, and ministry officials where they share experiences and learn about each other's successes and challenges," Plato's vice president John C. Super told journalist Alec MacGillis in an e-mail.[1]

One way the merry band of educators and software executives kept their minds off business was by taking a free safari on an 80,000-acre reserve. Many of the costs for the junket that weren't picked up by Plato were covered by the computer company Gateway, which also does a tremendous amount of business each year with schools.

Faced with the opportunity to have a good time on someone else's dime—particularly someone who would love nothing more than inking a six-or seven-figure deal with their school system—our two school leaders made completely different choices.

The first, Montgomery County deputy superintendent John Q. Porter, must have thought the trip would be a blast and recognized it as a good networking opportunity, yet ultimately decided against attending. "I can't speak to the learning that takes place on the trip," Porter said. "But it raises the question, if you come back from a trip with an organization that wants to do business with you and they're funding the trip, does that influence your decisions of what products you choose? I can't answer that question."[2]

What he meant, obviously, was that it just might be possible that the needs of students might be forced to take a backseat to the natural inclination to do business with a vendor who pays for these kinds of junkets. And while Plato officials claimed that trips like this one are for educational purposes, we have to remember that Plato Learning exists to do one thing: sell software. That's not a bad thing; it's just reality. If vendors like Plato didn't think that the junket would be good for business, they wouldn't be able to justify paying for it in the first place.

Our other administrator in this example made a completely different choice. Andre J. Hornsby, the superintendent of Prince George's County Schools, attended the junket, which didn't cost him a cent. His spokeswoman told the *Baltimore Sun:* "This was a project that he was proud to be involved with, that afforded an opportunity to be involved with an evolving educational system in South Africa that is providing all children with a comprehensive educational system that they didn't have before. It was a rewarding trip for all involved."[3]

There's no doubt it was rewarding for Plato Learning, who paid the $2,500 fee for Hornsby to participate. Despite the fact that business supposedly wasn't discussed on the trip, by the fall of 2004 the Prince George's Schools were testing the Plato product in preparation for a possible districtwide contract worth millions of dollars to use Plato's algebra program in all of its high schools. It is entirely possible that Hornsby and his administrative team selected Plato for the potentially lucrative test run because it is the best product available, and because they make all of their decisions based on "the kids." It is also possible that the vendor was selected for no other reason than that it had established such a cozy relationship with Hornsby when its sales people were socializing on their African safari. The public has no way to know for sure.

The case clearly illustrates the problem as it exists in the battle over precious resources for schools, and how the interests represented by those fighting for (and dishing out) a piece of the pie are often something other than the actual needs of children. Vendors have a responsibility to their investors to sell as many products as possible. Period. The education of students is not a vendor's primary responsibility, and when administrators and elected officials make decisions about doing business with vendors for anything other than improving educational opportunities for children, public education fails kids once again.

Stories of children and taxpayers getting ripped off by people doing business with school systems fill the pages of newspapers across the country on a daily basis. It's always the same scenario: The grownups get paid and the kids come last.

Concerned that officials at the Bret Harte High School District, east of Stockton, California, weren't giving their son the special education services he needed, the parents of Robert Moser sought legal relief in 1997. They were represented by Orange County attorney Maureen Graves, who took the case because it seemed like an open-and-shut case in her client's favor. The law firm hired by the school district dug in its heels, taking the case to federal court and spending more than seven years litigating. What could have been an $8,000 case ended up costing the taxpayers an estimated $500,000 once the district's law firm submitted its legal bills.[4]

The student went on to receive tutoring services and counseling from the foot-dragging school district, but he was 23 by the time it was ordered. The exorbitant legal fees came to light after a judge in the case became so incensed that he handed down a fine to the law firm representing the district and ordered that its lawyers attend ethics training. The firm, Lozano Smith, represented most of the school districts in the Monterey County region at the time and was accused of playing loose with the facts during litigation in order to bury the special education student and his case. Remarked Graves, the boy's attorney: "I think a lot of school district attorneys push the ethical envelope and sometimes they tear the envelope."[5]

It's not just lawyers whose bank accounts are getting fat while students suffer. In New York City alone, the public school system spends $2.5 billion per year on contracts for over 200,000 different items, from crayons to band equipment.[6] Despite the tremendous buying power that comes from a system with 1,300 schools and more than a million students, taxpayers—and students—are often getting ripped off. In the spring of 2004, schools were paying more for dozens of items purchased through their central office with contracted vendors than if principals were allowed to order it themselves over the Internet or through wholesalers like Costco or Sam's Club. The school system was paying $785.95 for a Panasonic 27-inch TV-DVD-VCR combination that was available for sale on the Internet for $479.98. A steel folding chair that cost taxpayers $12 through the centralized ordering system could be purchased on the Internet for $9.99; the same make and model flute that school bands must buy for $811 was available over the Internet for $575.[7]

## VENDORS FIRST

One of the most embarrassing examples of how greedy and/or incompetent grownups can't be trusted to put kids first in the current education system played out in a series of public hearings in Congress in the summer of 2004. The boondoggle of the summer: the federal E-Rate program. Widely known as the Gore Tax, the E-Rate program uses money from fees secretly collected each month from every American who has a telephone or cell phone to wire schools so that they can link to the Internet. It was added to the Telecommunications Act of 1996 to meet then–vice president Al Gore's goal of bringing the Internet to the classroom of every smiling child in America.

Administered by a little-known corporation called the Universal Service Administrative Company, E-Rate distributed $8.1 billion to local school districts between 1998 and June of 2004, when Congressional investigators uncovered a trail of waste and fraud by greedy telecommunication contractors and clueless school administrators.

In Brevard County, Florida, school officials used E-Rate money to install a $1 million server in a 650-student elementary school, even though that kind of server is better suited for major corporations and massive government agencies. "Was the server appropriate for that school?" asked Lee A. Berry, the district's deputy superintendent. "In our mind it was. It allowed each teacher and child to have a Web site."[8] Investigators thought otherwise, suggesting that the school system bought itself a souped-up Cadillac when a basic Ford Taurus would have been more than adequate. They stopped short of determining whether the decision was based on incompetence or corruption. The end result was that precious school resources were wasted.

The E-Rate investigation opened a can of worms all over. In Puerto Rico, where taxpayers spend about $2 billion per year on public education, Congressional investigators found that schools had spent $101 million in E-

Rate grants to wire the island's 1,500 public schools, yet actually succeeded in connecting just nine schools.[9] The problem was that once schools were wired, they lacked basics like computers, which aren't funded under the federal program. Investigators found that more than $23 million of the total E-Rate money in Puerto Rico had been blown on wireless computer cards that were purchased but never installed, once again showing that the needs of students simply were not being addressed.[10] It is unclear how much the manufacturer of the equipment profited from the dubious sale to the schools, but it is clear that students will never benefit from equipment that is sitting in some warehouse gathering dust.

When school officials are doling out that much money, contractors and vendors practically start foaming at the mouth as they daydream about how such a large and captive market could help their bottom line. The needs of students are easy to forget when the salesmen are meeting their quarterly sales goals. In May 2004, technology giant NEC pleaded guilty and paid a $20.6 million fine for rigging bids at six school districts under the E-Rate program.[11] In 2003, five contractors were charged with billing E-Rate for $1.2 billion in products and services in Milwaukee and Chicago that were never delivered. The indictment alleged that some of the school money ended up in Pakistan to buy a house and several cars.[12] In each of these cases, whether it was because of greed or incompetence, massive sums of money earmarked for our children never got to them because the larger system allowed it to get sidetracked. A startling investigative series on the E-Rate in the *Atlanta Journal-Constitution* newspaper in 2004 found at least $4.5 million worth of warehoused computer electronics, plus other equipment that was installed but not actually in use, and evidence that the Atlanta Public Schools district routinely overpaid for what it bought.[13]

As bad as the reports of E-Rate waste were nationwide after such a small-scale investigation, H. Walker Feaster III, inspector general for the Federal Communications Commission, hinted that things would get even worse if the audits were broadened. "Every rock we turn over, we find stuff," Feaster said.[14]

Writers at *USA Today* summed up the problem: "Consultants and public-interest advocates say blame is shared by everyone involved in the program: public officials so eager, they say, to get the much hyped program going that they imposed few safeguards; school administrators who welcome the federal largesse but who often have little expertise in setting up high-tech systems; vendors who prey on wide-eyed school officials in hopes of feeding at the trough of taxpayers' money."[15]

The goal of connecting classrooms to the Internet across America was a noble one, and all of us who have a phone line or a cell phone chipped in our fair share. Still, like so many other expensive programs involving public education, America's children don't always have much to show for all of that good will, thanks mainly to adults whose interests lie elsewhere. The adults, including the sales people and the manufacturers of the computer equipment, continued to get paid while the children continued to come last.

It's not just high-tech stuff where the school funds are wasted with vendors. In April 2000, the New York City Board of Education began shelling out $10,929 per month for a heap of rusting metal that served as a protective sidewalk shed outside Public School 225 in Rockaway Park, Queens, while the school's exterior awaited repairs.[16] Sidewalk sheds, often called scaffolding, are the unsightly structures that annoy neighbors but protect pedestrians from falling debris from old buildings that either haven't been properly maintained or are in the process of being renovated. In the case of P.S. 225, the scaffolding was erected because of repair work needed on the building's façade— postponed projects included in the school system's five-year capital plan.

New York City government, including the schools, went on a scaffold-erecting bonanza in 1998 after a passerby was killed by a brick that was blown off the roof of a Brooklyn school that was under construction. It was what most would consider a legitimate response to the tragedy, even if the accident itself was a statistical oddity. The scaffolding bonanza not only affected schools that were under construction or renovation, but schools whose building exteriors were deemed unsafe. Unfortunately for taxpayers and students (but great news for the small handful of scaffolding firms that got contracts to install them around schools) the scaffolding craze coincided with a period in which the city's School Construction Authority (SCA) was blowing their budget in epic fashion.

The SCA builds and repairs schools using the city's five-year capital budget for schools. It is kept separate from the school system's operating budget because it relies on long-term bonds that are issued to pay for the projects. At the time, the $7 billion capital plan was *prepared* by the Board of Education's Division of School Facilities, *approved* by the appointed members of the Board of Education, and *implemented* by the School Construction Authority, a quasi-independent entity whose board was run by the schools chancellor, an appointee of the mayor, and an appointee of the governor. The SCA itself was created by the state legislature in 1988 after a series of school building corruption scandals within the Board of Education. At the time the scaffolding was going up at P.S. 225, none of the three groups involved in the capital budget process—the SCA, the Board of Education, and the Division of School Facilities—was getting along with the others, to put it mildly. Their representatives didn't even like to be in the same room with one another, something that several independent evaluators later pointed to as one of the sources of the utter dysfunction that existed in the city's school building process. In the 14 years after the SCA was created, it had been unable to come to a formal agreement with the Board of Education as to what each group's responsibilities should be. The SCA and the board frequently gave contractors and vendors conflicting information, making contractors and vendors feel as if they were working for a divorced couple. Mayor Michael Bloomberg in 2002 referred to their relationship as a "two-headed monster."[17]

The Board of Education consisted of seven members, one appointed by each of the five borough presidents and two appointed by the mayor. The deliberations over the capital plan tended ostensibly to be political. Occasionally, there were discussions about which parts of the city actually needed or didn't need new schools or repairs, but much of the deliberations involved representatives of each borough duking it out to bring home the bacon. The chancellor and his staff in the Division of School Facilities, therefore, needed to craft a budget that was capable of getting four of the seven board members to vote for it, and it had to be done at an overall cost that the mayor and his two appointees could support—meaning the board didn't have a blank check to build and repair with reckless abandon. Chancellor Rudy Crew in 1999 proposed an $8.1 billion plan that was ultimately rejected by a faction of board members led by then-mayor Rudy Giuliani's appointees and representatives from Staten Island and Queens. They sent Crew and his team back to the drawing board with orders that they chop $1 billion worth of projects out of the plan.

They emerged with a $7 billion plan that managed to keep intact most of the planned projects that were in the original $8.1 billion plan—something made possible by revised (and critics later said unrealistic) cost estimates for many projects. Because the School Construction Authority and the Division of School Facilities weren't talking about whether the projected costs in the plan were reasonable, the plan became a nightmare for those involved, including the politicians. The SCA proceeded to build the projects on the capital plan list, but by the summer of 2001, only two years into the five-year plan, the Board of Education was forced to go back and slice $2.4 billion worth of projects from the rest of the plan since the first round of construction and repairs cost so much more than had been budgeted.[18]

The end result is that the leased scaffolding at schools like P.S. 225 sat there rusting month after month while the necessary work on the building itself got pushed further and further down the project list. The delays had a compounded cost. By the summer of 2003, taxpayers had paid out $426,231 and counting to a private scaffolding company, and the repair work at the school had still not been completed. At the time, the city had $4.1 million in current scaffolding contracts with vendors and $1.75 million in annual scaffolding lease agreements at about a hundred schools—most of which had repairs that were not addressed, in part because there was no money left in the capital budget to complete them.

The high price of scaffolding became a priority for Mayor Bloomberg in 2003. "We've got to catch up, but that was exactly what was wrong with the system," Bloomberg said.[19] Bloomberg blamed the School Construction Authority and the old Board of Education's Division of School Facilities for putting up the expensive scaffolding and then leaving it there while the work was never done. "You saw what happened—they put up the scaffolding and never did anything," Bloomberg said. At P.S. 225, his new School Construction Authority president, William Goldstein, was able in the summer of 2003 to negotiate the price of the scaffolding rental down to $3,700 from the $10,929 per month it had paid since April 2000. In acknowledging that the $3,700 figure was the going rate for the scaffolding, the new administration was tacitly admitting that the old contract was a complete rip-off to taxpayers.[20] By paying thousands of dollars more than market value every month, school officials made sure that children's needs weren't the top priority in a public education system that was simultaneously begging for more money from taxpayers.

## BEDDING DOWN WITH BIDDERS

The former superintendent in Queens Community School District 29, Celestine Miller, was indicted in 2000 on charges that she and her husband accepted nearly $1 million in bribes in exchange for steering $6.3 million in computer contracts to a Melville, Long Island, computer company. In one instance, the superintendent was given a brown paper bag filled with $50,000 in cash.[21]

There were several things that made Miller's case stand out from the usual school corruption cases in the city. For one, Miller conspired to rig the computer contracts with a real estate developer who leased property to the Board of Education. The developer gave Miller and her husband four properties in exchange for rigging the bid. For serving as the intermediary, the developer and an associate pocketed $2.2 million in kickbacks from the computer firm. Doubly enraging investigators in the case was the fact that after the bids were rigged, the computer company supplied inferior equipment that broke easily. Two years after the indictments were handed down, Miller and four other defendants pleaded guilty and agreed to repay $4.85 million to the Board of Education.[22]

The central board, headquartered for years at 110 Livingston Street in Brooklyn, away from the watchful eye of the rest of city government, had its share of corruption problems involving vendors. In the summer of 2000, the United States Justice Department charged 11 of the Board of Education's top 12 vendors with rigging bids on things like bagels and pizza. The scandal involved 13 different companies and 22 individuals and involved at least $21 million in school funds over nine years—money that could have gone toward feeding, if not educating the city's youngsters.[23] Interestingly, Joel Klein, as head of the Justice Department's antitrust unit, prosecuted the case. Two years later he became chancellor of the city's schools.

The companies involved in the bid-rigging scandal would meet in hotel rooms near New York's LaGuardia Airport and figure out who would be set up to win which bids. They were crooks, but they were equitable about it. They agreed who would get to be the low-bidder for each item and how much they'd bid. This guaranteed a steady stream of cash at inflated prices.

It is a pattern that seems to continue no matter who is trying to clamp down on schemes that divert money from the classroom. Investigators in New York City in 2004 reported that two employees in the food and transportation department accepted improper gifts from vendors doing business with the schools, including laptop computers, baseball tickets, and boxes of meat, chicken, and hot dogs.[24] The real scandal in the case, however, was that the employees either incompetently or deliberately allowed vendors to charge tens of millions of dollars more than they were really owed for school meal programs.

Sometimes the fights over school money and power were violent and deadly. In 1987, as the New York City Board of Education was considering a plan to allow central administrators to contract out some work done by custodians, the plan's strongest critic, custodian union president Dan Conlin, was shot by two gunman as he started his car outside his home in Bay Ridge, Brooklyn. Described by the *New York Times* as a "gangland-style slaying,"[25] the murder occurred at 6:57 A.M. Witnesses told cops the assailants parked their car a half-block away, walked over to Conlin's 1983 Jeep Wagoneer, pumped five slugs into his skull, and then fled the scene. Cops later arrested four men they said had been hired to do the killing. Another man, believed to be a middleman in arranging the murder, was found shot to death a short time later in a vacant lot on Staten Island.[26]

Described as one of the most powerful insiders at the Board of Education, Conlin was involved in intense collective bargaining negotiations with the Board of Education at the time. A major sticking point in the negotiations was whether the central board could use its own contractors to do work at schools or whether custodians could select their own subcontractors, as Conlin reportedly wanted. Former schools investigator Lydia Segal connected some of the dots in the tragic case: "Although the person who masterminded the killing remains at large, police evidence pointed strongly to a window contractor who stood to lose hundreds of thousands of dollars if Conlin's wishes prevailed. . . . A 1994 investigation sheds light on what the fuss may have been about: those who controlled the contracting process were taking kickbacks from vendors. The window contractor was among those busted."[27]

## WASTED OPPORTUNITIES

While schools in Fort Worth, Texas, were busy cutting their budgets to make ends meet, the school district's Tommy Ingram had as much as $700,000 in school funds stashed in a lettuce bag in his bedroom closet after participating in a slimy scheme that ripped off students and taxpayers. The scheme, which involved Ingram and a local concrete vendor named Ray Brooks, had a "far-reaching impact on the district and will affect future generations of schoolchildren," U.S. District judge John McBryde told the defendants when they were sentenced in 2004.[28] Basically, as sometimes happens in school districts all over the country, the pair paid each other from massively inflated bills for concrete work at schools, taking money that could have helped students directly out of school budgets. Brooks submitted overpriced bids for concrete work and then shared the wealth, in the form of a kickback, with his friend who controlled the contracting process.

In courtroom testimony, Ingram described the $700,000 in school cash that was stashed in the lettuce bag and how he had gambled away another $540,000 in school funds, tucked another $350,000 in a safety deposit box, and took trips that cost a total of at least $30,000.[29] At their sentencing, Judge McBryde complained that federal guidelines limited the prison sentence he could impose to eight years each for the educrat and the contractor, a sentence he considered too lean considering the impact on students that was described by school superintendent Thomas Tocco.

In a letter to federal court officials estimating what $15.9 million might have funded for students, Tocco estimated that, in that school year alone, the stolen money might have saved several popular budget items that instead had been cut due to a lack of funding. Among the budget casualties: $7 million that would have kept intact a planning period for high school and middle school teachers; $500,000 for band equipment; $1 million for tutoring; and $1.5 million for art, music, and Spanish instruction in elementary schools.[30]

Every dollar wasted on vendor fraud—and on "legitimate" contracts for supplies that don't address the needs of school children—contributes to the reality that kids often don't come first in public education. Fixing the problem requires true transparency, so that the public can monitor how resources are being allocated and evaluate whether these allocations put kids first. More importantly, however, it requires that the public raise the bar for school leaders and politicians, so that the pressure to meet the needs of students is more forceful than the pressure from vendors to make an easy buck.

# 6

## THE ELEPHANT IN THE ROOM

It was billed as one of Milwaukee's hot new innovative programs for the 1997–98 school year and chosen as the site for the public school district's back-to-school kickoff press conference that September. But within months, the Milwaukee Sign Language School would be recognized as a poster child for the concept of Children Last.

The brand-new school, located in what had been the Irving Elementary School on the northwest side of the city, was designed to immerse deaf and hard-of-hearing students in a program where everyone (including those who could hear) would be taught sign language as part of the curriculum. At a time when many parents were opting to leave the city schools for the suburbs, it was the kind of innovative program that actually attracted parents of deaf students to the city.

But the first year was a horrible fiasco, one that highlighted some of the systemic problems that often make it difficult for public schools to ever get good ideas off the ground. Lauded as the first of its kind in the nation, the school was unable to bring in teachers who actually knew sign language, because the city's teacher contract required hiring based on a teacher's longevity in the system, not on what unique skills teachers could bring to the school. Since the program was housed in a building that was formerly another school, the teachers who had been at Irving Elementary had first dibs on teaching positions: They had earned them by putting in their time, even though they didn't know sign language.

Many of those senior teachers (to their credit) agreed to learn sign language as they went along, and some participated in after school training sessions. Still, the reality was that the Milwaukee Public Schools in September 1997 opened a sign language school staffed by teachers who didn't know sign language. By the end of the school year parents estimated that less than half of the staff was fluent.[1]

To make matters worse, top school administrators, who had always been lukewarm to the idea for the school, removed in mid-year the assistant principal, who had developed the idea and fought for its creation in the first place. Lisa Kujawa, who had once overseen the school system's programs for the deaf and hard of hearing, also had been the school's most learned signer. Without an explanation to the parents who had enrolled their kids in her school, she was abruptly denied tenure, demoted, and uprooted from the building. "She was the one who knew how everything was supposed to work," said parent Christine Carpentier.[2] The decision to uproot Kujawa in the middle of the year compounded the problems that came from a school filled with deaf students and no teachers who could communicate with them. "For now, if we could get one person in there [who knows sign language] it would help," Sherri Goodwin, the parent of a first grader told me at the time, proving once again how low parents are forced to set the bar for their own children's education.[3]

Because the school was run by people who didn't seem to have a clue about the needs of deaf children, minor matters turned into major annoyances before the year was out. Several parents told me that their kids were sometimes stranded outside the building because they couldn't hear the buzzer that is used to electronically unlock the security doors. The buzzer would buzz, but the children couldn't hear it, so they didn't know when to push the door open. Some deaf children were disciplined by nonsigners and therefore had no idea what they had done wrong; their frustration ended up causing other disciplinary problems.

Conditions were so bad for the students that at an assembly at the conclusion of the school year, the "regular" children booed every time a deaf child was called to receive an award. "I don't think there has been a big breakthrough with the kids," one upset teacher told me, in what might have been considered the understatement of the school year.[4] That same month, more than a hundred parents from the school packed a Milwaukee School Board committee meeting to demand changes that would bring people who understood sign language into the school. They got little traction until they threatened to start their own charter school; then, all of a sudden, they were treated with a sliver of respect. "This is an indication that this district is out of control," said furious school board member Leon Todd.[5]

The school system started a sign language school for deaf children and allowed it to be staffed by people who didn't know sign language because the teachers contract in place at the time was concerned more with the seniority rights of teachers than the education rights of students. Few dispute the need for teachers to receive contractual protections from an often incompetent school system run by uncaring administrators on a power trip, but cases like the Milwaukee Sign Language school show what happens when those protections bump up against the needs of students. The union that negotiated the contract for the teachers was within its rights, and certainly had a responsibility, to insist that teachers who had been used to working in that particular school building be allowed to stay there even after the school was given a new focus. Some teachers had gotten used to the commute from their homes to the school and didn't want to start new assignments that would alter their routines. The teachers contract ensures that these desires are given first priority whenever school leaders make changes at a school. But neither the deaf students nor the hearing students had a contract or a union to protect their interests. When all was said and done, they were the ones to suffer the most from the debacle that played out throughout the school year.

Teachers unions have an obligation to fight for their dues-paying members, and their interests must be focused there. They don't exist to fight for our kids, nor should they be expected to be their champions, as that is a job best suited for parents, who are in the best position to put their children's needs first and foremost. The unions obtain their power in many ways, namely through negotiating successive labor pacts (which often accumulate protections over the years in lieu of adequate pay raises) and by actively working local, state, and national political networks.

While the issue of the unions' tremendous power over school issues is usually presented as a negative, it is important for parents and the larger community to understand how effective the unions are at accumulating and using that power so they might better understand how to steal (or steer) some of that power in directions that can better help kids. As we've already noted, parents often tend to be too nice, when push comes to shove, on issues pertaining to their children's schooling. The teachers unions, in contrast, certainly didn't get the power they have today by asking politely. They fought hard, organized themselves, sometimes spent time in jail, and never, ever thought twice about issuing a subtle threat or two. They decided that power was worth its costs, and they now are reaping the benefits, even if it means kids sometimes suffer because of it. My hope here is that school activists will look on the tactics of the unions with the same awe that I do and understand that in order to get our kids first in line for the attention of school leaders, parents too may need to turn into schoolyard bullies from time to time. Our kids have to matter that much.

The issue for policymakers and school leaders, meanwhile, is differenti-
ating between a union that protects the needs of teachers who work in an extremely stifling bureaucracy and one that insists on actually having a say in
how schools operate. At a time when the public needs to hold someone accountable for education, management of school systems is best left to actual
managers, who can be ousted if necessary, rather than union leaders, who are
accountable only to dues-paying teachers. Those of us who normally support
the concept of collective bargaining in the private sector wish things could be
clean and simple in the public sector: labor should be labor and management
should be management. That is, labor should represent workers and management (elected school boards, mayors, school superintendents) should represent the shareholders, in this case, the taxpayers and voters.

It doesn't really work that way, however. The unions are able to bring
out members to vote in typically low-turnout local school elections, helping
give labor a say in who gets to wear the management hat on the other side of
the bargaining table. Stanford University professor Terry Moe notes that
the unions usually benefit from holding school elections on separate dates
from higher turnout primary and general elections. Turnout in Dallas, Texas
for the 2002 general election, for example, was about 37 percent of eligible
voters—almost ten times higher than the 4 percent turnout for the July 27
school board elections the same year.[6]

In this sense, this kind of public sector bargaining relationship is unlike
anything we ever see in the private sector. Through labor contracts, state
and local laws that the unions have had enacted by politicians they helped
elect, and their sheer power on the local and national political scene, teachers unions often have a strong hand in the management of the nation's
schools and hold a de facto form of veto power over the actions and decisions of the people supposedly in charge. Even when they know it makes
them look bad publicly, the unions don't hesitate to squelch anything that
will weaken the contract or their power. "Their attitude is: What's mine is
mine and what's yours is negotiable," said San Diego schools superintendent
Alan Bersin, a labor-friendly Democrat and nontraditional school leader
who battled mightily with the San Diego Education Association. "Their
idea of collaboration is: Unless we all agree, we can't do anything."[7]

## THE UNION IS EVERYWHERE

In his book *Breaking Free*, writer Sol Stern, who like me sent his children to
the New York City schools, describes how the United Federation of Teach-

ers (UFT) managed to involve itself in the day-to-day operations of the central administration. "The UFT is everywhere and they know everything," Stern quotes former deputy chancellor Harry Spence as saying. "Their people sit on planning meetings in several departments."[8]

In fiscal year 2003, the United Federation of Teachers employed 18 people whose job titles were listed as either "communications," "writer," or "editor."[9] This is in addition to high-powered, private for-profit public relations and image consultants hired by the union and the teams of communications professionals shaping the message at the state and national level. Furthermore, the unions usually hire good, effective people to get their message out to the press and the community. Often former reporters, the press agents for the teachers union are frequently among the most effective spokespersons in the public sector.

Through its amazing communications machine, the union not only defines the terms of everything having anything to do with public education, it also establishes the criteria for who is a friend of public education and who is an enemy. As former Madison, Wisconsin, school board member Rick Berg notes, a "friend of public education" is anyone who does whatever the union says, including turning over more and more tax money with no expectation that it be used in any way to improve education for children. An enemy is someone who isn't willing to write the union a blank check.[10]

School board members in Milwaukee used to joke that when board meetings stretched past 1 A.M., anyone still sitting and watching in the auditorium was getting paid to be there. They were referring to reporters and the staff people from the Milwaukee Teachers Education Association, who almost never left before the meetings were officially adjourned. Even if they did bolt early, I'm quite certain someone from the union was always busy listening to the meeting on the radio. This isn't to suggest that the watchful eye of the union itself is a bad thing. The Milwaukee union did an excellent job sitting on top of the often-ineffective human resources people at the central office when I worked in that city, making sure that teachers were getting every penny they earned in their paychecks and that each was properly paid for their continuing education credits. Reading the union's regular newsletter *The Sharpener,* I couldn't help but think the teachers were getting their money's worth from their dues, if for nothing other than having an advocate who could walk across the street to the human resources office and effectively raise some hell on a teacher's behalf when necessary.

In New York City in 2003, the United Federation of Teachers was the first to raise issues about severe overcrowding in high schools and rampant increases in school crimes due to the system's inability to suspend unruly students. Management tried to reject the union's warnings as "politics from the status quo crowd," but the data quickly began to substantiate the union's anecdotal complaints.[11] Red-faced city and school officials were forced later in the school year to take massive steps to address the situation—including assigning 150 armed cops to patrol the city's worst high schools.

One of the best words to describe the work of teachers unions in terms of their influence over public policy is "effective." Teachers unions know how to throw some elbows if and when it becomes necessary to fight for their members. New York State comptroller Alan G. Hevesi, back when he was a professor at Queens College in 1975, wrote a book called *Legislative Politics in New York State: A Comparative Analysis*, in which he said the United Federation of Teachers "employs a wide range of pressure tactics" to get what it wants out of legislators in Albany. During the contentious battles over decentralizing the New York City schools and granting community control in the late 1960s, he wrote, the UFT "was able to intimidate very high public officials on all levels."[12] (Once Hevesi was elected to political office, however, he—like nearly every other Democrat in the state—became much more conciliatory with regard to the requests and demands of the teachers union. When you're a Democrat and you serve in New York, you are expected to do what the teachers union asks you to do.)

Even when the UFT loses battles with Republicans, it often is able to win enough concessions from legislators that their opponents can rarely declare a slam-dunk victory. In 1998, New York City Chancellor Rudy Crew teamed up with UFT president Randi Weingarten to keep a lid on any talk about creating legislation that would allow for the creation of charter schools, independent public schools that would be allowed to operate outside the constraints of the traditional system.

That same year, however, Assembly speaker Sheldon Silver and other legislators who took their marching orders from the UFT had an opportunity to vote themselves an impressive 38 percent pay raise. Governor George Pataki, who had been unsuccessfully pushing for a charter school law, let it be known that he would veto the legislature's hefty pay raise unless they gave him a charter school law. Legislative greed trumped UFT dominance and the law was passed, but with significant concessions designed to hamper the ability of the charter school movement to prosper, such as a cap that limited the number of new charters that could be granted.

Sometimes politics can lead the unions to eat their young—or even their unborn. As the University of Wisconsin-Milwaukee contemplated establishing publicly funded charter schools in 1999, a university official told me that the local teachers union was threatening to ban the college's student teachers—future union members—from getting any required classroom experience in the Milwaukee public schools if any charters were approved that would be managed by Edison Schools, the for-profit company. Essentially it would have made it extremely difficult for education students at the university to gain state certification to work in public schools. The issue was eventually resolved[13] (after I began calling around to get on-the-record comments from the union and university), but the union made it clear behind the scenes that it was willing to harm its own future members in the process of fighting larger political battles.[14]

Teachers unions have a responsibility to fight for the people who pay their dues now, not those who will do so in the future. Their power tends to be concentrated within the ranks of the oldest, most experienced teachers, who often are the most active union members. In this regard, the unions are limited in their ability to represent the teaching profession at large; they must represent the people who constitute their power base, not new or prospective teachers.

The unions don't exist to help kids or improve education, despite what marketing-savvy union leaders may claim. Many teachers union members dedicate their lives to helping children learn, but the union's responsibility is to protect employees, not children. As such, the union often must be willing to throw its weight around to bully anyone standing in their way. Sometimes, however, the bullying reaches a level that those of us on the outside consider shocking. As noted earlier, while San Diego's Alan Bersin was delivering his "state of the schools" speech in 2002, teachers protesting outside brandished signs comparing the superintendent to Hitler and likening his classroom reforms (such as requiring mandatory three-hour literacy and math blocks in the school schedule) to Nazi repression. One sign, summing up how completely out of control the union protesters had gotten, read, "Heil Führer Bersin." You almost had to wonder whether any of the protesters was a history teacher or if any of them knew that Bersin is Jewish.

Bersin understood that he was at war with the union soon after he started on the job in 1998. The venom reached its nastiest point in 2002, during a round of high-profile and costly school board elections. State and local teachers unions started running television campaign ads billed as "The Alan Bersin Puppet Show," claiming that Bersin steered a sweetheart deal to the architect-husband of a school board candidate and saddled the district with $30 million in debt. After Bersin claimed the ads were false and defamatory, National Education Association lawyer Cynthia Chmielewski wrote to Bersin explaining that the statements made in the ads were "amply justified."

What was telling, however, was that California Teachers Association president Wayne Johnson—one of the most powerful men in the state and often critical of Bersin's policies—included his own handwritten slam at the top of his copy of Chmielewski's letter, which he forwarded to Bersin. "Dear Alan," Johnson began, explaining that he agreed with the lawyer's letter, "I think you are the worst thing to happen to public education that I know of. I think you are one of the biggest jerks I have ever met."[15] These are the people at the other end of the bargaining table.

## THE ANACONDA IN THE CHANDELIER

Like many modern-day leaders, Bersin had a lot of trinkets and trophies in his school district office: gifts given to him by students at schools he had visited, pictures of himself and various dignitaries, and plaques bearing his name from his days as the czar of the Mexican-American Border in Bill Clinton's administration, to name just a few. I met Bersin in the spring of 2004 as we began a series of discussions about his relationship with the 10,000-member San Diego Education Association, the union representing teachers in his district. Two items near his desk stood out more in my memory than anything else in his second floor office on Normal Street.

The first item was the vicious handwritten note to Bersin from Wayne Johnson, a copy of which was later given to me by a district staffer. Bersin, a lifelong Democrat and college-era chum of both Bill and Hillary Clinton, joined a growing list of liberals who learned firsthand that the industrial-style unions representing teachers are one of the biggest obstacles when it comes down to trying to make fundamental changes that could improve the struggling school system. Bersin's reforms included establishing a citywide curriculum, hiring literacy coaches, and requiring teachers to participate in intensive professional development sessions designed to improve their teaching skills. The union resented an outsider coming in and bringing reforms that assumed the problem with the schools was the teachers' skills. It resisted his reforms almost from the start and wasn't afraid to play hardball.

The second item that interested me wasn't plainly visible, for it was tucked away inside Bersin's desk, but he quickly produced it for me as we discussed the teachers union–dominated passive-aggressive culture in the schools. Specifically, we were talking about the contractual grievances and threats of lawsuits under which Bersin had to operate. What he showed me was a copy of an essay published in the *New York Review of Books* in 2002, by Princeton University professor Perry Link, on the subject of censorship in modern Communist China. One passage in particular described the way Bersin felt school leaders often were forced into submission by union leaders who essentially had veto power over any reforms with which they disagreed. Link wrote:

> In sum, the Chinese government's censorial authority in recent times has resembled not so much a man-eating tiger or fire-snorting dragon as a giant anaconda coiled in an overhead chandelier. Normally the great snake doesn't move. It doesn't have to. It feels no need to be clear about its prohibitions. Its constant silent message is "You yourself decide," after which, more often than not, everyone in the shadow makes his or her large and small adjustments—all quite "naturally." The Soviet Union, where Stalin's notion of "engineering the soul" was first pursued, in practice fell short of what the Chinese Communists have achieved in psychological engineering.[16]

After six years at the helm of California's second largest school system, the otherwise labor-friendly Bersin was convinced more than ever that the "anaconda in the chandelier" for American education was the teachers union, omnipresent and quietly waiting to lash out whenever their interests were threatened. The silent message, "You yourself decide," could be applied to every school decision maker in America: You yourself decide whether it is worth the inevitable pain that could come from stepping out of line.

The teachers unions certainly aren't the only special interest group that has gotten us so far off track from serving our kids, but their fingerprints are indisputably all over the mess. If your local community school board includes the lists of guests who attend board meetings in their official minutes, chances are you'll find representatives of the union have perfect attendance. They simply are always there, acting the part of the anaconda, watching closely and reminding those making the decisions whose support really matters in the end. Elected and appointed decision makers in the school system come and go, but the anaconda remains.

Since Albert Shanker was elected president of New York City's United Federation of Teachers in 1964, the powerful union had been led by only three presidents by the time of this writing: Shanker, Sandra Feldman, and Randi Weingarten. In the same time period the New York City schools had 17 politically appointed schools chancellors: Calvin Gross, Bernard Donovon, Nathan Brown, Irving Anker, Harvey Scribner, Frank Macchiarola, Richard Halverson, Anthony Alvarado, Nathan Quinones, Charles Schonhaut, Richard Green, Bernard Mecklowitz, Joseph Fernandez, Ramon Cortines, Rudy Crew, Harold Levy, and Joel Klein.

This is not an insignificant difference. The unions understand more than management that knowledge is power. They have amazing institutional memory. Not only do they tend to retain people with detailed knowledge of their labor contracts (including specifically how certain things got in there in the first place) over the long haul, they often hire away the key people from the top ranks of the school system once they retire, adding to their informational arsenal. Unlike the way it would be viewed in the private sector, when the union hires away a top administrator from the system, it is rarely seen as "crossing over to the dark side," because many administrators began their careers as teachers and members of the same teachers union. It's more like a natural progression back to the union they never really left in spirit.

When management changes hands as often as it does in urban school systems, it's easy to understand why there is seldom any clearly articulated long-term bargaining strategy that represents the interests of students and taxpayers. I once sat down with staff members of the Milwaukee Teachers Education Association after a contract was settled, and they explained how years earlier they had come up with a list of basic issues they wanted addressed in their contract. They viewed each successive contract negotiation as a way to knock things off the list, and they were extremely effective at doing so. They were amazingly organized, realistic in their expectations that it wouldn't all be achieved at once, but sharply focused on their long-term strategy.

## KNOWLEDGE IS POWER

It is hard to imagine how management can ever manage when labor seems to always know more about what is happening than management does. In September 1998, after a prolonged period without a teacher contract, Milwaukee superintendent Alan Brown found that his negotiating position during bargaining was frequently undermined after union-friendly school board members leaked information across the street to the Milwaukee Teachers Education Association (MTEA) offices. In the end, school board president Joe Fisher, a former teacher who was endorsed by and very friendly with the MTEA, personally took over the negotiations in what another union-backed board member described as an awkward attempt at Kissinger-style shuttle-diplomacy.

Superintendent Brown technically was the spokesman for management in the negotiations, representing the school board. In this case, he was put in the awkward position of representing a bargaining stance that was changing behind his back during private meetings between Fisher and union negotiators. Administrators said they literally watched out the window as Fisher walked into the union's offices across Vliet Street and emerged a short time later with a new bargaining position for management. "Basically, Alan Brown goes in and says, 'This is the district's position,' and (MTEA executive director) Sam Carmen tells him, 'I don't believe you,'" said one union-friendly source, whose account was confirmed by board members. "The funny thing was, Carmen was absolutely right."[17]

Fisher, who was thrown out of office by voters in his district seven months later—in part because of his role in what was widely considered a contract that gave away the store—had been strongly supported by the teachers union when he was first elected in 1995. Both the MTEA and the state union, the Wisconsin Education Association Council, gave his campaign $600, the most allowed by law at the time. Carmen and other MTEA employees also gave directly to Fisher's campaign, and the union used its phone banks to contact voters on his behalf and created promotional material to help Fisher get elected. The undermining of Brown's contract negotiations by a president of the school board created what was at the time one of the most costly teacher contract settlements in Milwaukee history in 1998. When school boards are stacked with people like Fisher, however, who had been a member of the union as a teacher and who was elected with the union's considerable assistance, we can hardly expect that management will put the needs of our kids first and foremost.

Because they can get away with it, teachers unions are always telling school board members how things should be, and school board members are expected to report back to the union on what the boards are doing behind-the-scenes. The United Teachers Los Angeles had such a grip on its school board in 2004 that union leaders made no attempt to hide their hand signals to school board members during meetings, instructing them how to proceed on important policies. The hand signals were in addition to phone calls and e-mails being sent by the union to board members right in the middle of the meetings. "It's so blatant. It's like a baseball game—people are giving signals out there. It's ridiculous," said board member Mike Lansing. "These guys are puppeteers, and we've got board members who can't think for themselves."[18]

San Diego's top labor negotiator, Willy Surbrook, told me he also noticed occasions when things discussed in closed session in his city made their way to leaders of the San Diego Education Association. Superintendent Alan Bersin said he sometimes even played the union by telling things to board members who he knew would squeal to the union.

## THE CONTRACTS

If it's not union leaders playing hardball, it's the contracts they have successfully negotiated with management over the years that put the needs of children after the wants of adults. Teachers who are assigned to schools based on seniority, not on their fit with the school; custodians who earn more than principals but who don't paint above ten feet high (a different union handles anything above ten feet); teachers who don't have to do lunchroom duty, et cetera—such contract provisions constrain change and directly affect our children and their families on a daily basis. From students who are forced to learn in classrooms without adequate working lights (New York City custodians are allowed to change light bulbs, but the contract prevents them from changing the ballasts) to the parents whose parent-teacher conferences are cut short because teachers aren't required to stick around beyond a certain time period—the contract impacts almost everything.

Parents in New York City were particularly irked by the time limits on their evening parent-teacher conferences to discuss their children's performance in the fall of 2003. Some overcrowded schools limited the parents' time with their kids' teachers to two or three minutes each, enforced by intrusive kitchen timers. "The timer went off, the teacher stood up, and I was booted out the door," one mom at Gramercy Park's Public School 40 told me.[19] The cap was set at five minutes at Middle School 54 on the Upper West Side, three minutes at Bay Academy in Sheepshead Bay, Brooklyn, and two minutes at Manhattan's Stuyvesant High School, parents said. The teachers contract in effect at the time required management to negotiate with the teachers union whenever substantial changes were proposed for school policies. Because the schools always have set aside one afternoon and one night session for the twice-a-year-meetings, any change to make the meeting times more parent-friendly would have to be negotiated with the teachers union.

School labor contracts are privately negotiated documents that have very public implications. Union leaders and school officials will occasionally bargain in public (while claiming they don't) if they feel it serves their purposes, but generally speaking, seldom is much light ever shed on what exactly is in the contracts. Teacher contracts, in particular, take on a rather mysterious quality and school leaders themselves aren't always familiar with exactly what the contracts do or don't allow. It is not uncommon for a possible plan to be shot down by administrators "because of the contract," even if the contract wouldn't actually prevent the plan from rolling out. For the people who run schools, however, the contracts and the grievances they spawn are a part of nearly every workday in one way or another. Interestingly, despite labor's regular appeals to the public to support their members in the quest for pay raises, union leaders seldom welcome any sort of public examination of what is actually contained in their contracts.

In one high-profile instance in New York City, in 2003, a city councilwoman was branded "antiworker" for asking probing questions about how school labor contracts affected children and the operation of good schools. Public hearings on the impact of work rules and job protections for teachers, principals, and custodians, called by Democratic councilwoman Eva Moskowitz in November 2003, hammered home the point that it took far too long to unload incompetent employees from the system. Other work rules were silly and counterproductive: Custodians can't repair more than 75 tiles at a time, can't paint anything higher than ten feet, and can "spackle" but not "plaster." As *Newsday* columnist Joe Dolman noted afterward: "Few outfits could run the way the school system runs and not find themselves unceremoniously hooted out of town."[20]

Over the course of a tense and dramatic week, Moskowitz, a former teacher herself, picked apart a generation's worth of negotiated contractual work rules that were clogging up schools. Her hearings attracted hoards of reporters and columnists who didn't normally wallow in the kinds of public school issues addressed by the oversight committee. The hearings had a year's worth of City Hall drama packed into several days. UFT President

Randi Weingarten, who was furious that the Democratic-controlled council allowed the hearings to take place at all, showed up for her testimony joined by Brian McLaughlin, the intimidating head of the New York City Central Labor Council. "I wanted to remind the City Council members that the entire labor movement in the city is watching them," McLaughlin told me afterward, in a tone that just about made the hair on the back of my neck stand up. Playing the part of the thug, McLaughlin sat at the table next to Weingarten, staring intently at city council members during Weingarten's often caustic exchange with Moskowitz. At the time, Moskowitz was the only Democratic official in New York City who was elected without the UFT's endorsement. McLaughlin's stone-cold message to the council members was clear: Labor got you all elected and we can get you all unelected as well if we have to.

Enormous pressure was placed on council members to back off the probe in the weeks leading up to the hearings. Moskowitz said she would not call off the hearings or tread lightly on the contract issues. When Moskowitz was done dissecting the contract, her colleagues tried to use the hearing to sheepishly heap praise on Weingarten for her work for education.

Some witnesses at the hearings were so fearful of retaliation or black-listing by the powerful unions that they agreed to speak only on audiotape and after their voices were recorded and distorted so that they couldn't be identified. Other witnesses agreed to testify in person but backed down on the morning they were scheduled to appear, out of fear that their careers would be ruined if they crossed the unions. While Weingarten and other union leaders denied there was any intimidation going on, two things became obvious.

First, despite the fact that neither Moskowitz nor the council's education committee staff had publicly released the names of those school employees who would be blowing the whistle on the contractual language that hurt kids, the UFT somehow had advanced knowledge of who was on the top-secret witness list. Weingarten's prepared remarks on the morning of her appearance named the school principals who were scheduled to testify. The union president's prepared remarks were designed to serve as a rebuttal for what she expected those school principals to say, even though neither the union nor the public was made aware of their identities. Two of the witnesses backed out at the last minute under the pressure, and Weingarten's prepared speech—which mentioned their anticipated remarks—rebutted testimony that, in the end, never existed.

Second, the labor movement—and the United Federation of Teachers in particular—made it clear they were out for Moskowitz's scalp for putting so much public pressure on the union to explain itself. For months following the hearing, the union attacked Moskowitz in their regular union newspaper, *New York Teacher*, calling her names and accusing her of trying to grab headlines at the expense of teachers' working conditions. Rumors quickly spread through City Hall that Moskowitz would be ousted as chairwoman by her fellow Democrats who were being lobbied behind the scenes by union leaders.

Moskowitz had been warned for months that it would be foolish for a Democrat like her to take on this "third rail of politics." Top city officials, including some education officials, urged her not to go forward with the hearings. (More than one official warned her it would be the end of her political career if she shined a light on the powerful unions and their contracts.) Colleagues on the City Council, elected with the considerable help and resources of the unions, tried to sink the hearings before they were even officially scheduled.

Council speaker Gifford Miller, a close ally of Moskowitz, was under enormous pressure from Weingarten to soften the tone of the hearings, council aides told me at the time. The controversy came at a time when Miller was preparing to run for mayor in 2005 against Mayor Bloomberg, a run that would be made much easier with support from the teachers union. The Moskowitz hearings shattered the status quo in the council. Usually in New York City the teachers union tells the elected council members how things are going to work, not the other way around. The union raises the issues and the politicians respond to them. Moskowitz ignored the protocol and put her political career in jeopardy.

McLaughlin, thinking that the normal rules, with the union calling the shots, still prevailed, sent a letter to Miller on behalf of organized labor ordering him to "cease and desist" from poking into the school labor contracts.[21] Miller, despite the pressure, allowed Moskowitz to proceed, but she was clearly out there on her own. "I'm looking at this topic because I honestly believe that parts of the contract affect children in a negative way," Moskowitz said. "I just didn't feel that I could be chair of the Education Committee and knowingly ignore a topic that affects kids."[22]

Mayor Bloomberg on the eve of the hearings called Moskowitz a "gadfly" for stirring up the hornet's nest of labor politics. By the end of the week, however, after a steady spotlight on the real-world implications of the contracts, the mayor praised her courage and blasted her colleagues on the council for kissing up to big labor rather than trying to have an honest discussion about the impact of the labor contracts on schools. "Everybody else for the last two days in the City Council has stood there and pandered [to labor leaders] and said, 'Aren't you wonderful,'" Bloomberg said on his weekly radio show.[23]

Her critics in the unions, meanwhile, accused Moskowitz of trying to generate publicity for herself to prepare for a run for citywide office, such as Manhattan borough president or city controller—a charge she deflected by noting it would be much easier to win those races with the unions' support than by ending up on their hit list.

At a speech to union members in December 2003, Weingarten declared war on Moskowitz's political career and urged her 120,000 members to vote against the former teacher in any future election. "I don't think we've ever gone through anything like the Eva Moskowitz hearing," Weingarten admitted.[24] For months, the UFT hammered away at Moskowitz in internal newsletters to members. One mailing compared her to the Disney character Cruella De Vil. The official union newspaper *New York Teacher* featured an extremely unflattering picture of Moskowitz under the headline, "Why is Eva Going After Teachers?" In early 2005, Moskowitz announced she would run for Manhattan borough president in the fall of that year. Not only was she expecting to run without the union's support, it was widely anticipated that the union would actively work against her to punish her for her deeds.

## THE APPEARANCE OF CHANGE

Republican presidential candidate Bob Dole had complained on the campaign trail about the teachers unions as major obstacles to reform. In 1997, months later, the Washington-based National Education Association commissioned a consultant to probe the reasons why Dole's message—while it hadn't helped him to beat the incumbent, Bill Clinton—seemed to resonate with so many people in national polls.

"What the NEA now faces is a crisis," reads the report prepared for the union by the Kamber Group. "But one cannot handle a crisis in a business-as-usual mode. And despite its best intentions, the NEA continues to operate in a business-as-usual mode."[25]

Based on interviews with the NEA's own central staff and staff in the union's state offices, the report clearly laid out the idea that the mainstream public had essentially begun to view the union as little more than a pain in the neck. Interviews with state union employees, for example, "reflected a belief that NEA had focused on its traditional union role for so long and had said 'no' so often in the educational debates of the last 10 to 15 years that they had allowed themselves to be cast as the 'less reform-minded' of the two teachers unions."[26] The smaller American Federation of Teachers, with its popular former leader Al Shanker, had established itself as a union more in tune with the modern realities of classroom teaching. Under Shanker's leadership, the AFT even pushed for raising standards in schools and promoted a strong curriculum to improve student learning.

The report called on the union to do two things: dominate the public debate so that non-union-friendly reform ideas (like paying teachers based on performance) can't get in a word edge-wise, and begin the process of shifting the union's approach "from that of an industrial union to one that embraces attributes of craft unionism, in which ensuring *quality* workers is just as important as raising wages and benefits at the bargaining table."[27]

The Kamber Group report advised NEA president Bob Chase to publicly unveil a kinder, gentler direction for the union in a speech in which he "says some things for their shock value . . . (e.g., there are bad teachers and our job is to make them good or show the way to another career)."[28]

Weeks later, in a widely covered speech at the National Press Club, Chase declared: "There are indeed some bad teachers in America's schools. And it is our job as a union to improve those teachers or—that failing—to get them out of the classroom."[29]

The speech marked the launch of what Chase would come to call New Unionism, NEA's short-lived attempt to professionalize the teaching profession by policing itself and focusing on quality schools. The NEA had been so widely seen as bully obstructionists that the story immediately took on "man bites dog" significance. Chase began speaking across the country and proposing reforms such as peer assistance and mentoring for substandard teachers, and calling for less conflict and more collaboration with management. Within a few years, however, due in large part to a lack of support among the NEA delegates who get to determine the union's official policies, the New Unionism movement lost most of its steam.

Chase's calls for reform were often shouted down by his own members. His effort to open the door to the concept of merit pay for teachers in 2000 resulted in the door being slammed shut and locked even tighter than before he started making his push. At the NEA's annual Representative Assembly in

Atlanta, Georgia, in 1997, Wisconsin delegates from Milwaukee, Racine, Madison, and Green Bay (the old school unionists) actually got up and walked out of the convention hall in protest after the union, at Chase's urging, passed a measure that endorsed the practice of peer review, in which teachers would have the ability to identify struggling colleagues and show them the door to another profession if they didn't improve. Many of the protesting delegates felt that the New Unionism concept represented a complete abandonment of "unionism" itself, and made their disapproval known. "We are opposed to a system that puts a teacher in the role of firing other teachers," said Pat O'Mahar, assistant executive director of the Milwaukee Teachers' Education Association, explaining the concerns of the group.[30]

After the protest, the NEA put me in touch with John Grossman, the executive director of the Columbus (Ohio) Education Association, which had a successful peer review pilot program under way at the time. He was frustrated that the dissenters hadn't given the issue as much thought as he had hoped. "Our friends there in Wisconsin seemed to get into the heat of the battle before we could ever talk about the substance," he told me. Grossman and Chase were frustrated that so many union members themselves considered these attempts to modernize and reform the union to be antilabor because they were initially designed to save the union from extinction.

The presidents of all four local unions whose members walked out of the Atlanta Representative Assembly had given Chase a written warning soon after he delivered his New Unionism speech at the National Press Club the previous winter. They urged him to follow the example of the AFL-CIO and return the union to its traditional labor roots. "It's time that the NEA join the labor movement, renew its commitment to its members, and move forward in its quest on behalf of education employees across the nation," the letter stated.[31] Basically: Take your pretentious new unionism and shove it.

Parent-activist Leah Vukmir, who several years later would be elected to the state legislature, accused the Wisconsin unions of shooting themselves in the foot by opposing Chase's plan. "Every profession has a peer review process, including doctors and lawyers," Vukmir said. "The teachers unions are always complaining that they are not treated like professionals, and this isn't going to help."[32]

Great care must be taken to separate the unions from their individual members, as was pointed out to me by Milwaukee teachers who specifically chose *not* to walk out of the convention hall that summer. In fact, most teachers who are members of the National Education Association have no idea what the union's official policies are or how the union spends its $240 million annual budget, nor do they care, so long as they have someone advocating on their behalf before a bureaucratic and often incompetent system that throws teachers into classrooms with little support.

The unions are filled with these well-meaning people, but that doesn't mean that the union itself collectively cares as much about children as its individual members. As Randi Weingarten, the president of the United Federation of Teachers in New York City told new teachers in 2004: "Our number one legal responsibility is to represent you."[33]

Another tactic employed by the unions in their attempts to counter the widespread belief that they obstruct reforms is the careful coordination with outside groups to do the obstructing for them, for appearance sake. Kamber Group's report to the National Education Association in 1997 advised that "third party coalitions must be formed to fight the NEA's battles" on issues such as vouchers so that it doesn't interfere with the union's attempts to reconstruct its public image as obstructionist. What the NEA took the advice about forming "third party coalitions" to mean was this: Find a group with a nice name like People for the American Way (PFAW), pay them well, make it clear what you need from them, and give them a script to work from so that they say all the right things to make it look like it's not just the teachers unions who feel that way. To make it even cozier, top officials from the union will also sit on the PFAW's board of directors to keep an eye on things.

Delegates at the 2000 NEA Representative Assembly in Chicago complained that as much as $200,000 per year in their dues money was going to the PFAW and that they weren't getting enough in return.[34] The reality, however, is that it's a very nice arrangement for the union from a public relations standpoint. When secretary of education Rod Paige called the union a "terrorist organization" in February 2004, for example, PFAW quickly was able to issue a statement expressing outrage so that the powerful union could play the role of the stunned victim.[35] The gaffe proved to be a major political setback for Paige, who was pushed out of the job after President Bush won reelection later in the year.

Groups like the PFAW can also get themselves muddied in school politics on the local level on the union's behalf. A contentious 1999 school board race in Milwaukee pitted a slate of union-endorsed candidates against a slate of voucher-supporters endorsed by Mayor John Norquist, a Democrat. Norquist successfully painted the union as an obstacle to reform, and the election came one year after the Wisconsin Supreme Court upheld a program of taxpayer-funded vouchers that could be used in private and religious schools. Because the voucher issue had national implications, the National Education Association pumped $25,000 from its contingency fund to the left-wing People for the American Way to operate a phone bank to contact voters in Milwaukee and provide them with information on the election from the union's point of view. PFAW worked with the group Wisconsin Citizen Action to campaign against the mayor's slate. The NEA also pumped $50,000 in contingency funds to its state affiliate, the Wisconsin Education Association Council. The Wisconsin union used the money for a "Great Schools" campaign of issue-advocacy television ads in the race. But it backfired. The voucher-supporting slate was able to use the union support as a campaign issue and soundly defeated the union-backed candidates in a stunning election.

The unions also routinely fund academics who issue reports that support their initiatives. In 2000, University of Wisconsin-Milwaukee records showed that both the NEA and American Federation of Teachers were supporting the school's Center for Education, Research, Analysis, and Innovation.[36] The center, at the time, was host to professor Alex Molnar and researcher Gerald Bracey, both of whom are well known nationally for supporting pet union issues, such as smaller class sizes, and for criticizing efforts to privatize education services. Molnar, a passionate advocate for smaller classes, not only chaired a state commission that recommended a statewide smaller class size program in early grades, his research center later was awarded the state contract to evaluate the same program he originally recommended. Perhaps not surprisingly, the research group found his program to be a smashing success and recommended even more funding for it.[37]

## UNIONS AS A POLITICAL FORCE

The teachers unions are extremely good at reminding candidates for office that they carry a big stick. In 2004, the United Federation of Teachers hired political consultant Scott Levenson, of the Advance Group, to determine how the rank-and-file turnout in New York City elections compared with the city as a whole. The results were astonishing. Calling the union a "political powerhouse," Levenson found that from 1999 to 2003 turnout rates at the polls were consistently higher among teacher union members than the public at large. In one low turnout election year, 1999, 32 percent of the union's members voted in elections for city council, compared with 7.81 percent of the public citywide.[38] The union's newspaper, *New York Teacher,* noted that the findings were something "all candidates ought to bear in mind." The study also highlighted races in which UFT members almost certainly determined the outcome. In the 2001 Democratic primary election, for example, city councilman Mike McMahon won by just 170 votes in a district in which 668 teachers union members voted. Councilman John Liu won the same election by 202 votes in a district where 352 UFT members voted.[39]

It isn't just on the local scene that the unions are influential. For the 2004 presidential election, a little-known group called Communities for Quality Education popped onto the national political landscape to run television advertisements critical of the federal No Child Left Behind law. Although the law was a bipartisan bill in Congress, it was closely associated with President Bush who made it one of his most important domestic policies.

The law, which was supported in the Senate in 2001 by Democrat John Kerry, for the first time required that local school districts and schools achieve measurable results for the billions of dollars the federal government shelled out for K through 12 education across the country. (See chapter 7.)

In the Communities for Quality Education advertisements, schoolteachers identified only as Michelle, Nanci, and Rosemary complained that the law forces them to "drill students for standardized tests" but doesn't fund smaller classes.[40] Anytime you hear someone say the phrase "smaller classes," or "smaller class size," you can pretty much bet your mortgage that the teachers unions are behind it, especially when smaller classes are offered as an alternative to things that have nothing to do with large class sizes like, in this case, standardized testing. Whether you have 35 children and a testing requirement, or 10 children and a testing requirement, you still are left with a testing requirement. In this case, the unions were behind the ads and they were spending a fortune in teachers' dues money to get the message out. An analysis conducted for the *Los Angeles Times* by the TNSMI Campaign Media Analysis Group found that the unions and their Communities for Quality Education group had spent almost $3 million to air the ads in presidential swing states[41] in the month of June 2004 alone.[42] By July, the NEA had donated $4 million to Communities for Quality Education, all of which came from a national media fund financed by a $2 special dues add-on that NEA members pay each year.[43]

The National Education Association, in particular, is able to deploy what it calls Uniserv directors to work on major political campaigns. These positions, located in each congressional district, are funded with dues. The NEA and American Federation of Teachers regularly pay for phone banks, printing, and other campaign costs—including get-out-the-vote drives—for candidates. By law they are supposed to be spending teacher dues money to inform their members of the union's positions and endorsements and to get out the union vote. And yet it's hard to conceive of how this could be monitored.

In contrast to 2000 when the NEA didn't roll out its political operation until after Labor Day, in 2004 it got the political wheels turning early in the year to try to defeat President Bush. Political operatives from the union were sent to ten key battleground states—Florida, Iowa, Michigan, Minnesota, Nevada, New Hampshire, Ohio, Oregon, Pennsylvania, and Wisconsin—to help the state activists and union leaders get their acts together earlier for the campaign. By the summer, the NEA added five more states to its list—Arizona, Arkansas, Missouri, New Mexico, and West Virginia.[44]

The NEA, in particular, is so active in the presidential campaigns that it almost doesn't matter what the Democratic candidates they support have to say about education. The message is clear: We are the ones providing the foot soldiers, and we'll make you remember that once you are in office. In 2004, the presidential election season following the messy ballot recount in Florida that helped send Republican George W. Bush to the White House in 2000, the NEA attempted to make sure such a loss didn't happen again in the Sunshine State. The union was the single largest contributor to a political group called Floridians for All Political Action Committee, providing $250,000 so that the group would campaign in favor of a proposal on the statewide ballot to raise Florida's minimum wage by $1 to $6.15 per hour. While many NEA members no doubt support plans that would raise the minimum wage, organizers made no secret of the fact that the ballot measure and the Floridians For All PAC were designed not so much to actually raise the minimum wage but to mobilize low-wage workers to get to the polls on election day.[45] The union was hoping that, in addition to voting themselves a pay raise, low-wage earners would cast their ballot for the Democratic presidential candidate.

The relationship between the Democrats and the teachers unions is longstanding. Linda Chavez, a former civil rights commissioner in President Ronald Reagan's administration, had previously served as the editor of publications for the AFT. She later claimed she was regularly called upon to print extra copies of campaign endorsement flyers, which were then given to the candidates' campaigns to use as they saw fit.[46] "In 1980, when the AFT endorsed Edward M. Kennedy in the Democratic presidential primary against incumbent President Carter, the union delivered tens of thousands of such fliers to the Massachusetts senator's campaign headquarters for general distribution," Chavez wrote in the *Los Angeles Times* in 2004.[47]

Chavez also says she witnessed paid union staff running phone banks from the union's headquarters, making calls to registered Democrats, not necessarily just to union members as the law requires. She noted that because union dues are tax deductible, we are all paying for these political activities. Businesses, in contrast, are not allowed to do what the unions also do on federal campaigns.

It is noteworthy that for the second presidential election cycle in a row, the teachers unions failed to deliver for the Democrats in 2004. Commentators on the left, like the *New Republic*'s Martin Peretz,[48] and Dan Gerstein, former aide to Senator Joseph Lieberman, argued that the teachers union played a role in the Democrats' loss, the latter referring to the teachers unions as a "progress-blocking interest group."[49] In an election in which the hot election issues appeared to be gay marriage, abortion, and other "values," it is entirely possible that the busloads of in-your-face teachers union field workers from the blue states who canvassed in the suburbs of Cleveland, Ohio, did more harm than good. Many pundits felt the election turned on moderates who were swayed by the Republicans over these issues, issues on which the teachers unions tend to fall in the far left quarters of the party. The future of the Democratic Party, as we will see in chapter 7, may rest, in part, on what it decides to do about the high-profile role the teachers unions play.

## BEATING THE UNIONS AT THEIR OWN GAME

Former Milwaukee school board member John Gardner drove the Milwaukee Teachers Education Association nuts from the day he was sworn in after the spring 1995 elections. Not only was Gardner a strong supporter of private school vouchers and charter schools, he was a strong voice for more student-friendly changes in the teachers contract. But even more problematic for the union, Gardner was a radical liberal at a time when the union drew strength by branding their opponents as right-wing profiteers. Gardner was an activist who had strong flirtations with socialism and who had cut his teeth as a community organizer with Cesar Chavez in the United Farm

Workers union. He was dangerous for the union because he knew their play book by heart, and he often was able to beat them at their own game.

The union made Gardner the focal point of their campaign efforts for the spring 1999 school board elections in Milwaukee. Not only did they spend hundreds of thousands of dollars in their attempts to unseat him, they did it in a manner that shows how low the union is willing to stoop to take out someone who gets in their way. Using Gardner's vote in 1997 against a zero-tolerance policy to expel students who commit crimes, the teachers attempted to portray Gardner as a reckless leader who looked the other way while violently dangerous African-American students disrupted schools. Gardner is white and was running against an African-American woman who had been a school principal. At the time of the 1997 vote, Gardner accused the district of being irresponsible by turning unruly students out onto the city streets without any supervision or any programs to monitor drug use or other issues confronting students.

Gardner's stance on the policy issue was certainly fair game, but the MTEA managed to go completely overboard and it backfired on them. The union produced television ads showing pall bearers carrying a coffin out of a church to suggest that children were dying because of the vote. Another glossy mailing produced by the union appealed directly to racist elements in the electorate, showing a white cop in front of a school. Another showed a picture of a school kid toting a handgun, an open bottle of beer and a marijuana cigarette. A vote for Gardner, the union would have had voters believe, would turn Milwaukee's schools into pistol-packing versions of Woodstock.

The day after the ads aired, Gardner went on the offensive, calling a news conference directly outside the teachers union headquarters on Vliet Street. As union staff members watched, he dared the city to compare his record on crime with his opponent's and noted that he had been endorsed in the race by every law enforcement group in the city. Then he cut loose on the union itself, in what became a theme that eventually propelled him and his entire slate of five reform candidates into office: "The MTEA routinely defends child-molesters, thieves and drug pushers who teach in our schools," he charged.[50]

It is possible to take on the powerful teachers unions and win, as Gardner showed, even if they amount to only incremental gains. It is also possible for competent school managers to find the kinds of loopholes in teachers union contracts in their attempts to run the schools in ways that put kids first. In the summer of 2004, New York City schools chancellor

Joel Klein, a lawyer, found a way within the contract to hire the best teachers possible to help struggling summer school students pass exams that would help them get promoted to the next grade. The city's summer school program had performed extremely poorly over the years, prompting Klein to drastically cut the size of the program. Teachers had long treated summer school assignments as an entitlement that allowed the most senior teachers to increase their salaries so that they could earn higher pension payouts in retirement. New York City teachers didn't think the chancellor had the right to make those kinds of managerial decisions, and more than 1,400 grievances were filed by teachers who did not get the summer school jobs they wanted.

But Klein had a trick up his sleeve that led to some positive results. Because Mayor Bloomberg had recently instituted a third-grade retention policy, by which kids couldn't be promoted to fourth grade unless they were slightly proficient in math and reading, Klein was able to create a new Summer Success Academy to help second- and third graders pass the tests. He argued that it was a new program and not part of the old summer school, and therefore the teachers' contract allowed him to staff those summer classes with the best teachers available, not merely those with the most longevity in the system. Klein was able to hire teachers who were skilled in math to actually teach math.

The results showed that having a good teacher in front of kids might actually have some academic value. On a scale of 1 to 4, with 4 being the most proficient and 1 being the least, more than 4,200 third grade summer school students in the city scored at least a 2 under the new Summer Success Academy. The previous summer, only about 2,500 performed as well. "This year we said: Enough is enough," Bloomberg said in announcing the summer school scores.[51]

For years the teachers unions have used their contract to the advantage of their members. Klein, in this case, was able to use his skills as a lawyer to use the same contract to the advantage of students. And that's the whole point here. Rather than lamenting the role of the unions and ending the discussion there, education advocates (at least the ones who want to put kids first) are best advised to study the unions and emulate their success in advocating for their dues-paying members. They should join the union on issues when doing so benefits children, and they should be willing to go to the mat against the same union when their policies and contracts get in the way of our kids' education.

Parents and students in Warwick, Rhode Island, had it exactly right in August 2004 when they actually formed a picket line outside the offices of the Warwick Teachers Union over what they charged was the union's hard-line stance during that round of bargaining over a contract. Teachers had worked without a contract for a year, and protested this by refusing to proctor SAT tests, to chaperone homecoming dances, or to attend school open houses. Roughly 40 parents and their kids decided they had had enough: They took a page from the union's play book, and embarrassed the union by attracting news coverage of their protest outside the union hall.

In addition to beating them at their own game, parent reformers should fight hard for greater transparency with regard to the teachers' contract. Like New York City councilwoman Eva Moskowitz's hearings on the school labor contracts, reformers should know and understand the contracts and tactics of the teachers unions. Politicians usually like to say that they don't negotiate labor contracts in public. But why not? When those who stand to win and lose the most in teachers' contract negotiations are our children, can't a sound argument be made that such a public contract should itself be negotiated publicly? It's obviously quite difficult to negotiate with people watching, but we have unfortunately witnessed what can happen when the public is closed off from these negotiations.

At the very least, the public should insist that school systems begin to publicly post on their web sites the disposition of all the contractual grievances. Let the public read for itself why a teacher accused of molesting a student has gotten his job back and decide where the problem is in our schools. We make kids take tests all the time and publicize their results, yet we allow the grownups—the administrators, the employees, and the union lawyers—to operate without being closely examined. The public's disenfranchisement from the process has allowed the unions and management to operate in the dark for too long, and too many children have paid the price.

Teachers unions have an obligation to fight for better wages and job protections for their members. That doesn't make what they are fighting for wrong, but the public has a similar obligation to make sure that we get the best possible schools and the best possible teachers in front of our children. Parents can play a role in helping make that happen, particularly if they understand that education is inherently political and engage in political gamesmanship themselves.

The issue of smaller class-size is a perfect example, an issue that is very important to many parents and educators. Class-size reduction programs just feel right to many parents and teachers who envision a more easily man-aged classroom and enhanced learning for children. The idea of adding teachers to reduce the teacher-to-student ratio also has a significant finan-cial impact for the unions in the form of increased revenue from dues and enhanced strength in numbers. Because unions often recruit parents to work as foot soldiers in political battles for smaller-class-size funding, par-ents should consider entering into the same kinds of arrangements often employed by the unions to get something out of the partnership that goes beyond just smaller classes. Organized parents, for example, could insist that teachers agree to add additional time to regular parent-teacher conferences. (The contract typically controls the amount of time allocated for such after-school meetings.) Or, even better, parents should demand that once they get smaller classes, the union and school leaders agree to quickly get rid of in-competent teachers.

Parents have an important stake in what happens to their children in schools and must understand that their concerns are just as important—I would argue more important—as the concerns of teachers and other people who earn paychecks in school systems.

# 7

# DEMOCRATS AND REPUBLICANS
# (BUT MOSTLY DEMOCRATS)

In late February 2000, the political jumble that is public education was on display for the world to see in a sometimes raucous debate in the Harlem neighborhood of New York City, widely considered the heart and soul of African American culture. The debate inside Harlem's famed Apollo Theater between Democratic presidential candidates Bill Bradley and vice president Al Gore included sharp jabs and accusations by the two candidates on such issues as health care, affirmative action, and community renewal. Yet, questions and answers on the topic of education showed the disconnect between Democratic candidates and party constituents.

The complaint is commonly aired by political campaigns that "celebrity journalists" tend to suck the life out of televised debates with their overly self-indulgent babbling. But in the case of the showdown at the Apollo, two reporters were refreshingly willing to "tell it like it is" while prefacing their questions on school reform and the influence of the powerful teachers unions. The questions also shone a bright spotlight on the problems Democrats have when trying to square policies that are popular with traditional party constituencies but are opposed by the unions that provide the manpower and cash for elections.

*Time* magazine writer Tamala Edwards, a young black woman who seemed to have more in common with the largely African American crowd than either of the two white Ivy Leaguers on the stage, posed a question about school vouchers that genuinely seemed to stun the vice president. Vouchers, already in place in Milwaukee, Cleveland, and Florida at the time, allow students to attend private schools at public expense and are vehemently opposed by the nation's teachers unions.

Noting that a majority (60 percent) of African Americans supported vouchers at the time, Edwards noted that Gore had been taught in private schools and that he sent his own children to private schools such as the expensive Sidwell Friends in Washington. "Is there not a public or charter school in D.C. good enough for your child? And if not, why should the parents here have to keep their kids in public schools because they don't have the financial resources that you do?" Edwards asked.[1]

Gore felt the question was too personal. "You can leave [my children] out of this if you want to," Gore said, before reiterating his belief that school vouchers drain money from public schools at a time when public schools need to be uplifted. He sharply criticized Bradley for supporting experimental voucher plans "every single time they came up for a vote during his 18 years in the Senate." Showing his money was where his mouth was, he called for a 50 percent increase in federal spending on schools, including more federal money for local school construction. For his part, Bradley backed away somewhat from his previous support of vouchers for low-income families and also talked about his plans to double the amount spent on Title I funding for the nation's poorest schools, to increase early childhood education programs, to hold teachers accountable, and to give parents more public school choices.

Later, CNN reporter Jeff Greenfield revisited Edwards's question and suggested that the reason Gore's education plan wasn't particularly bold was the enormous influence the teachers unions have on the party's platform.

> Mr. Vice President, when Tamala asked you about schools and your children, you bristled a bit, so let me depersonalize this. You and Mrs. Gore, Senator Bradley and his wife, me—any parent of means has the choice. You can send your child to public or private school. But when the public schools fail our children, we don't wait for new legislation. We protect our kids' future by pulling them out of those public schools. There are tens of thousands of parents, disproportionately black and brown, who do not have that choice. And I would put on the table one of the staunchest opponents of that choice are the two major teachers' unions that happen to supply one in nine of the delegates to the Democratic National Convention. The question is, after 35 years and $100 billion in Title I money, why shouldn't these parents conclude that the Democratic Party's opposition to choice is an example of supporting a special interest rather than their interest?

Gore responded that his stance on vouchers was not based on the opinions of the National Education Association and American Federation of Teachers—there are no stronger opponents of private school choice than these public sector unions—but on the opinions of the American people. He then reiterated his plan to double federal spending on public education. "Now, if I felt that the only alternative to vouchers was to continue things the way they are, then I would feel perhaps the same way [as the voucher supporters]," Gore told the crowd. "That's why I think that the alternative must not be this same kind of gradual change, much less status quo that we've had."

What was problematic about Gore's response from a political perspective was that he had been in the White House for the previous eight years, not to mention having served eight years in the U.S. Senate, and before that as a U.S. congressman for nearly a decade. He was calling for an end to the status quo, but from the perspective of parents he *was* the status quo. Many low-income and middle-class Democrats in the Apollo and watching on television understood this.

Bradley's response was a bit more interesting:

> Well you know, Jeff, I think you raised a very important point. There's not a parent in an urban area in America that doesn't think about it. And in fact, the reason I voted for experiments in vouchers on several occasions was because I was listening to those parents. I represented New Jersey, second-highest per capita income in the country, with five of the poorest places. I would do town meetings in Newark and Jersey City. And African American parents would come up to me and say "Our school is a disaster. Drugs, violence, teachers that aren't qualified. Nobody cares. What are you going to do about it?" And I'd say, "Well, you ought to join the school board." They'd look at me like I just descended from Mars. They'd say "Wait a minute. We join the school board? We can't. We go to work at six, get home at nine." So I voted to give them a chance with a couple of experiments. . . . But I think the answer is not vouchers, because the system isn't big enough. The answer is a major new investment in public education under Title I, but not the money just flowing in, but the money flowing in making the schools accountable for results and qualified teachers.

Bradley, who had been a supporter of school vouchers when he only needed to get reelected to the U.S. Senate by voters who adored him in New Jersey, was forced to back away from that support because he understood it's not the best way to win a low-turnout primary election where the teachers unions hold considerable electoral power nationwide. Perhaps to prove that Gore knew who was buttering his bread, Gore responded to Bradley's remarks by reminding the crowd that he supported federal hiring bonuses for new teachers. Weeks later, New York teachers showed their thanks by distributing more than a million pieces of campaign literature supporting Gore during the New York primary.[2]

At an August 2000 speech in Carthage, Tennessee, Gore explained why he thought school choice was so popular, particularly in low-income areas and the central city. "If I was the parent of a child who went to an inner city school that was failing . . . I might be for vouchers, too," Gore told the crowd.[3]

There in a nutshell is one of the major problems facing the Democratic party. What many of its constituents desperately want, the power structure of the political party simply will not allow. At best, the problem represents a political pickle for Democratic politicians. At worst, it creates a veneer of hypocrisy. As former *Washington Post* editorial writer Peter Milius once wrote: "You know the Democrats are the party that cares most about the poor because they tell you so, world without end, and bask in the glow."[4] And yet when given the option to choose between meeting the needs of schoolchildren and meeting the needs of school employees, they opt for the big people almost every single time. Democrats often allow their education policies to be entirely driven by the teachers unions, whose interests aren't necessarily the same as parents who simply want their kids to get a good education. The symbiotic relationship between the unions and the party assures that the needs of children will only be addressed after the needs of school employees.

The teachers unions have an enormous amount of power on the national, state, and local level when it comes to influencing policies and debates. They get this power because they are extremely effective political campaigners. They have discipline, long-range vision, and access to enormous amounts of money from teachers' dues to help keep their machinery operating from election to election.

Many Democratic candidates for office find themselves in a political dilemma: What the teachers want is often so out of touch with what the general public wants that candidates have to twist themselves into pretzels to please both constituencies. Up-and-coming politicians risk premature political suicide by offering any bold plans that might upset the education applecart. Any ideas that don't match the party line risk branding a candidate anti-education, antiteacher, or extremist. The unions are so effective, they not only can flex their muscle on the national level for presidential and Congressional elections but often play a crucial role in helping candidates get elected to local positions, which are often the launch pads for higher office.

Particularly in the inner city, the unions are very good at allocating their resources to control who gets to run for office—and win—as a Democrat. And it's not just the money that the unions can give to campaigns. "When you look at the young black and Latino politicians, you'd be surprised at how little money it takes to get elected when they have the backing of the unions," said Howard Fuller, former Milwaukee schools superintendent who became a national leader in the school choice and charter school movement. "What they get from the unions are the mailings and the telephone calls, and the volunteers."[5]

The unions often operate what Wisconsin political consultant Bill Christofferson calls a "turnkey campaign operation" for the candidates they support in local elections. "Typically, once they find the candidate, they run the entire campaign," Christofferson said. "They file the papers, do the phone banks, put up the yard signs, and do the fundraising. It's very difficult for a regular person who is not a teacher-backed candidate to take them on."[6] One school board member in Milwaukee, who was a Democrat, told me that during her campaign for office she received motivational calls from the teachers union almost daily, asking her whether she had knocked on any new doors doing campaign work.

The teachers unions' constant presence on the local and national political scene through the Democratic party makes it too easy for Republicans to refrain from having to come up with many creative plans for education reform as well. It becomes difficult for the education debate to ever get beyond calls for more money from Democrats and calls for more testing and lower taxes from Republicans—none of which addresses the problem that too many children aren't getting the education they need from our schools. Former Washington, D.C., Councilman Kevin Chavous, a Democrat who has been called "antiteacher" in television ads because of his support for charter schools, said it is almost impossible to convince other politicians to support radical reforms that aren't supported by the unions. "They say 'I want to do it, but I can't offend the union. They'll run me out of office. They'll run someone against me,'" Chavous said.[7]

What we see then is a political party whose leaders are unable to even discuss making fundamental changes to public education that might offend the teacher employees. John E. Coons, a retired Berkeley law professor, believes that the political and ideological left has completely lost its way on the education issue by failing to consider the needs of the least powerful citizens. As Coons describes it: "The rich choose; the poor get conscripted."

> Here is an educational system which prides itself on being "public" but which provides access to the best schools only for the rich, meanwhile herding the workers and the poor into the state schools that operate in those neighborhoods where they can afford to live. . . . Where were—and where are—those Democratic politicians who so constantly assure us of

their deep concern for the not-so-rich? So far as I can tell, the Democrats (my own party) are either running these state schools that warehouse the poor or—with the help of the teachers' unions—are busy in the legislatures and Congress making sure that nothing in this system changes except its ever-expanding cost.[8]

The problem for children in the school system is that the Democratic party is so closely linked to the teachers unions that its candidates for office often emerge as the strongest advocates for a status quo that continues to abandon and neglect the educational needs of students. An internal NEA document in 1992–93 celebrated the fact that the union "now participates in all political and senior staff meetings held by the Democratic Party."[9]

But the union's strangle hold has been starting to wear thin with some on the left. Voucher systems, which are anathema to the unions, wouldn't exist in places like Milwaukee and Cleveland were it not for support from elected Democrats who were willing to ignore the orders of party leaders.

Former Wisconsin representative Antonio Riley, an African American Democrat who represented a north-side Milwaukee neighborhood where a third of the households were on some form of public assistance, was one of the Democrats who broke with the party in 1995 to approve the expansion of the city's school choice program to include religious schools. Riley spoke on the Assembly floor challenging the party leadership and joined with the Republicans to back the measure, which was requested by governor Tommy Thompson. "I don't regret that decision whatsoever," Riley said in 1999. "I think most of the people in my district applaud my support for school choice and charter schools."[10]

Other African American Democrats in Milwaukee like representative Annette Polly Williams and senator Gary George occasionally caused their party fits by supporting school choice (see Chapter 11). "From a black perspective, this has always been about: Do you put your party before your people?" said Mikel Holt, editor and associate publisher of the *Milwaukee Community Journal*, Wisconsin's largest black newspaper.[11] Outside of Milwaukee, many other African American leaders have been faced with the same choice and made the same decision to support their constituents over their party: former Newark councilman Cory Booker, Philadelphia representative Dwight Evans, former New York representative Floyd Flake, Cleveland councilwoman Fannie Lewis, and D.C. mayor Anthony Williams.

Vouchers aren't the only education problem for Democrats. The party's willingness to let the employee unions dictate its stances on school issues bolsters the efforts of the unions to stop major changes from affecting their members. San Diego superintendent Alan Bersin and New York City chancellor Joel Klein are both Democrats who served in Democratic presidential administrations, and Los Angeles superintendent Roy Romer, a former governor of Colorado, used to be the chairman for the national party. All three have a new understanding for how frustrating the unions can be when you are trying to revive lifeless school systems. All three, in their attempts to bring major changes to their struggling school systems, have come to understand that the teachers unions and their contracts actually stand in the way of their reforms. Each has resorted to high-profile battles with the teachers unions over school policies.

Reforms like vouchers in Washington, D.C., wouldn't have become a reality without the support of Democratic mayor Anthony Williams. Other Democrats such as California senator Dianne Feinstein provided major credibility to the D.C. voucher movement early on, an action many observers felt killed her chances to run as a Democrat in the 2003 recall election of governor Gray Davis because her position so angered the California Teachers Association. Feinstein's support for Washington's most disadvantaged students showed "there's a crack in the dam among Democrats," said Lance Izumi, of the Pacific Research Institute's Center for Innovation in Education. "There will be a lot more pressure on Democrats to see school choice as a true civil right."[12]

A key question in the future will be whether the Democratic party will be run by people who favor defending institutions that clearly are not advancing the needs of children or by leaders willing to place the needs of the students first. Andrew Rotherham, a former Clinton White House aide on education issues, refers to the problem as "interest group liberalism" versus "ideas-based liberalism." He notes: "The cause of this incoherence and exhausting affinity to tired shibboleths is painfully obvious—interest group rather than ideas-based liberalism. Liberals have become beholden to institutions and organizations so today's liberal universe is essentially delineated by constellations of interest groups rather than core principals or ideas. . . . When the issue is not school spending, liberals, in no small part because of politics, too often end up siding with the adults and not the kids."[13]

It isn't difficult to understand why the unions have so much power within the party. Approximately one out of every hundred Americans is a dues-paying member of either the National Education Association or the American Federation of Teachers.[14] At the 2000 Democratic Party Convention in Los Angeles, slightly more than 12 percent of party delegates were card-carrying members of the National Education Association, which explains in part why vice presidential contender Joe Lieberman, upon being tapped to be Al Gore's running mate, was twice forced to meet privately with NEA president Bob Chase to make clear that he was quickly abandoning his past support for private school vouchers.[15] But holding 12 percent of the delegate slots only matters when the general Democratic voting population is willing to let teachers unions dictate education policy. Surely there are some delegates among the other 88 percent who believe that children should come first and adult employees second. Until their voices are raised, the minority will continue to dominate party platforms.

Conservative flame-throwing columnist Ann Coulter, reporting on the 2004 convention in Boston, joked (at least I think she was joking): "The traditional greeting at the Democratic National Convention is 'Where do you teach?' On rare occasions, the greeting is modified to, 'Where does your husband teach?' or 'Where does your gay lover teach?'" She remarked that the party could save a lot of money by holding its convention in conjunction with the NEA convention, usually held a few weeks earlier.[16]

The teachers simply have a strangle hold on the Democratic Party—something that isn't lost on others within the party, even other nonschool labor leaders. At the same 2004 convention in Boston, Andrew Stern, president of the 1.6 million-member Service Employees International Union (SEIU), the largest union in the AFL-CIO, stirred a controversy by suggesting that the party was so bankrupt that it might be better over the long term if Democratic nominee John Kerry lost the election.[17] Practically lost in the ensuing controversy over Stern's remarks were his particularly stinging comments about education—an issue very important to his low-wage earning members since their kids are the ones who are taught in the nation's struggling public schools. The *Washington Post* posted on its Web site the audiotape of Stern's remarks, which specifically mentioned the teachers union as a group that was holding back the party in terms of advancing new ideas to make schools better: "I think we are a stale party of ideas. We can't talk about education. We can't discuss when it is failing our members' (children) in public schools in urban areas. You know, we're the experiment. Maybe vouchers aren't the only answer, but then what is? I'm tired of hearing if we just pay teachers more, you know, life will be terrific. It's a huge problem."[18]

The fact that prominent Democrats were starting to talk about the party's teachers-union problem is a good thing. But it could take years before the party gets back to its roots and concentrates on meeting the needs of children over the needs of school employees. When you look at all the work the teachers do for the party as a whole, it's easy to understand why. "It's really hard when the public employees are the only growing force in the labor movement and they can provide a strong revenue stream for the Democratic party," said former Milwaukee mayor John Norquist, who himself was on the teachers' bad-boy list for years for supporting school choice and charter schools.

It's more than just money that the unions provide. The teachers unions themselves provide crucial foot soldiers for national elections, transporting union members to key swing states to assist local political workers. Because heavily Democratic New York is usually a lock for the teachers union, in the summer of 2004 city teachers were bused to Pennsylvania to do campaign work in that neighboring swing state. In the union's newspaper, an article seeking volunteers was headlined "Spend your summer helping dump Bush."[19] Teachers were also asked to volunteer over the summer if they were vacationing or passing through Arizona, Arkansas, Florida, Iowa, Maine, Michigan, Minnesota, Missouri, Nevada, New Hampshire, New Mexico, Ohio, Oregon, Pennsylvania, Washington, West Virginia, and Wisconsin. "The AFT is also targeting work in Missouri around the Aug. 3 governor's primary, where a progressive win there could take the state out of the Bush column in November," the article said. "Travel, housing, and food costs will be defrayed."[20]

Lee Cutler, a teacher at Nanuet Middle School, in the suburbs of New York City, went door-to-door in working-class neighborhoods in Wilkes-Barre, Pennsylvania, trying to register voters and drum up support for Democratic nominee John Kerry. Cutler told his union newspaper: "There's a poison in the White House and we have to get rid of it." New York City math teacher Stu Davis pounded the pavement in Bristol, Pennsylvania, and reported back that he was impressed with the union's political operation. "They had a real high-tech set-up," he said. "They knew every union member on the street. They gave us territories to cover and records that identified everyone by name and address and their party affiliation."[21]

## DEMOCRATIC DILEMMA

In 2004, Democratic nominee John Kerry hoped to dispel the popular and widespread notion that he was a traditional tax-and-spend liberal from the Northeast. Kerry initially used education to portray himself as a take-the-bull-by-the-horns leader with new ideas. Calling his school plan a "new bargain for America's teachers and children," Kerry issued the well-worn liberals call for more money for teachers while simultaneously embracing a more centrist call for results in exchange for higher pay. The "bargain," from the candidate representing the party that had long before been hijacked by the powerful teachers unions, caught some observers by surprise because it represented a sharp departure from the usual party stance and proved to be very disappointing to the union leaders.

Specifically, Kerry proposed more federal money to boost teacher salaries while requiring that states that received it loosen protections that prevented school managers from firing incompetent or ineffective teachers. "I believe that we need to offer teachers more pay, more training, more career choices, and more options for education," Kerry said on May 6, 2004, during a visit to Colton High School in San Bernardino County, California. "And we must ask more in return. That's the bargain."[22] Essentially, the bargain was between government and the nation's teachers: We'll pay you more, but you give us better results. On the need for managers to be able to fire poor teachers, Kerry told the crowd: "No one can have a lock on the job forever. . . . It's not fair to the teacher. It's not fair to the other teachers. It's not fair to the parents. And of course, it's not fair to the children."[23]

Making matters even more intriguing, Kerry's campaign released a press statement declaring that the candidate "will establish new systems that reward teachers for excellence in the classroom, *including pay based on improvement in student achievement*" (emphasis mine). The statement was striking because, as we saw in the last chapter, the national unions are hostile to any merit pay or performance-based pay that gives some teachers more than others on the same pay scale, based on the quality of their work.

For its part, the NEA, which had been specifically ordered by teacher delegates at their 2000 Chicago convention to oppose performance pay in all forms as an official union policy, released a statement saying it looked forward to finding ways to "strengthen" Kerry's proposals. By "strengthen" the union apparently meant dropping the idea that teachers should be paid based on some measurable degrees of success.

Weeks later, Mike Antonucci—who writes about the internal workings of the NEA and AFT (as well as their state and local affiliates) for an outfit he runs in California called the Education Intelligence Agency—got his hands on a confidential memo from NEA president Reg Weaver to top union brass. At a meeting union leaders had with Kerry the previous week, according to the memo, the Democratic candidate backed away from the "pay-for-performance" language in his education platform. Antonucci reported that Weaver, executive director John Wilson, and director of government relations Diane Shust met with Kerry in Washington days after Kerry floated his proposal. Weaver described what he called "a very positive meeting in which the Senator expressed strong interest in working closely with NEA and outlined his support for a number of NEA priorities."[24]

Wrote Weaver: "We raised our concerns that the Kerry campaign used the language 'pay-for-performance' in his press release, although the Senator himself did not use those words in his remarks and the formal policy document did not use it. The Senator clarified that the campaign did not intend to use that language and would not do so in the future. He asked that I convey this point to NEA leaders."[25]

Prominent Kerry education advisors denied any backtracking and brushed off the memo as a way for Weaver to save face with union members, but the message was clear: The national teachers unions still feel that they have the right to tell Democratic candidates how things are going to work as far as education is concerned. From that moment forward, merit pay was never discussed by the campaign.

Others wondered why Kerry even felt the need to tiptoe around the unions at all. "It's not like the teachers are going to withdraw their support and suddenly support Bush," one education leader who advised Kerry told me weeks later. "As long as the teachers are going to be a liability, they should start getting used to this kind of dissent."

A rift between Kerry and the NEA, whether genuine or itself perhaps contrived for political purposes to make Kerry look like he wasn't a puppet of the unions, continued to play itself out into the summer. For reasons that some attributed to stupidity and others claimed was smart politics in the war over moderate voters, Kerry chose to announce that he had selected South Carolina senator John Edwards to be his running mate on the same day that he was scheduled to appear before the National Education Association's 10,000-delegate Representative Assembly as it was meeting in Washington. The union had even postponed votes on changes to its bylaws to accommodate the busy candidate. Kerry made the tactical decision to back out of his scheduled speech before the union as he basked in the media glow of his veep selection. Some observers noted that such a decision was a clear sign that the Kerry campaign had come to view the teachers' support as a liability in a nation that was increasingly hungry for dramatic change in its schools.

NEA president Reg Weaver was furious at the snub. "Are we disappointed? Yep. Are we angry? Yep," Weaver told delegates from the podium where he presided for the entire day without once even uttering Kerry's name. Weaver's lack of enthusiasm was noteworthy because election-year teacher conventions usually serve as pep rallies for the party's major candidates. Later in the day, in a display of histrionics designed to save face for the union's political clout, Weaver took a call on his cell phone while he was standing at the podium. Holding the phone up toward the delegates, Weaver said: "I'm not going to tell you who this is, but tell them who you are." At the prompt, directing their chants toward what they assumed was a high-ranking Democratic party leader, delegates began chanting, "We are NEA!"[26]

After getting yipped at by union leaders, Kerry and Edwards a day later beamed themselves into the Washington assembly via satellite television from Cleveland, Ohio, where they were campaigning. Weaver assured the crowd that he wasn't the only one from the NEA who had been flexing some union muscle with party leaders and the Kerry campaign. "I believe the campaign heard from many of your state presidents," Weaver told the crowd.[27]

The scorned union found itself in the unusual position of having to remind the party how much power it held in its hands, another sign that the party leaders were aware of the problems the union was causing its candidates. Weaver, for instance, opened his summer convention by saying, "Our message to the Democrats is going to be: 'Don't take us for granted. We'll support you if you demonstrate support for public education.'"[28] Kerry, meanwhile, spent the rest of the summer trying to carefully keep the teachers off his back while trying to appeal to a larger public that had grown impatient with the organized obstacles to school reform.

Antonucci, who for several years has provided gavel to gavel coverage of both national union conventions on his Web site, picked up on one tactic that Kerry used when he addressed American Federation of Teachers delegates at their annual convention in Washington a few weeks later. He found that Kerry's speech to the teachers was written in a way that loaded the first half of his sentences with his calls for more spending, which produced loud applause from the crowd that often drowned out the calls for reform included in the second half.

The script played out something like this:

> Kerry: Pay for teachers in America today is a national disgrace. We need to raise it . . .
> AFT delegates: (wild, enthusiastic applause)
> Kerry (amid the applause): . . . starting in the poorest schools and in the subjects where we face the most serious teacher shortages.
> Kerry: We need to offer teachers more . . .
> AFT delegates: (more wild, enthusiastic applause)
> Kerry (amid the applause): . . . and ask more of them at the same time.

Kerry: Teachers deserve due process protection from arbitrary dismissal . . .

AFT delegates: (more wild, enthusiastic applause)

Kerry (amid the applause): . . . but we must have fast, fair procedures for improving or removing teachers who aren't performing.[29]

Critics might call it talking out of both sides of your mouth, but such criticism ignores the simple fact that it is next to impossible for a Democrat to run for president without bowing to the NEA and AFT. This is a major problem for the party and crippling in terms of its ability to come out on the children's side on education issues. More than one prominent Democratic education policy person told me that their advice to Kerry at the start of the election season was simply not to say anything at all about education since the unions had no one else to support anyway. Reg Weaver and AFT president Sandy Feldman were never going to share their podium with President Bush, the thinking went, so why bother making it sound like you are offering something to the unions that simultaneously alienates mainstream voters? Before Kerry's snub of the NEA, union delegates voted 7,390 to 1,153 to endorse him as a union the following November. There wasn't much chance that number would change in favor of a Republican, no matter how Kerry treated the union.

## REPUBLICANS ON THE HOOK, TOO

Much of this chapter has focused on the Democratic Party because, honestly, it seems natural that the Democrats should be the ones to champion the plight of those underserved by our education system. Much of the current system's dysfunction is concentrated in urban areas, which tend to lean Democratic. While education in the Republican suburbs also has its share of problems, the problems tend not to be as severe as in the cities.

If the problem with Democrats is that they allow themselves to be co-opted by the teachers unions, the problem with Republicans over the last several decades is that they have managed to be co-opted by their own hatred for those same teachers unions and their apparent disdain for spending tax money on schools in general. If the Democrats have been defined by their opposition to major system-shaking reforms, the Republicans have been defined by the opposition to paying any of the bills that come with education. If the Democrats are unwilling, or unable, to take bold steps on education issues, Republicans have shown a tendency to talk a big game when it comes to schools, even though they rarely deliver anything meaningful.

Just like the union's constant negativity within school reform discussions, the Republicans' 20-year drumbeat against education spending has done little to improve learning for students. From the moment president Jimmy Carter created the U.S. Education Department as a cabinet-level position—itself a political gift to the National Education Association in exchange for work done on the campaign trail[30]—the right wing's obsession over the intrusion of the federal government into the realm of education was hardly a stance that would revolutionize modern school systems. Republicans also got sidetracked by their own pandering to religious conservatives by suggesting that allowing prayer in schools would somehow make things better.

Too often, the education politics of Republicans seems focused on winning incremental political battles with the teachers union and not on making the kinds of reforms that effect wholesale change in school systems. In fact, some Republicans view weakening the teachers unions to be an end in itself, helping to weaken the organizational support of their partisan opponents, rather than as a means to helping kids learn in better-functioning schools.

Republicans occasionally have offered support for school choice, but fell short in offering solid solutions to problems within the system. Some Republicans viewed programs such as vouchers both as a way to avoid the public schools, rather than a way to give parents the power to jolt the existing system into a more customer-friendly mode of operation, and as a way to avoid arming the system with the supports necessary to compete in a way that meets the needs of all students. The reality is that even with a competitive education marketplace, most students still will be educated in public schools. By not addressing the problems within the public school system, school choice simply won't be able to provide a majority of students the education they need. As Frederick Hess argues, market-driven school reforms are not self-executing, meaning someone still needs to orchestrate the reform of the larger systems to make them appealing choices within the marketplace. "In the absence of broader organizational and institutional changes, choice-driven competition is unlikely to deliver the results that its proponents desire," Hess notes.[31]

In large part, Republicans viewed vouchers as an answer to the question of whether private schools are better than public schools, rather than a question of who is best suited to make that decision for each child. The views of many Republicans are in line with their general support for privatization, not with a movement to improve public education by offering more choices.

Some Republicans don't appear to understand the policies they supposedly endorse. Consider the case of Harvey Milk High School in New York City. The alternative school's conversion to a full-fledged public school in 2003 caused a major uproar from conservatives who seemed bothered by the fact that the school specifically caters to gay, lesbian, and transgendered students.

Prominent Republican school choice supporters like former Florida Representative Joe Scarborough (now a television commentator) sneered at the school, despite the fact that the school's enrollment showed that the "school of choice" was entirely supported by the marketplace. The editorial pages of the *New York Post*, normally friendly to the idea of choice, quickly trashed the entire concept of the school. Suddenly, conservatives like New York Conservative Party leader Mike Long, who are usually quick to talk about the virtues of market forces, felt that the choices of these particular students didn't count. School choice, it seems, is only good when the right wing approves of all the options.

In New York City in 2004, the right-leaning *New York Post* also editorialized in favor of closing Harlem's Reisenbach Charter School after its fifth year of existence because it had low test scores. It was a position that many Republican charter school advocates supported, based on the notion that high standards needed to be coupled with tough-minded accountability. The same editorial, however, called for tuition vouchers for students—a curious departure from the rest of the editorial since voucher programs generally rely on parents (not editorial writers) to decide which schools are best for their kids. In the case of the Reisenbach parents, they had done their homework and their argument against closure of this charter school was that even with its acknowledged shortcomings, it still was better than then surrounding public schools that the students would be forced to attend once it was closed. "We know what's out there and it isn't much," parent Beverly Patoir told me as the fate of the school was being considered. In the end, the power of the Reisenbach parents was ripped away from them by the state, the school was closed, and the students were forced to enroll in public schools whose performance in many cases was rated lower than the closed charter school.

I have met Republicans who understand school choice; many others, like the editorial writers at the *Post*, seem to think that parental choice shouldn't really be in the hands of parents but in the hands of an elite group of decision makers. This attitude ignores the most interesting (and powerful) segment of the school choice constituency: African American and Hispanic parents who are sick of substandard schools and policies thrust upon them by the white establishment. Attracting these parents to a larger political constituency will require a complete rethinking of the approaches used by each political party on education issues. The party that is first to recognize school parents as consumers will find itself with a ground swell of new support.

## RIGHT IDEA, LAME IMPLEMENTATION

Republican president George W. Bush in 2000 took his party in a different direction entirely on education issues, several times stealing centrist issues that probably should have been embraced long ago by Democrats. Rather than proposing the elimination of the U.S. Education Department and reduced federal funding for education, Bush showed an understanding that there could be a productive role for Washington to play in local schools. His calls for testing of all students, tied to federal funding for schools, allowed him to vividly explain that his brand of compassionate conservatism would battle "the soft bigotry of low expectations."[32] Because the Democrats were such staunch supporters of a status quo that allowed those low expectations for special education, minority, and non-English speaking students, it was an easy void for Bush to fill.

Democrats have made it very easy for Republicans to take the high road, even if the GOP does a lousy job of taking advantage of it. Democrats, for example, use up political capital advocating for more money for costly programs like Head Start, which assists low-income and other at-risk students in preparing for kindergarten. It makes it easy for Republicans to propose "reforms" with specific targets such as more intensive use of research-based early childhood literacy programs in Head Start classrooms. Basically, the Republicans force Democrats to argue in favor of more blank checks without accountability, reinforcing the notion that Democrats don't care about quality or results. It's a maddening practice.

Education has typically been an issue owned by the Democrats in national races. Republican nominee Bob Dole self-destructed in 1996 after he criticized teachers unions in debates and stump speeches but offered little more than a plan to abolish the federal Department of Education as a way to improve America's schools. Only 16 percent of voters polled that year believed Dole was stronger on education issues than the incumbent, President Clinton.[33]

The gap was nearly closed in 2000, however. Bush, whose own children attended public schools in Texas, used education to help show he was a "compassionate conservative," pushing plans for greater accountability of school systems and even private school vouchers for students trapped in failing schools. In an election that was so close it came down to a few hundred votes (and a controversial recount and Supreme Court decision) in Florida, Bush was able to cut away at the Democrats' dominance on the education issue. Exit polls showed Bush captured 44 percent of voters who made education an issue, compared with 52 percent for Democratic vice president Al Gore. "The Republicans went from minus 62 to minus 8," Republican pollster David Winston told the *National Journal*, describing the change in the gap between the parties on election issues. "That difference would have been enough for Gore to outright win."[34]

I know many Democrats who cast ballots for Bush in 2000 because they felt he would do a better job of moving power from bureaucrats to parents. Pilar Gomez, a single mother of four whom I knew when I worked in Milwaukee, was even asked to be a prime-time speaker during the 2000 Republican National Convention in Philadelphia, despite the fact that she had been a Democrat for many years. "Parents know what works: more flexibility, more accountability, and more choice," Gomez said in her televised speech, which helped portray what was supposed to be a kinder, gentler GOP. Gomez, one of many parents I met who had children in both public and private schools (under Milwaukee's voucher program), had been hoping that Bush would help put parents in charge of their kids' education. She was willing to break ranks with her party because she felt that parents have an obligation to fight for their children rather than accept the status quo. "On the issue closest to my heart, the education of my children and my right to choose their schools, party lines fade," Gomez told the cheering delegates.

Bush's platform eventually became known as the federal No Child Left Behind Law and required states to continue mandatory testing for all students while offering students in schools deemed "in need of improvement" either tutoring outside of the schools or transfers to other schools that weren't failing. Democrats like Gomez, who switched parties because of Bush's support for vouchers, would emerge profoundly disappointed by the Republicans' inability to deliver. In order to have the law pass Congress with bipartisan support, Bush quickly caved on the issue of including private schools in the mix of schools that could receive transferring students. This severely limited the choices available to low-income parents with kids stuck in educational disasters in inner cities.

When Republicans don't live up to their rhetoric on the education issue, it makes for some good political theater when reform-minded Democrats call them on it in public. One day after Republicans stripped private school choice from No Child Left Behind, Milwaukee mayor John O.

Norquist ripped President Bush for not taking school choice seriously enough to expend political capital on the controversial cause. "It's not easy to do, but he hasn't tried," Norquist said at the time.[35]

Not only did the Republican administration not fight the good fight for parents of kids in failing schools in the deliberations, it also failed to stick up for parents when it came time to implement the law. Foot-dragging bureaucrats all over the country showed little inclination to make the limited, public school choice portion of the laws available, and the Bush administration largely remained silent. Opponents of the law (often led by the teachers unions) attacked it from all directions while Republicans during Bush's first term sat back without offering much of a spirited defense.

The Bush administration's ineptitude on the No Child Left Behind issue made national headlines in early 2005 when *USA Today* reporter Greg Toppo reported that the U.S. Education Department had secretly paid $240,000 to pundit and syndicated columnist Armstrong Williams, an African American conservative, to actively promote and support No Child Left Behind. Months before the propaganda scheme was revealed, the department admitted that it had maintained a secret ranking of journalists based on how friendly to the law they were perceived to be. Observers noted that if they had spent as much time implementing the law as they spent ranking the news reporters (not to mention the hundreds of thousands of dollars spent on outside consultants to compile the rankings), thousands of children nationwide might have benefited in the process. Furthermore, since Williams had already been a supporter of the law before the administration secretly offered him the $240,000 propaganda payment, critics suggested that the Bush administration didn't even understand how to bribe people. The money, they said sarcastically, should have been given to an *opponent* of No Child Left Behind. Both Education Department public relations scandals, the rankings, and the Williams payment, caused former Clinton aide Andrew Rotherham to refer to the federal educrats as "the gang that can't flack straight" in the *New York Times*.[36]

There were legitimate concerns raised in school systems in the wake of No Child Left Behind, issues that would have been better addressed by departments other than public relations. Some critics argued that allowing concerned parents to free their children from failing schools, combined with the practice of demanding results in exchange for federal funding, would make it extremely difficult for those failing schools to ever work themselves off the failing list. Taking the most engaged families out of failing schools at a time when the schools must show improvement was counterproductive, they said. Some also worried that an influx of kids from failing schools would bring down the test scores at good schools, helping turn them into failing schools. This is a good example of the kind of thinking that places the needs of institutions ahead of the needs and desires of the students and families they are supposed to serve. (Imagine this alternative version of the same argument: It's not fair to judge inner-city public schools because all of the best students and their families decided long ago to move to the suburbs where the schools are better.)

Another common complaint regarding No Child Left Behind in its first two years was that good schools were often being unfairly tainted because various subgroups of the student population weren't faring so well. In the summer of 2004, a group called Communities for Quality Education (launched by the National Education Association) called a press conference at Reno High School in Reno, Nevada, to complain that the law could lead to sanctions for the popular school because it tested its way onto the state's list of failing schools. "Reno High School is widely acknowledged to be one of the best high schools in the United States," said Dan Geary of Las Vegas, a spokesman for the group. "It has been featured in *Newsweek* magazine twice as one of the top high schools in the nation for preparing kids for college. It has many distinguished alumni who are state leaders, scientists, doctors, and lawyers. And along comes the federal government and gives it a failing grade."[37]

How did such a good school make the failing list? For starters, the percentage of special education students at the school who took the state's math and reading tests didn't reach the 95 percent mark, as required by the law. Second, those special education students who did take the test scored very low and were not making "adequately yearly progress" as the law provides. The whole concept of adequate yearly progress has been controversial from the start. Schools in which student scores are low but improving won't necessarily make the list, while schools in which student scores are high but slipping, might. Still, the complaint raised by the teachers union at Reno High School sends a clear message that some educators don't expect much from special education students in terms of achievement.

By breaking down the scores by race and type of student, parents are able to look at school performance in new and possibly more meaningful ways. While the critics wondered how such a good school could end up on the failing list, it's not difficult to imagine a special education parent at Reno High School wondering why the school had ever been singled out by *Newsweek* if it was allowing so many special education students to fall through the cracks. Surely those students count too. Reno High School journalism teacher Dan Halcomb told reporters that the No Child Left Behind Law was hurting teacher morale. But what about the morale of those special education students? It's a question we're not used to asking because we've been conditioned to judge various school reforms over the years based on how teachers feel about them, not by how parents and students feel about them.

For an entire generation, parents have been told to sit still and be patient while school leader after school leader rides into town and promises reform. Such calls to cool their jets are nothing short of enraging for the parents and their children who must attend the substandard schools that are always being reformed in one way or another. Bush and his administration talked a big game about radical change, but when it came to enforcing their own law, they were nowhere to be found.

The federal government spends an awful lot of money on local public education around the country. Since the passage of the 1965 Elementary and Secondary Education Act (later altered to become No Child Left Behind), federal education spending ballooned from around $25 billion (using inflation-adjusted figures for comparison) to more than $108 billion in 2002, yet student achievement has generally remained flat.[38]

Since the U.S. Constitution says absolutely nothing about the federal government's role in education, states have always had the right to turn down the federal government's money if they didn't wish to follow the mandates from Washington. While many local critics have complained of unfunded mandates and unfair requirements under No Child Left Behind, the original 1965 law was considered one of the main methods of enforcing the Civil Rights Act of 1964, which prohibited discrimination based on race, color, or national origin. Basically, back in 1965, if you wanted to get a share of federal funds, you had to do something about your segregated schools.[39]

Rooted in the education reforms President Bush oversaw as governor of Texas, the original purpose of the federal No Child Left Behind Law was to attach some accountability strings to all that money. The feds were to provide significantly increased grants to districts that would use "scientifically based" reading programs, require annual testing in reading and math to measure student progress, and provide an escape hatch so that students in perennially struggling schools could take their federal money with them to another public or private school of their choice.[40]

The Bush administration quickly decided in negotiations that the private school choice remedy was a deal-killer for many of the Democrats whose support was needed in order to pass the law. It was dropped in favor of a public school choice provision.

*City Journal* writer Sol Stern wrote that a second concession in negotiations over the law changed the definition of a failing school. The original definition pushed by the Bush administration judged schools based on school-wide test scores, but liberal Democrats, Stern wrote, wanted to include schools in which a small racial or ethnic subgroup had poor scores, even if the majority of students were performing on grade level.[41] "Some of the Democrats on the other side didn't want to say that it's OK to have one group falling behind in a school," the administration's point man Sandy Kress told Stern. "In effect, they were telling us that if you really want to say, 'No Child Left Behind,' then let's really leave no child behind."[42]

No Child Left Behind was supposed to both force school systems to improve—or shut down—their failing schools over the long term and offer an educational lifeboat to a better school for students and families in the short term. One of the biggest failures of President Bush's education administration, however, was its failure to get tough with school leaders who dragged their feet.

On September 25, 2002, U.S. education secretary Rod Paige appeared at Samuel Gompers High School in the Bronx, along with New York mayor Michael Bloomberg and schools chancellor Joel Klein. The visit came just weeks after New York State had released its schools-in-need-of-improvement list and parents were told they would not be allowed to exercise their rights to transfer. Parents were furious that they were not able to take advantage of the new law because local school officials wouldn't let them.

In a move that showed the federal government, New York State, and the city Department of Education weren't really serious about the law, both Mayor Bloomberg and Secretary Paige urged parents to once again pipe down and be patient while their kids wasted their time attending failing schools. "Joel Klein and I are here to ensure that there is no need to get tutoring or to move their child to a better school," Bloomberg told reporters with Paige and Klein at his side. "We have said we will make the schools better and we will."[43]

Both Bloomberg and Klein sent their children to elite private schools, exercising their right and responsibility as parents to seek the best possible education for their offspring. Their message to parents who earned as much in a year as top private schools charge for tuition: Quit your moaning, we politicians are working on it.

Perhaps it was because Bloomberg is nominally a Republican and because Paige worked for a Republican administration, but the Education

Secretary allowed a golden opportunity to put his foot down pass him by right then and there. In an instant, New Yorkers understood the No Child Left Behind law was meaningless in their city. "We know there are some problems, but this has never been tried before," Paige told reporters, who egged him on for several minutes, trying to get him to criticize what was widely acknowledged to be a horrible implementation by city school leaders.

To Bloomberg's credit, several months later he publicly acknowledged that his 32 school districts had done a lame job serving parents and implementing No Child Left Behind. Bloomberg and Klein centralized the transfer process for 2003–04, but they made it harder than necessary for parents to avail themselves of the opportunity to transfer their children. Parents needed to first apply in order to get a second "transfer application" and were sent letters (with a Virginia return address) informing them about the process that didn't actually even use the word "transfer" until the second page. School officials did process transfers for all 7,000 students who went through the arduous procedure of requesting them.

A year later, however, in the summer of 2004, Klein announced that for 2004–05 the department would do less to comply with the law, because he worried that too many transfers would "destabilize" the city's few good schools by flooding them with students from failing schools.

New York City's experience with free tutoring, or Supplemental Educational Services was even more disappointing than the transfers. One of the biggest problems in New York City was simply the incompetence of administrators at the Tweed Courthouse headquarters in informing parents about the tutoring programs. Educrats held informational forums on the Friday night and Saturday morning of Yom Kippur weekend but didn't send the flyers announcing them to students until that Friday at the earliest. The flyers were stuck in students backpacks on the start of the holiday weekend and no one seemed to know about them.

I showed up at one of the Saturday forums, held at Manhattan's Washington Irving High School, and I was the only one there who didn't work for the education department. More scarcely attended forums were held two weeks later, which also happened to be Columbus Day weekend, though attendance was sparse at those as well. "We're not getting enough information early enough," complained Maria Dilworth of the Brooklyn neighborhood group Cypress Hills Advocates for Education. "Using children as a delivery service just doesn't work."[44]

Critics accused education officials of botching the notification process to keep private tutoring costs low, thereby freeing up federal money for other projects. "It's mind-numbing, because this is one of the most critical choices a parent can make about a child's education—and these are kids who are already in failing schools," said lawyer Charlie King. King pursued a lawsuit on behalf of parents who say they were denied school services; the suit was dismissed on jurisdictional grounds.[45]

On October 14, 2003, while I was visiting Walton High School in the Bronx, students told me they had just been given the booklets containing applications for the Supplemental Educational Services tutoring. The application deadline was October 15. It was no wonder then that the response was less than stellar. To add insult to injury, after many uninformed parents missed the deadline for applying, educrats offered parents a "grace period" to respond, implying that it was the parents who had done something wrong. "To me it means forgiveness," explained Andres Alonzo, the chief of staff to deputy chancellor Diana Lam, at a City Council hearing on No Child Left Behind implementation. Councilwoman Eva Moskowitz, chairwoman of the Education Committee, retorted: "Forgiveness is something parents should be giving to DOE,"[46] because she felt it was the parents who had been treated poorly, not the bureaucrats.

Clearly, the controversial law for the first time introduced the novel notion that school spending is supposed to be somehow linked to student performance, something that was controversial in itself. What was problematic, however, was the Bush administration's apparent belief that passing the law was somehow more important than implementing it. After the law was signed in 2002, the feds were extremely slow in issuing guidelines and other advisories, which allowed foot-dragging bureaucrats, who never seemed eager to implement the law, to delay giving parents any new rights regarding their kids' schools. Even after three school years under the law, education secretary Rod Paige continued to use a laissez-faire approach to its implementation, sending mixed messages to both bureaucrats and parents about the administration's sincerity. As the *New York Times* editorial page opined during the 2004 presidential race: "The government agency in charge of the most important education reform in 100 years lacks the capacity, courage, and leadership to do its job."[47]

So here is the dilemma for parents who want more power over their children's education: The Democrats don't seem able to even talk about giving it to them, while the Republicans seem to be all talk and no action.

Parents must continue to make the case, however, that they are the ones best equipped to put the needs of their kids first—and they must start punishing politicians of both parties who stand in their way. Without this parental resolve, education reform will continue to involve tinkering at the margins.

# 8

# FRIENDS WITH DEEP POCKETS

Education philanthropists provide enormous sums of money for schools, whose leaders often are not in a position to look a gift horse in the mouth. In 2002 alone, donors gave nearly $1.7 billion to education causes (excluding libraries and higher education)—more than twice what had been given only three years earlier.[1] Their donations help school officials across the country implement reform strategies, such as pay-for-performance schemes for school employees and administrative restructuring, that would be difficult if not impossible to afford using their regular operating budgets. This reliance on private money adds yet another other level to the politics of education, and creates yet another potential hurdle for those who wish to make sure kids really do come first in schools.

The big buzz in recent years has been the creation of small schools and the conversion of large high schools into smaller "schools within schools." The movement has been almost entirely driven by philanthropy, particularly the Bill & Melinda Gates Foundation, which has dangled millions of dollars in front of school leaders all across the nation to promote the cause. Other prominent foundations like the Carnegie Corporation of New York have joined in as well.

In New York City, chancellor Joel Klein made the creation of new small schools one of his first priorities upon taking the job in the summer of 2002. Speaking at a luncheon sponsored by the Carnegie Corporation in early October of that year, Klein pledged to build 200 new small high schools over the course of the next several years. "There is a great deal of wisdom in the concept," Klein told the crowd. Several things were odd about the announcement of such an ambitious plan, one that would obviously consume the energy of the system's top people for years to come. The first was that up until that point, there had been very little public discourse in the city about the desirability of small schools or even about their effectiveness. In fact, there didn't appear to be a clear public consensus as to which of the many problems facing the city's high schools the small schools plan was meant to solve: low graduation rates, a lack of rigorous college-prep type programs, rampant violence and crime, et cetera. In fact, the most popular public high schools in the city—places such as Stuyvesant and Bronx Science—are large high schools and people were willing to shell out big bucks for tutoring to help give their kids an edge on the annual entrance exams. What's more, the complaint that some of the city's large high schools were persistently horrible had much more to do with the fact that they were persistently horrible than that they were large. If anything, parents in New York City at the time Klein announced the small schools push were much more interested in smaller class sizes than smaller schools.

The city's Department of Education officials treated the small school movement as if it was a solution to what had ailed the city's high schools for years—namely, a dangerously low graduation rate of only about 50 percent. But the cries for reform from the public seldom appeared to be "Give us smaller schools." It would be 20 months before the fast-moving small schools plans would be formally debated in public. Even then, it wasn't the Department of Education that conducted the hearing, but the City Council's Education Committee. Top educrats, after working in the dark for so long, were forced into a defensive stance at the oversight hearings.

Even more noteworthy than the lack of discussion or the apparent lack of parental demand for the small schools was the notion that a great deal of the hype behind the movement had been generated by foundations that favored the small school idea. The findings of years' worth of studies on the impact of small schools varied from highly positive to little impact. New York's own experience was filled with successful and unsuccessful small schools. Yet, there was the cash, dangling in front of the faces of school leaders in New York and across America. Millions and millions of dollars were there for the taking, with the only strings attached being an arranged marriage with the small school concept.

There is considerable debate over whether reforms like smaller high schools are evidence-based or merely fads that pick up steam because there is free money behind them. U.S. education secretary Rod Paige warned philanthropists in 2002 that too many schools were "jerked off center" by people offering private cash to needy schools to advance their pet reforms.[2] Paige urged school districts to turn down private money if it didn't fit with their mission.

The Gates Foundation offered New York City more than $50 million to turn large, out-of-control high schools into smaller schools-within-schools. The money was used to develop specialized programs (like environmental studies or law enforcement), each of which has its own principal and staff and, ideally, a floor or corner of the larger building.

Gates is certainly not alone. A growing number of well-heeled and well-meaning philanthropists are influencing important policies in school systems nationwide by simply opening up their checkbooks. Paige's advice of caution is important to heed if you view public education as a public service where the decision makers are accountable to the public. It is one thing to seek philanthropic help in implementing reforms that a local community and local school leaders have decided are a priority; it is another to allow outside philanthropic contributions to drive the policy decisions that affect a local community.

I am not alleging here that Chancellor Klein based his policy decision on the small schools money. In fact, his selection of Michele Cahill, who researched small schools for the Carnegie Corporation, as one of his top aides was a signal that the small school movement likely would have a prominent role in his reforms. I also don't mean to imply that Klein and his team didn't have their own goals for the small schools; over time it became apparent that they were focused intently on improving the city's dismal graduation rates. That said, the question of "where did this plan come from?" is an important one for voters and local taxpayers to strongly consider. If the pet project of the moment turns out not to work, for example, will the private entities endorsing them be held accountable? And while funding may be "private," if seed money is eventually expected to be replaced by tax money, the act of philanthropy has very public purposes and should be treated that way by policymakers.

A valid question that was constantly raised by observers of New York City's school system during this time period was whether or not the city was sacrificing quality by moving so quickly to establish so many of these new programs. In the fall of 2004 alone, the city created 53 new small high schools, many of them located inside existing large high schools. In a city whose high school problems were substantial, the fast pace was more than justified. But some of the city's new small high schools for the 2004–05 school year weren't even unveiled in time for the first rounds of the city's high school admissions process the previous fall. Some observers questioned if the city was moving so quickly because of a sense of urgency for the needs of the students or because the Gates money came with its own set of timelines that were driving the policies.

Other concerns have been raised nationally about the potential civic impact on such policy-driving gifts from wealthy donors, the most compelling being whether or not such reliance on philanthropy further disenfranchises the public from its public school system. Barbara Dudley, former executive director of Greenpeace USA, caused waves in philanthropic circles in 1999 when she penned an opinion peace for the *Chronicle of Philanthropy* in which she decried the public's reliance on Gates to make reform happen in high schools. "The flaw . . . is that Bill Gates isn't accountable to anyone—and when important decisions about public policy are made by wealthy individuals rather than by local citizens or elected officials, people lose faith in our system of democracy," Dudley wrote. "They no longer believe that their opinion, or their vote, or their participation in civic life matters."[3]

The history of the small schools movement is fascinating in this regard. What is noteworthy about the Carnegie Corporation's interest in small schools, for example, is that Carnegie was also primarily responsible for breathing life into the "large school movement" of the 1960s, which the new "small school movement" was seeking to reverse.

Using a grant from Carnegie for his studies, James B. Conant in 1959 published *The American High School Today: A First Report to Interested Citizens*, which was a call to arms against high schools that he considered too small to offer an adequate education for both college-bound students and those for whom high school would be the peak of their academic experience. Conant by no means invented the concept of the large comprehensive high school—for much of the twentieth century it was in play to varying degrees. Still, his work, backed by additional Carnegie grants that followed, set in motion a philanthropic drumbeat for the idea as a way for America to remain strong internationally in the cold war era. Carnegie president John Gardner, in the foreword to Conant's book, described such a high school as being "responsible for educating the boy who will be an atomic scientist and the girl who will marry at 18; the prospective captain of a ship and the future captain of industry."

Conant, who had just finished his stint as ambassador to Germany during its post–World War II reconstruction, argued that it wasn't the large size that would automatically improve the quality of education, but the system's increased ability to efficiently provide lots of options for students in terms of academic and elective course offerings. He noted that if a senior class was too small, and only a quarter of the students were capable of taking advanced subjects, it would be difficult to justify offering those subjects. "To provide adequate teachers for specialized subjects is extremely expensive," Conant wrote. "Furthermore, to maintain an interest in academic subjects among a small number is not always easy. Wide academic programs are not likely to be offered when the academically talented in a school are so few in number."[4]

To be sure, American education followed Conant's and the Carnegie's lead, the end-result being the creation in the 1960s of large high schools that often resembled small universities. To understand and appreciate the role that philanthropists play in policy, one must understand that it was foundation money that drove the large high school movement in the 1960s, and today some of the same foundation's money is driving the small high school movement.

Even more curious in hindsight, Conant, in a chapter titled "Elimination of the Small High School—A Top Priority," offers this conclusion: "Citizens who wish to improve public education might well devote their energies to mobilizing opinion on behalf of district reorganization directed toward the reduction of the number of small high schools."[5]

If foolish consistencies are truly the hobgoblins of little minds, as Ralph Waldo Emerson contended, then education philanthropists have proven over the years that they know the secret to exorcising those hobgoblins: the simple flip-flop. Like many of the situations described in this book, the flip-flop itself is not a bad thing if it is based on newer and better information that becomes available. The interested public should understand, however, that the same high-powered donors who today may declare that children would be best taught in classrooms with blue walls just may be the same people who insist that we repaint the walls yellow a quarter century from now.

## MODERN SCHOOL PHILANTHROPY

At the time, it was hailed as the largest ever gift of its kind to public education. In 1993, publisher and philanthropist Walter Annenberg (a former ambassador to Great Britain) announced at the White House that he was giving $500 million to improve public education systems in the United States. Annenberg explained that he was bothered by violence in schools, and that he believed that improving education itself might have an impact on reducing classroom violence. Said Annenberg in his brief remarks:

> I do not believe the Annenberg Foundation's $500 million challenge grant over five years will do the whole job. This must be a challenge to the nation. At this point I can't see any other way to guarantee our nation's future. A number of foundations and corporations already are providing

funds to aid schools in what has become a nationwide education reform movement. It will take individual giving, corporate giving, and foundation giving to do the job. I believe those who control sizable funds should feel an obligation to join this crusade for the betterment of our country.[6]

Annenberg dubbed his philanthropy a "challenge to the nation," and his subsequent grants to projects in 35 states became known as the Annenberg Challenge. More than 1,600 businesses, foundations, colleges, and fellow philanthropists contributed more than $600 million in matching grants over the course of the challenge, which lasted until 2003.

Despite the word "challenge" in its name and mission, the grants represented a very nonconfrontational approach to reforming the education system. School leaders had nothing to lose by endorsing the efforts of local universities and community groups who were required to work together to enhance the work of the overall public school system. The "challenge" was directed at other donors and community groups, not at the status quo of the school systems Annenberg was trying to assist. As Frederick Hess notes, this type of education philanthropy generally promoted "capacity building" within the existing system and presumed that the chief cause of educational failure was a lack of expertise or funds within the system.[7]

Most of the Annenberg money went to nine large, urban school districts: San Francisco, Boston, Chicago, Detroit, Houston, Los Angeles, New York City, Philadelphia, and South Florida. It funded arts education, leadership development, consultants, and other programs that provided school's leaders with technical assistance from intermediary groups.

In New York City, Annenberg provided a $25 million grant over five years to stimulate the creation of new small schools beginning in 1995. It required matching contributions of $25 million each from local philanthropists and city government, and was designed both to increase public school choice and to transform the overall system. The requirements of the grant were such that the mayor, Rudy Giuliani, the schools chancellor, Ramon Cortines and the teachers union were required to work collaboratively together and with several other partner organizations (including the nonprofit New Visions, which served as the fiscal agent) to implement the small schools reform. Requiring the collective buy-in of all of these divergent groups essentially eliminated any chance that radical change would occur from their work; reaching a consensus often required finding a lowest-common denominator of agreement.

Because the small school movement in New York City predated Annenberg's challenge, much of the Annenberg grant went toward strengthening existing small schools rather than stimulating a new supply. The grant did, however, give more legitimacy to the small schools, particularly those housed in larger buildings. Prior to the grant, for example, test scores and other demographic data at the small schools were lumped together with the larger schools that housed them, a condition that began to change under the grant. By the end of five years and beyond, however, the grants could hardly have been seen as having driven major change, and certainly did not transform the New York City schools system in as radical a way as Annenberg had intended.

In 2003, a decade after the grants were first announced, researchers from the Annenberg Foundation wrote a generally positive self-evaluation of the efforts. "The independent researchers tracking the challenge . . . are accumulating substantial evidence of student gains, including examples of student accomplishment not easily captured in a test score," wrote national coordinator Barbara Cervone.[8] But independent evaluations of Annenberg's largesse were less complimentary. Wrote the Thomas B. Fordham Foundation's Chester Finn in a 2000 analysis of challenge grants in New York, San Francisco, and Philadelphia:

> While students in some schools surely benefited from this unprecedented private generosity, the system as a whole was largely unresponsive. Our conclusion is that the main reason these grants didn't accomplish more was because the essential idea on which they were based—that what public schools most lack is expertise and that talented and motivated outsiders working with the system can provide this—is itself erroneous. . . . One could simply conclude that Ambassador Annenberg didn't get much for his money, at least not by way of improved student achievement or the kinds of systemwide changes or policy revolutions that hold reasonable likelihood of yielding major gains in the near future.[9]

At the very least, however, many philanthropists—including those at the Annenberg Challenge—believe the effort set a road map for those who followed, with important lessons about what works and what doesn't. "I think they've learned some lessons from us," said Mary Neuman, national coordinator for the Annenberg Challenge, in 2003. "They've learned to be focused and not have a bunch of initiatives at once."[10]

The vibrant economy of the late 1990s combined with a heightened awareness in the private sector that public education needed a major jolt translated into millions of new dollars making their way to schools around the country. New donors, such as California developer Eli Broad, John Walton of Wal-Mart fame, and Bill Gates, developed a brand of what is often termed "muscular philanthropy," a type of giving with a clear focus on change and a sharp eye toward measurable results.

## CITY SCHOOLS AND THE PRIVATE SECTOR

When mayor Michael Bloomberg assumed control of New York City's schools in 2002, he quickly turned to philanthropists like Eli Broad and Julian Robertson, who wrote big checks with the understanding that their donations weren't intended to support the status quo. One of the key features of Bloomberg's structural reforms for New York City has been the elimination of the city's 32 community school boards, which were long considered patronage mills and beds of corruption. He did so by hiring a team of high-priced consultants with private money that was donated to the Children First effort. It is worth noting that the community school boards themselves were crafted in the 1960s in large part by the Ford Foundation, whose representatives not only participated in the policy planning and drafting, but also supported academic papers that were used to argue in favor of decentralization of the school system. The Ford Foundation, under the direction of McGeorge Bundy, had already assisted three neighborhood-based experiments in increased parental decision making when Mayor John V. Lindsay appointed Bundy to chair a blue ribbon panel to create a plan to decentralize the entire New York City school system.[11] Because the eventual plan for 32 community school districts needed to be approved by the New York State Legislature, the United Federation of Teachers (UFT) was able to flex its considerable political muscle in the Albany statehouse to water down Bundy's plan to create decentralized elected boards across the city so that all residents of a district—not just parents—could vote to elect school board members. The Bundy panel felt that parents should be the ones choosing their representatives, but the union, for obvious reasons, wanted no part of that scenario.

UFT president Al Shanker was so incensed by the Ford Foundation's role at the time that he went on a nationwide speaking tour to warn educators in other cities of the "irresponsible intervention" of philanthropists that threatened their public education systems.[12] The teachers union used the threat from philanthropy to its political advantage in the negotiations over the state law change in governance, in return getting other changes in the law that made it nearly impossible to fire an incompetent teacher if he or she had tenure.

By the time Mayor Bloomberg dismantled them 30 years later, the community school boards were known more for patronage, corruption, and incompetence than for empowering parents to run schools that put their kids first. Former Bronx borough president Fernando Ferrer in 2002 (who at the time was president of the Drum Major Institute for Public Policy, a Manhattan-based civic group) testified before a state task force on community school district governance reform that he believed one of the most important lessons learned from the 1969 legislation—and from the 1996 changes to the law that created School Leadership Teams—is that governance reforms alone don't improve public education.

"In the late 1960s, the Ford Foundation asked a question that they didn't stay around to answer," Ferrer testified. "What should the relationship be between schools and communities? Our city has attempted to legislate the answer. That is, in large part, why the history of who governs the New York City schools is one of conflict. The perennial struggle of top-down versus local control versus all of the above has distracted us from developing the deep, sustained relationships between schools and communities that could actually improve public education and elicit support for reform."[13]

The evidence does indicate that in New York and elsewhere the philanthropic and political obsession with the way systems are structured has "distracted" school systems, to use Ferrer's terms. Still, reformers who choose to focus on communities, and not individual students within those communities, promote a distraction from what should be the schools' core mission to educate students. We've tried both top-down management and decentralization, but we've strangely still never been willing to give real power to the people by letting parents vote—not on a local school board or School Leadership Team, but with their feet as consumers.

Aside from real parental choice, we also don't know what would have happened if parents could have controlled the community school boards (though I think we can guess it still would have had its problems). Richard Magat, who served on the staff of Bundy's Committee on Decentralization of the New York City Schools, wrote in *Education Week* in 1997: "One can only speculate whether a school-parent-only system would have prevented community school boards from being controlled by politicians and special interests, malfeasance, and corruption."[14]

## TRANSFORMING THE SYSTEM

California philanthropist Eli Broad has had more say in the long-term direction of Mayor Bloomberg's city schools than anyone who actually lives and pays taxes in the city. He was one of the first people to meet with Chancellor Klein after he was tapped to lead the New York City schools in 2002.

Klein's first-week visit to Los Angeles and San Diego set the stage for his eventual reform effort known as Children First, which was funded in part by a multimillion contribution from Broad and modeled after San Diego's Blueprint for Student Success. The effort in both cities seeks to streamline the administrative bureaucracy and focus resources on classroom learning.

(Personal disclosure: In 2002 I participated in a conference for education journalists in San Antonio, The Future of School Boards, that was hosted by the Hechinger Institute on Education and Media. The conference was underwritten by the Broad Foundation. In addition, Broad was one of the funders for the 2004 San Diego Review, a research team on which I worked.)

Broad, one of the top contributors to former president Bill Clinton's legal defense fund, has also personally funded the campaigns of reform school board candidates in his hometown of Los Angeles, as well as in San Diego and elsewhere. Broad, chairman of SunAmerica Inc., a financial services company, and founder of home-building giant KB Homes, has also played a role as an advisor in helping select school leaders for districts he has funded.

The Broad Foundation first got involved in education funding in the early 1990s, but seemed to get much of its traction at the turn of the century by "investing" in projects to train new school leaders and highlighting successful turnaround efforts in urban systems. As Broad told Frederick Hess: "I believe the infusion of a new generation of leadership from outside the overly bureaucratic environment of public schools will bring marked improvement in student achievement."[15] Broad noted that, by his estimates, 98 percent of the nation's superintendents were trained within the school system and received little education in the area of management and/or leadership. In 2003, Broad became a major donor to New York City's nonprofit Leadership Academy to recruit and train new and dynamic school principals.

Broad's personal and foundational investment in these education management reforms made him a player with policymakers. In Oakland, California, in 2003, Broad worked closely with mayor Jerry Brown to screen candidates for the superintendent job there and is said to have been the person who first approached former Democratic Party chairman Roy Romer about taking on the job of running Los Angeles's school system. I happen to admire Broad's willingness to shift the focus of reform to improving the management and governance structures of school systems. I believe they do matter. Yet, the public's responsibility remains the same: since no one elected Broad to part with millions of his hard-earned dollars, accountability for what his donations are doing to schools needs to be transferred to those in power who accept his largesse. Someone must be held accountable, and it's impossible to make it the gift's giver.

## PHILANTHROPY THROUGH THE PROPER LENS

The point here is not to indict the men and women who give generously to support public education, but to note that by simply writing the checks, they insert themselves as major players into a public—and political—climate. Education philanthropy is by no means a bad thing. In fact, it is a critical way for school leaders to try new things in the face of budget cutting. Also, people like Eli Broad (another Democrat) have done exactly what I am suggesting the overall public should do: he has set high expectations for school leadership, demanded competence from the people in charge, and has been willing to stand up to an often relentless teachers union. Like everything discussed here so far, however, philanthropic efforts must be viewed through a lens that begs the question: How does this help students? Or more precisely: Should our schools do what this donor wants because we think it fits in with our plans and we believe it is best for students, or are we considering it just because it is "free money"?

If "free money" comes with strings attached, the public and transparent school leaders must decide whether or not it is worth it in terms of the short- and long-term impact it will have on student achievement and parental satisfaction. In addition, like all forms of educational public policy, philanthropically driven reforms should be evaluated to determine whether they are having an impact. And while it may sound obvious, the people footing the bill should not be the ones conducting (or even funding) the evaluation. Foundations and policymakers should be mindful of the lack of credibility that comes when the donors are involved even in informal evaluations of the projects and programs they are funding.

New York City Schools chancellor Joel Klein's nonprofit Leadership Academy to train principals using philanthropic dollars, for example, got glowing reviews in a public television documentary series called "New York Voices" in the 2003–04 school year. The series ran on Channel 13/WNET. But when you understand the funding mechanism for both the show and the Leadership Academy, you understand that there was pretty much zero chance that the documentary would have been anything but positive.

The Wallace Foundation (formerly known as the Wallace-Readers Digest Foundation and based in New York) was one of the original donors to the Leadership Academy when it was unveiled in early 2003. The academy, which was run by former telecommunications executive Robert Knowling, recruits and develops aspiring principals through an intensive, corporate management type of program. Although the academy came under attack early on for paying extremely high salaries to its employees, in the summer of 2004 it graduated its first class of 77 new principals. The model is premised on the notion that turning around 1,200 schools in New York City will require 1,200 change-agent principals. The small number of graduates is a drop in the bucket in terms of what the system needs, even if you buy the philosophy, but it appeared to be an encouraging start.

In the fall and spring of the first year of training, public television ran a series of positive programs looking at the academy and its work. The programs themselves were paid for with a $375,000 grant from the same Wallace Foundation that had provided the academy's initial grant. After the academy's first year of operation, in August 2004, the Wallace Foundation awarded another $5 million to the Leadership Academy, as well as another $440,000 grant to Channel 13 (through the Educational Broadcasting Company) to follow the new principals through their first year on the job.[16]

Like many educational projects funded by philanthropists, the Leadership Academy offered some glimmers of hope, but cannot be fully evaluated until years down the line when these new principals have had enough time to have perhaps affected the educational lives of their students. (This didn't stop Klein from declaring the academy a success after just a few months of operation.)

(Additional personal disclosure: I participated in a 2004 conference on educational leadership in Washington, D.C., that was sponsored by the Hechinger Institute on Education and Media and underwritten by the Wallace Foundation.)

## THE PUBLIC HELD HOSTAGE

Using private money to play public politics can be a mess, however, and policymakers should be willing to look a gift horse in the mouth if they feel like the horse is holding a gun to its head. In 2002, months before San Diego superintendent Alan Bersin's contract was set to expire, the Bermuda-based Atlantic Philanthropies offered the district a $5 million grant to help support the district's Blueprint for Student Success, a plan that established a common, citywide curriculum and invested heavily in intense teacher training to improve instructional skills. The grant, however, was contingent upon Bersin's continued employment with the district. "We are investing in the leadership team that is in place in San Diego and the reforms that have been implemented," said Alan Ruby, a senior vice president for the foundation.[17]

The elected school board had yet to make its decision about whether or not to keep Bersin on, so such an offer for private money with major strings attached represented an offensive encroachment on the public's representation on an important policy decision. All told, $27.5 million in private contributions to the district that year were contingent upon Bersin remaining in office as superintendent, including $22.5 million combined from the Bill & Melinda Gates Foundation and the Flora Hewlett Foundation.[18]

It's easy to understand why a philanthropy would want to safeguard its investment, but it should be equally obvious why these kinds of restrictions have no place in public education governance. Even if you are a huge fan of Bersin as a school leader, the elected school board should have been able to make its final decision about extending or not extending Bersin's contract based solely on the merits of his job performance. If philanthropic contributors to public education have such little respect for the "public" nature of the system, elected school boards should be willing to simply say "no thanks."

This also isn't to say that philanthropists shouldn't attach strings to their donations. Those strings must be made clear, however, and evaluated along with the other policy implications attached to the donations. In 2002, for example, the Broad Foundation made clear that it reserved the right to take back its $2 million planning grant for the New York City schools if Chancellor Klein were to leave his job early. This scenario was somewhat different from what we saw in San Diego, however, as it came to light at the start of Klein's chancellorship, rather than right before a crucial vote on whether or not to renew his contract, as was the case in San Diego. "This is an insurance policy," Broad's managing director Dan Katzir said of the New York City situation. "If a key player is removed or leaves, we think it's important to put a grant on hold and take a closer look."[19]

## CUTTING OUT THE MIDDLEMAN

In Milwaukee, philanthropy played a crucial role in helping sustain the school choice movement while it endured political and legal attacks from the powerful teachers unions. A nonprofit scholarship organization called PAVE (Partners Advancing Values in Education) enhanced its fundraising to provide scholarships to the low-income students who anticipated using the new state vouchers. Cochaired by John Stollenwerk, president of Allen Edmonds Shoe Corp., and Donald Schuenke, retired chairman of Northwestern Mutual Life, PAVE raised millions of dollars from local business leaders and philanthropies to enable more low-income Milwaukee students to attend the school of their choice while the court battles were carried on. One local foundation that stood out in its generosity was the Lynde and Harry Bradley Foundation.

Steered by then president Michael Joyce, long a school choice advocate, the Bradley Foundation funded $8 million in PAVE scholarships, as well as countless related research projects and legal costs. When the challenge to expand the voucher program reached the state supreme court, the Bradley Foundation funded attorneys Kenneth Starr and Clint Bolick (of the Institute for Justice) to defend the program on behalf of the State of Wisconsin. But from the start, Bradley made clear that its acts of charity were intended to be replaced by government funding of the program already passed by the legislature.

On June 10, 1998, the Wisconsin Supreme Court deemed the expanded voucher program constitutional. Parent activists and other choice supporters heaped praise on Joyce, who sat quietly in the back of the room as they celebrated the news in the basement of St. Joan Antida High School on Milwaukee's lower east side.

"After 13 years of struggle and over ten million dollars of investment, we had helped to make what had been an abstruse intellectual construct, a talking point, and translated it and transformed it into a concrete reality," Joyce later explained. "A powerful educational reform involving real flesh and blood human beings exercising freely the bedrock principle of a self-governing republic—that the parent is the primary educator of the child."

Once expanded school choice was a reality, it became clear that the new demand it created would require more private school seats than even the inclusion of extant religious schools could provide. Private resources were needed to help strengthen and expand existing private and religious schools and also to create new schools for voucher-bearing students.

Investment manager Ronald Sadoff knew he wanted to get involved in a project that would help low-income residents of Milwaukee's central city, but he didn't want to be the kind of donor who sat on the sidelines writing checks. He wanted to be sure that his involvement was making a difference. "I had concluded that education was the way to go," Sadoff recalled.

In 1996, Sadoff and his wife, Micky, saw a *60 Minutes* update of a late 1970s piece about Chicago educator Marva Collins. The Sadoffs were

FRIENDS WITH DEEP POCKETS

moved to learn that students who had attended the no-nonsense educator's school beat the odds by escaping their housing projects and gaining meaningful employment as adults. Ron Sadoff made the 90-mile trip south to visit with Collins and tour her school, Marva Collins Preparatory, and knew right away that he wanted to bring that kind of school to Milwaukee's inner city. "I told her, 'I'm not leaving here until I get a license,'" Sadoff said.

While attorneys thrashed out a 20-page licensing agreement ensuring that the Marva Collins Preparatory School of Milwaukee would follow the Marva Collins method to the letter, Sadoff found other charitable individuals willing to assist him, most notably Junior Bridgeman, a former Milwaukee Bucks star who had acquired a dozen area fast-food restaurants. In 1997, the new school opened its doors in Milwaukee's tough Metcalfe Park neighborhood to serve low-income students armed with vouchers. Today it is one of the most popular schools in the central city for students in the voucher program, even after it was forced to change its name in 2004 after a licensing dispute with Collins.[20]

In addition to starting new schools as the Sadoffs did, scores of private individuals provided funds to help existing schools increase their capacity, often by contributing to PAVE. Its scholarship program having served its purpose, PAVE turned to expanding the supply of private school seats. PAVE also took on the task of working with private schools, which were used to living hand-to-mouth, to plan for their future in an era of taxpayer-financed vouchers. Lastly, PAVE turned itself into a clearing house of information for schools participating in the voucher program and for officials administering the program. The Bradley Foundation continued to support PAVE in this new incarnation: In 1999 Joyce announced a $3.25 million grant to PAVE for development of new and better private schools, "without which the hard-won freedom to choose cannot be exercised."[21]

"It really is the next big horizon for education in Milwaukee," PAVE director Dan McKinley said at the time. "We're now moving from the demand side to the supply side and making sure there is a good supply of education options for students."[22] School choice supporters identified tens of millions of dollars in building projects planned or underway at private schools in underprivileged neighborhoods by the spring of 2001, thanks to the generosity of local citizens and foundations.

While few Milwaukee school board members and other choice supporters are known outside that city, one of the coalition members, Howard Fuller, former Milwaukee public schools superintendent, has gained national prominence. Fuller resigned his post in frustration in 1995, having concluded that real reform could not occur from within the system. He explained at the time that he was turning his efforts to putting pressure on the system to change from the outside, via school choice. Fuller has since emerged as the foremost leader for school choice in Milwaukee and—many believe—in the country. With funding from various philanthropists and foundations, Fuller created the Institute for the Transformation of Learning at Marquette University to advance effective education reform locally and around the country.

Not all of the institute's support came from local sources, however; national foundations such as the Walton Family Foundation and the Milton and Rose Friedman Foundation have provided significant funds, too. Fuller's institute now employs more than a dozen staff and operates a local, charter school resource center, technology learning centers throughout Milwaukee, an office of research, and a Web site, www.schoolchoiceinfo.org. Fuller also founded the Black Alliance for Educational Options (BAEO) to organize African Americans to fight for school choice for their children.

Among many early contributors to the Institute for the Transformation of Learning was Milwaukee's Helen Bader Foundation, which has provided more than $500,000 for various projects in recent years.[23] The Bader Foundation's Jeanette Mitchell said that her directors were pleased to play a role in pushing for change in Milwaukee's schools.

Like Howard Fuller, Mitchell once gave everything she had to working within the system. In the 1980s, she served on the Milwaukee school board, for a while as its president. But in the early 1990s she decided that there was a more powerful role for her to play on the outside. "When I left the school board, I understood clearly it would never change on the inside without outside pressure," said Mitchell. "My board of directors understands that a lot of our funding has assisted Milwaukee in becoming 'ground zero' for school reform," Mitchell said, "We now have more options for education in Milwaukee than anyplace in the country."[24]

The Bader Foundation, in part because of Mitchell's insider understanding of what really happens within the system, recognized the need for greater transparency to help educate the larger public. To this end, the foundation in 1996 provided Fuller's institute with a $45,000 grant to conduct a detailed study of the teachers contract: what's in there, how it got there, and what claims were made about what would happen to student achievement once collective bargaining was a reality. The study found that despite promises in the 1960s that teachers would be happier and student achievement would be improved under the contract, neither appeared to be the case.

The difference between education-related philanthropy in Milwaukee and much of the other education philanthropy around the nation is best summed up by what the American Enterprise Institute's Frederick Hess describes as the difference between old giving and new giving, or "status quo" giving versus "common sense" giving. The first relishes the notion of helping the current system improve by feeding the beast, funding professional development, and leadership development. "Funding the current system or the experts working with the system is the old education philanthropy," notes the Fordham Foundation's Chester Finn.[25] The new philanthropy pokes at the beast with a lance from the outside, funding standards-based reforms and programs that give greater power to low-income parents to prod the system to better serve the needs of its customers. Since, left to their own devices, school systems (even those getting financial help from donors with deep pockets) will naturally continue to place their needs ahead of the needs of students, the best route to effecting change is undoubtedly to create external pressures that challenge the very existence of the system and the mindset of those who operate within it.

# 9

## THE CORPORATE ROLE IN REFORM

If you added up the cost of all the designer suits worn by the men on the stage at Manhattan's School of the Future one spring morning in 2004, the total value would be considerably more than a starting teacher in the city earned in a year. These were some of the biggest names in the corporate world, gathered together by a group called PENCIL (Public Education Needs Civic Involvement in Learning) to demand that the state legislature pony up more money for New York City schools to settle a lawsuit that claimed city schools were underfunded.

The roster of corporate bigwigs gathered in the auditorium that morning included Time Warner chairman and CEO Richard Parsons; Andrew Tisch, chairman of the Executive Committee of the Loews Corporation; Anthony Cuti, chairman and CEO of Duane Reade; Stuart Suna, President of Silvercup Studios; Robert Johnson, President, chairman and CEO of Bowne and Co.; and David Coulter, vice chairman of JP Morgan Chase & Co. These were the people on the city's A-list, the movers and shakers whose opinions were thought to matter more than the average Joe.

Nearly a year earlier, an appellate court had ordered state officials to craft a new statewide education formula by July 30, 2004 that would result in more equitable funding of the city's schools. Legislators in Albany were showing signs that they wouldn't be able to reach an agreement. Republicans wanted to protect their largely suburban school districts from cuts; Democrats wanted more cash than the state could afford. The business honchos gathered that morning were delivering a message.

"We demand action," said Time Warner's Parsons, part of a chorus clamoring for more money that morning. Claims that improving education was important to the city's business economy and "the most important issue facing the state" were flying. If the issue had been anything other than education, their collective power might have mattered. But it didn't. When the organizers from PENCIL opened up the press conference for questions, I raised my hand and asked a simple question: What are you going to do about it?

The answer, or their lack of a clear answer rather, was illuminating and demonstrates how generally impotent the city's business leaders have been in terms of putting their collective feet down for major changes in the city's public school system. For several moments after I asked, there was silence, as they looked at each other to see how the question should be answered. It seemed as if these corporate titans had never considered this very basic question.

Viacom executive vice president Dennis Swanson took a shot at the question. He described how he had recently been at a breakfast for broadcasters at which he had seen Governor George Pataki and raised the issue of more money for city schools. "If we have to go back, we'll go back as many times as we have to until we get this settled," Swanson pledged.[1] The most significant corporate titans had gathered together that morning to declare that education was important to them and to the city as a whole, and yet none appeared to have done their homework. None had developed a clear strategy to translate their demands to action.

Try to imagine someone from the teachers union giving such a weak answer. It's impossible. When the unions feel something is important, they leave absolutely no doubts. Publicly they rally, write op-ed pieces, stuff mailboxes with postcards, and engage the assistance of friendly groups to mobilize others to generate pressure and support for their cause. Privately, they contact all the lawmakers they supported over the years and remind them how important the union support was, is now, and forever shall be. Like the anaconda in the chandelier I described in chapter 6, the union makes it crystal clear that it expects compliance, and often it often gets it.

Three months after the corporate honchos' press conference, the court-imposed deadline for Pataki and the legislature to come up with a plan had come and gone with nothing to show for it. Business leaders, as they long had been before their press conference, proved to be largely absent from the debate and the politicking in Albany.

There are plenty of people (including people close to Pataki) who don't consider simply pumping more cash to dysfunctional schools to be a "major systemic reform" and they may be correct. The point here is not that business leaders should have been out there twisting the arms of legislators or playing hardball politics behind the scenes for more money, but to illustrate what every elected official in New York already knows: business leaders have extremely limited pull when it comes to demanding changes in education.

In many ways their lack of punch on the issue is a shame, since, unlike powerful unions representing school employees, their interests are served by the adequate education that is delivered to children. Today's students are tomorrow's workforce and tomorrow's consumers. It isn't hard to understand what business leaders have to gain from improved schooling for children. Additionally, it is business leaders who are probably best suited to understand the frustrations of school management in dealing with labor contracts and labor-friendly state laws that make it hard to adapt school systems to the needs of all students. They are in a unique position to use their power and expertise to truly help school leaders put children first, even if it takes behind-the-scenes battles at the State House and City Hall. While other groups in this book share the blame for allowing their self-interests to shift the school system's attention away from students, business leaders in New York City and elsewhere get the blame for sitting on the sidelines when they could be helping shift that attention back to students. Unlike parents, corporate titans employ lobbyists and can flex considerable political muscle. They also tend to have acheived positions in their corporations because they understand the concept of power: how to get it and how to use it. If they believe that public education is important, they are in a position to use their power in ways that cause major change. Participating in a once-a-year Principal for a Day event (which is PENCIL's claim to fame) is a great activity for the community, but it does very little to improve the overall delivery of education to students. In short, when business leaders put their feet down in support of sustained measures designed to turn the system on its head, they can leave an imprint. But they have been largely absent in many cities.

Taking a controversial stand can be a major headache for business leaders, however. There are many members of the National Education Association, for example, who refuse to shop at Wal-Mart because founder Sam Walton's son, John, has given millions of dollars to support charter schools and private school choice. But business leaders need to understand that Wal-Mart isn't exactly dying in the revenue department, that it is possible to draw the ire of organized teachers' groups for the sake of meaningful changes to the education system without killing your core business. Business leaders have plenty to worry about with their everyday work without having to deal with headaches caused by pickets and boycotts from education groups. The teachers unions can be particularly bothersome because their members are usually done with work by 3:30 P.M., making it easy for them to gather large crowds for prime-time protests.

"I have worked with business guys on school issues who have dealt with unions like the Teamsters in their jobs," said Jerry Butkiewicz, secretary of the San Diego-Imperial Counties AFL-CIO. "The way I describe the teachers unions to them is this: They are as strong as the Teamsters, but even more organized."[2]

But business leaders who want and need better schools to improve their cities and the quality of their workforce, as well as those tycoons who speak of a "moral imperative" to improve the schools as our New York leaders did, have to be willing to put their own necks on the line and feel some short-term discomfort. When CEOs show they are taking a huge risk by taking a controversial stand, their requests for legislative assistance often carry more weight. They need to be able to tell a governor or a mayor, "Look, I'm putting my tail on the line by supporting this, either you are going to back me on this or I'm going to start looking for someone who will." This is, of course, what the unions do on a regular basis.

The people who hold elected office can hardly be expected to take business leaders seriously on education issues if there are no repercussions for *not* taking them seriously. You can stand up at a press conference, as Anthony Cuti, CEO of Duane Reade drugstores did, and say that "a well-educated workforce is an urgent priority for business." But if legislators have all met with your lobbyists during the current legislative session and the issue of education has never once been raised, your stance on schools is likely to be considered lip service by the elected officials who matter. Politicians are more likely to act decisively on an issue if they are feeling— or fearing—severe discomfort in one way or the other. Business leaders often have an ability to inflict discomfort in ways ordinary citizens can not because they have access to the two main ingredients of any good political soup—money and power.

It bears repeating that this discussion shouldn't serve to blame the teachers unions for the way they do business. In fact, I'd argue for exactly the opposite. The unions are breaking no rules and are doing nothing other that following a disciplined plan for action. Those who are fighting for school reforms that put kids and parents first (including business leaders who view such customer-oriented approaches as a form of system reform in itself) would be wise to observe the union in action.

Just like parents who are too nice when it comes to their kids' education, business leaders also tend to settle for much less from public school systems than they ever would allow in their own corporations. Business leaders are better poised to evaluate initiatives based on outputs (student learning), but they allow school leaders to evaluate themselves based on the inputs (how much they've spent or changes they've made). Even the shrewdest of business leaders can fall into this trap. New York City chancellor Joel Klein, who had been CEO of Bertelsmann Inc., for example, declared his nonprofit Leadership Academy to train new principals to be a success before a single applicant had even graduated from the program, much less secured a job running one of the city's 1,300 public schools. It's hard to imagine him taking the same approach at Bertelsmann. Schools are certainly not corporations and can't be run the same way businesses are run, but that doesn't mean business leaders should check their bottom-line mentality at the door when they get involved in schools. In an education system in which results are often an afterthought, business leaders can influence change just by asking the right questions.

Can you imagine what it would be like if business leaders got their act together for education, mobilized their army of lobbyists, called in their favors from legislators, and reached out to other groups with which they have little in common other than the desire for better performing and more parent-friendly schools? I've actually seen it happen.

## THE MILWAUKEE EXPERIENCE

In Milwaukee, business leaders in the early 1990s grew frustrated with years of what Metropolitan Milwaukee Association of Commerce (MMAC) president Timothy Sheehy called "polishing of the apple." Business leaders had adopted schools, engaged in partnerships with the system, and threw their support behind various superintendents, but little seemed to change. "We had put hundreds of thousands of dollars into well-meaning efforts and what we got was a lot of hand-holding and hand-wringing," Sheehy told me in 2001. Data released by the Milwaukee public schools at the time consistently showed that only 4 out of 10 high school freshmen stayed in school and graduated after four years. Members of the MMAC were losing patience. "There was a growing awareness year after year, as a new superintendent would come in and we'd watch another wave of reform efforts, that nothing was actually changing," Sheehy said. A consensus began to form that something bold needed to happen.

The MMAC's board of directors, under the direction of Richard Abdoo, then chairman of Wisconsin Energy, and Robert O'Toole, chairman of A. O. Smith Corporation, quietly made expanding school choice its number one lobbying priority. They also put MMAC money where its mouth was, spending more than $500,000 to help enact the legislation that would allow more students and schools to participate in Milwaukee's voucher experiment. "It was Bob O'Toole's power and energy that really drove that," said former Milwaukee mayor John O. Norquist, a Democrat and prominent school choice supporter. "He really saw it as an issue of whether or not education was being delivered competently or not."[3]

One of the first steps the Sheehy, Abdoo, and O'Toole team took in the early 1990s was to hire consultant Susan Mitchell to work with MMAC and with Howard Fuller, then the Milwaukee schools superintendent to find ways to effect meaningful education reform. Soon after, Mitchell compiled a report (published by the Wisconsin Policy Research Institute) entitled *Why MPS Doesn't Work*. This report described an administration and school board tied up in minutia and a monopolistic system in which ultimately no one was accountable for results. Her findings caused waves to ripple throughout the business community and motivated Abdoo and O'Toole to press their colleagues to support school choice reforms in Milwaukee.

Convincing a critical mass of business leaders that change through competition was needed took some delicate work, Sheehy recalls. But the idea began to percolate that expanding the school choice program to include more students and religious schools (of which there are many more in Milwaukee than secular private schools) just might provide the needed catalyst to improve all of the city's schools. This controversial expansion would mark the first time government funds would be provided to pay for tuition at private, K through 12 religious schools. (Government funds have been used to underwrite tuition at religious universities and colleges in Wisconsin and nationally for many years.)

"The effort to convince business leaders didn't happen overnight," Sheehy said. "There were lots of CEO-to-CEO meetings on the subject. We really probed the question of whether this was the right thing to do."[4] Some business leaders initially voiced reservations about the voucher expansion strategy on church-state grounds, while others wondered if the effort would be worthwhile if there was a chance that it would be judged unconstitutional down the line. Others had been burned by teachers union protests over earlier MMAC efforts, such as trying to reform the state's pension system, and were not eager to raise their ire again.

"We were trying to get people to understand what we wanted to do and why we wanted to do it," Sheehy said. "We didn't come to the table as

voucher advocates and we're not voucher advocates per se. We're here because there is a well-documented link between the school system and our
ability to draw from the talent pool that is out there."

MMAC also reached out to other groups, like the Greater Milwaukee
Committee, a group of influential business and civic leaders, to either gain
their support or ask them to quietly step out of the way on the controversial
issue of school choice, Sheehy said.

As a consensus emerged, business leaders asked Susan Mitchell to develop a legislative strategy to expand school choice to cover more students
and to include religious schools. She quickly started working to bring the
grassroots activists together with private sector leaders to build a coalition—
a project team—composed of supporters that crossed political, religious,
economic, and racial lines.

The project team's first task, in October 1994, was organizing a rally
that was attended by hundreds of minority parents to support Governor
Thompson in his school choice effort. Two weeks later, while Thompson
was touring Wisconsin Electric's Oak Creek power plant, south of Milwaukee, Sheehy and a group of prominent business leaders led by Abdoo and
O'Toole (both major campaign donors to Thompson) met with him behind
closed doors to explain that expansion of the voucher program was their priority, too. "He was a little surprised that it was that important to us," Sheehy
later recalled. Thompson told them what a difficult fight lay ahead, and the
business leaders pledged to develop the necessary framework and provide
the kind of support that would be needed for passage.

In early 1995, Governor Thompson publicly expressed his support for
expansion of the voucher program in his State of the State address. By then,
the coalition was already working at full speed. Individual business leaders
had been encouraged to twist legislators' arms to ask for their support, em-
phasizing that this was the business community's number one legislative priority. Parents were also organized to visit legislators to talk about their
hopes for their children. These combined efforts paid off. In 1995, the legislature voted to expand the Milwaukee voucher program to serve more low-
income students—up to 15 percent of the MPS enrollment—and to allow
religious schools to participate.

"A strong coalition was everything," said Susan Mitchell, now president
of the Milwaukee-based American Education Reform Council, which shares
the Milwaukee story with reform advocates throughout the nation. "The
people we were up against are too powerful to fight with anything less than
a unified effort,"[5] she said. In many ways, the story of Milwaukee's educa-

tion transformation depended on a disciplined adherence to the central strategy developed by the coalition. Business leaders and private foundations have played, and continue to play, an essential role in that group. The coalition of generally conservative business leaders and generally liberal parents created a powerful force that caused a major shift in the way education is delivered in Milwaukee—a shift that doesn't guarantee success, but removes traditional obstacles that prevent students from getting the most from adults in the school system.

Business leaders in Milwaukee also opened up their checkbooks and supported candidates for public office that supported school choice. Battles against the school voucher program didn't end with the state supreme court decision upholding its expansion. In the spring of 1999, the teachers union decided to turn the upcoming school board election into a veritable referendum on vouchers. The unions have a long history in Milwaukee and elsewhere of running candidates for school board seats and winning them with ease. This time, however, the school choice coalition stepped in to support a slate of reform-minded candidates, which was backed by resources raised by Sheehy and others, as well as the political machines of Mayor Norquist and Governor Thompson. The unions faced opposition they had not previously encountered. One of the pro-school choice candidates spent a record-breaking $190,000 on his race. A conduit organized by the MMAC and utilized by area businessmen (each individual can contribute a maximum of $3,000 per race) provided over $50,000 to that campaign. For the first time in Milwaukee history, the teachers union (using funds provided by the National Education Association) and the choice coalition squared off in dueling television ads.

Raising money from business leaders for school board races was difficult at first, said Sheehy, who took on much of the fundraising responsibility for the business community. "At first, many would say, 'I'm writing an $800 check for who?' They were much more used to statewide and congressional races. . . . Once they saw it as another piece in our support for education reform, then it came a lot easier," Sheehy said. The combination of money and organization resulted in a landslide victory for the choice coalition, sending five pro-voucher candidates to sit on a nine-member school board in 1999. The union had never lost this badly before.

The business community, through the MMAC, also remained active in school issues and frequently sent representatives to school board meetings to counter the ever-present teachers union representatives who were there to influence school policy. Milwaukee's business leaders took an unusual route toward improving the delivery of education in their city. Their involvement came after years of middle-class factory jobs leaving the city. Milwaukee looked toward a future in which more of its workers would need more than a very basic education to secure the same middle-class life that had been within the grasp of most factory workers.

By the 2003–04 school year, about 17,000 Milwaukee students attended private schools as part of the school choice program or independent charter schools, and thousands more parents exercised choices of schooling in the city's newly competitive public schools. There were also some early tangible results in the classrooms. Between 1990 and 2002, the annual high school dropout rate in the Milwaukee public schools dropped from 16.2 percent to 9.0 percent and student performance on the Wisconsin Knowledge and Concepts examination (WKCE) improved in 13 of 15 tests administered between 1997 and 2003 in grades four, eight, and ten.[6] Meanwhile, the school system's leadership was able to get concessions from the teachers union to ease school hiring based solely on a teacher's longevity in the system. Programs popular with parent-consumers (such as full-day four-year-old kindergarten, and specialty magnet schools) have been expanded.

## SAN DIEGO'S BUSINESS ROUNDTABLE

Short of advocating revolutionary measures like school choice, business leaders in some cities rolled up their sleeves and entered the school reform debate in a meaningful way. San Diego's Business Roundtable for Education, an arm of the local chamber of commerce, has played a crucial role in raising the bar and demanding more from local school leaders. Ginger Hovenic, the roundtable's president and CEO, has helped remind the public there that there are no good excuses for schools that aren't educating children. It probably makes a big difference that Hovenic happens to know what she's talking about when it comes to schools. A former educator once named National Distinguished Teacher of the Year, Hovenic said, "People throw all this dust into the air and it makes it hard to see. They say kids can't learn if they don't eat breakfast. So we feed them breakfast, and we give them snacks. Why aren't they learning now? People don't want to accept the reality that our schools aren't doing the job."

The Business Roundtable sees itself as a friendly critic of the San Diego City schools. It played a major role in getting Alan Bersin hired for the superintendent's job and actively campaigned against Bersin's critics and teachers union candidates in local school board elections. It also sponsored several charter schools to serve as models for change and hasn't been shy in pressuring Bersin to keep the bar high. One of the Business Roundtable's charter schools, High Tech High School, focuses on math and engineering and links students to industry mentors in the San Diego area who are desperate for workers with advanced math skills. Another charter school, the Preuss School, provides a college preparatory program for low-income students who represent the first generation in their families who will go to college.

The Business Roundtable isn't a bunch of San Diego business elites who are content to serve as Principal for a Day once a year. The chamber, which has sought to be an agent of change in the education scene in San Diego, also started a San Diego Charter School Consortium to bring charter schools in the area together and to offer technical and legal advice. After supporting a $1.51 billion school building bond known as Proposition MM, the Roundtable pushed to have a representative appointed to the Oversight Committee to make sure the school building money from local voters wasn't wasted.

"If we don't raise the bar, then shame on us!" Hovenic told me in her tenth floor office overlooking downtown San Diego. "We cannot allow our institution of schooling to continue to perform at such low levels. We've got to push the parents, we've got to push the kids, we've got to push the teachers, and we've got to push the administrators. We need to set high expectations for everyone involved."

## THE ROLE OF THE PRESS

One group of businesses in every community that must play a crucial role in the debate on public education reform is the media. All of the calls for transparency and accountability in the running of schools will mean nothing without a vigilant press assisting voters and parents to make sense of what is happening with our students. It's easy to cover meetings and elections, but since policymakers seldom deal with the kind of structural issues that emerge as obstacles to good schools, reporters too often don't write about them. The kinds of larger problems I am describing in this book are hanging out there for reporters all over the country to sink their teeth into. The reality of what our editors expect of reporters sometimes stands in the way of their ability to tell the real stories about schools.

I once discussed the New York City school bureaucracy with Richard Lee Colvin, a former *Los Angeles Times* education writer who had gone to work for the Hechinger Institute on Education and Media at Columbia University. We were talking about the fact that hundreds of teachers hadn't gotten their first paychecks until November of the 2003–04 school year. He asked a basic question which hadn't even occurred to me at the time: "Why is it we never hear about the firefighters and cops working for months without paychecks? What is it about the schools bureaucracy that makes its problems stand out even when compared with other bureaucracies?"

It was an outstanding question, and one that we as education reporters should be seeking to answer every chance we get. The short answer, of course, is that most police and fire departments view as their essential mission the act of protecting the citizenry and battling fires. There is a clear understanding in those organizations that their internal bureaucracies exist to support the people who actually catch the bad guys and put out the fires. In education, however, bureaucrats seldom see how what they do impacts whether or not children are learning. The press has an obligation to remind the public that one reason students are not learning to their fullest potential is that the systems themselves aren't set up with students as their top priority. That so many people believe that students are king in public education is actually an indictment of our nation's education and political reporting.

Any list of those worth blaming for today's school mess must include the media, I'm afraid to say. Reporters don't do enough in our daily reporting to describe how little of the system's energies are actually focused on children. We seldom even come close to explaining how work rules embedded in the school culture make it difficult for school leaders to actually lead. We also don't tell enough stories that explain how the many facets of the current system—particularly the widespread incompetence in management—profoundly affect classroom teachers.

For years we have defined "balanced reporting" as reporting that includes the views of "both sides." Yet, very often, children are not one of the "sides" represented. We've forgotten that having a point of view—especially one that looks at all school issues with an eye toward their impact on children and the system's ability to improve schools—is often necessary if we want to get past the "he said, she said" kind of reporting that dominates our trade. With a sharper focus on how issues may affect children and improve their schools, we are better positioned to bluntly and accurately describe what ails the schools.

Editorial writers too often buy into the great man theory of history, or more precisely the good guy theory of education reform. Editorials in the *New York Daily News* and *New York Post*, more often than not, have treaded lightly with mayor Michael Bloomberg and his chancellor Joel Klein, because they seem to believe they are good guys trying to do good things for the city's children. There has been a sense, shared by business leaders, that the mayoral control which these tabloids fought hard to help win represented the ends, rather than the means to the end—in this case, a better functioning school system.

The *New York Times* editorial page has been even more removed from what happened in the city's schools in the first two years of the mayor's reforms. At an October 29, 2004 speech at New York University, historian Diane Ravitch estimated that in the previous two years, when the city's public school system had been taken over by Mayor Bloomberg and in the midst of major upheaval, the *New York Times* only wrote two editorials on local school issues. This seemed like a bit of a stretch to me, so I checked and found she wasn't very far off. I found six editorials in the *Times* for the preceding two years, but four of them were written between November 18, 2002 and January 4, 2003, when Klein and Bloomberg were just starting to unveil their reforms. So to put this in perspective, for the first 22 months after the city's most important education reforms in over a century were launched, the editorial board of the most influential newspaper in the city only penned two editorials focusing on city education issues.

One type of free pass that is often afforded school leaders around the country by the press is what is referred to as a "honeymoon period." This is the period of time in which the press backs off the new school leader to give him or her some room to understand the layout of the system before holding them accountable for fixing it. Before school leaders lose their luster, many reporters and editors are more willing to give them the benefit of the doubt. But these honeymoon periods, which can sometimes last as long as a year, serve to shove the needs of children behind the desire to give the adults in charge a break. For children, honeymoon periods amount to wasted time.

In 1997, I covered the tumultuous hiring of Alan Brown for the job of superintendent of the Milwaukee Public Schools. His hiring was controversial because of some complaints about his treatment of black students raised by the local branch of the NAACP in Waukegan, Illinois, where Brown held the top schools job before being plucked by the Milwaukee School Board. Black activists in Milwaukee hurled raw eggs at the board members after the vote was finalized. In the days following the egg tossing incident, while Brown was making his rounds across the city to introduce himself to the movers and shakers, I discussed his hiring with a prominent African American leader in Milwaukee and I made the mistake of using the phrase "honeymoon period" to describe the leeway Brown would likely be given by the local media early on in his tenure. I was emphatically reminded that the children of Milwaukee couldn't afford another honeymoon period. The city had seen five superintendents (including acting superintendents) in the previous six years. We're talking about five distinct honeymoon periods during which the person running the system was considered immune from criticism. With America's schools in a state of crisis, we simply cannot afford to let anyone be immune from scrutiny for even a day. Considering the average American school superintendent's tenure lasts only two and a half years, it means a student who starts school in kindergarten and graduates high school on time will have endured five distinct honeymoon periods in his or her academic career. Reporters and editors owe it to those students to keep the heat on the grownups in charge of the system from day one.

The public *can* take back its schools, but only if school systems are truly transparent and if journalists and editorial writers work with the public to hold school leaders accountable for meeting the high standards we have set for them. In addition, newspaper readers and television viewers must demand that journalists and editors treat education issues with the seriousness they deserve. Political reporters at most newspapers around the country ought to develop a much better understanding of education; education reporters ought to develop a much better understanding of politics. What the grownups in the system do is just as important as how the kids do, and should be covered that way by the press.

Aside from the abilities and desires of individual reporters, the unwritten rules of daily journalism also contribute to the mess, since so much of what we consider news is based on parroting issues that are first raised by politicians. In that sense, the idea that schoolchildren are routinely left behind by our society isn't "news" because it has been happening for years and most politicians would prefer not to talk about it. But if a free press isn't reminding people of this tragedy, who else will? As reporters we have an obligation to let people know exactly what we see, even if it is news no one wants to hear. If we are demanding transparency and straight talk from school leaders, we need to be prepared to report frankly on how the political system really works or doesn't work. Much of this book argues for transparency on the part of the school system and brutal honesty on the part of the public about what it faces. The press must do its own job of furthering that transparency by holding school leaders and politicians accountable, while arming parent-warriors with the information they need to make the best decisions for their kids.

## BUSINESS AND PRESS INVOLVEMENT

Throughout this book, I call on parents to exert pressure on school systems by both exercising choice and by vocally demanding that the bar be set higher for politicians and school leaders to act in ways that put our kids first. In order for systems to be able to appropriately respond to that pressure, we will need some help from our friends in the business community.

If major cities like New York are going to make it to the next level with their education reform efforts, business leaders are undoubtedly going to have to take more risks by daring to rock the boat. Business leaders played an important role in taking control of New York's 1,300 public schools away from a dysfunctional Board of Education and giving it to Mayor Bloomberg, but it took ten years, largely because of the business community's inaction on education issues. Unfortunately, too many business leaders seem to view mayoral control as the ends and not merely the means to a better public school system. They need to help the mayor take the next step by setting high expectations for school management, demanding competent leadership (including transparency), and fighting for ways to break the school monopoly and shift the system's power to parent-consumers. Instead, New York City business leaders seem more concerned with having everyone in the system get along—whether or not the kids are better off in the process. The *New York Times*, for example, in a March 26, 2004 story on stalled contract negotiations between Mayor Bloomberg and the United Federation of Teachers, reported that Kathryn S. Wylde, president of the business group Partnership for New York City, found the breakdown discouraging because she had urged both sides to work more closely together. Such a soft position on education is particularly troublesome when it comes to supporting management during important labor contract negotiations. If anyone is poised to understand the need for management to be able to do its jobs unobstructed by burdensome work rules that get in the way of properly run, child-centered schools it would be business leaders. Their silence in New York City on this important issue is a major reason why the city is forced to settle for a status quo that doesn't work.

Business leaders and chamber of commerce types have been better positioned to bluntly tell politicians and school leaders that their excuses for poor performance over the years were 100 percent baloney. For reasons most of us cannot understand, these civic bigwigs tolerated decades of failure, even when the end result affected their ability to hire verbally and mathematically literate workers. The biggest problem with Principal for a Day events, for example, is that they bring the CEO out of the corner office and put him or her in the principal's office. This strikes me as backward. If we really want public education to survive in the short term and thrive in the long term, the people who run our schools need to understand concepts that the private sector takes for granted, concepts like performance, accountability, and competition.

In addition to demanding that school leaders get their managerial acts together and providing real-world guidance from time to time, business leaders can do something else in the spirit of providing a friendly jolt into action: they can support measures that give political cover to parents who wish to vote with their feet on the ongoing referendum over school quality.

# 10

## LEADERSHIP AND VOTERS

Chicago mayor Michael Bilandic was riding a huge lead in the polls in 1979 until his city was besieged by a snowstorm that exposed the weakness of his snowplowing operation. Voters months later threw him out of office. New York mayor John V. Lindsay was pelted with snowballs in 1969 when his plowing operation cleared the streets in Manhattan but left Queens a slippery nightmare. Voters are quick to blame politicians when the streets aren't plowed or when the trash isn't picked up, but why are we so willing to accept public schools that don't work for so many of our kids?

Whether or not individual taxpayers have kids in schools, they shell out a boatload in taxes for a service that—unlike snow removal—has an exponential impact on the future of the local and national economy, judicial system, democracy, and culture as a whole. Voters simply have a poor track record of demanding more out of their school leaders, but it's hard to blame them. Real accountability is so diffused in the public education system that when it comes time to throw the bums out, it's often difficult to tell which bums we're talking about.

It's not as if Americans are happy with what they are getting out of their public education system. A 2004 Gallup Poll found that while 61 percent of Americans surveyed said they were satisfied with their system of government and how it worked, when the subject was turned to public education, only 42 percent were satisfied with the overall quality of public education.[1] By way of contrast, our neighbors to the north in Canada are much more satisfied with their schools (62 percent) than they are with their system of government (51 percent).[2]

A June 2004 Washington Post-ABC News poll, less than five months away from the presidential election, found that only 9 percent of adults nationwide listed education as the single most important issue in their vote for president, far behind the economy (26 percent), the war in Iraq (19 percent), and the U.S. campaign against terrorism.[3]

While education is often the most costly public service on the local level, voters seldom head to the polls to hold elected officials accountable for their ability to place the needs of students ahead of education's special interest groups. Those special interests often play a crucial role in helping candidates get elected to public office in the first place. As voters, we allow candidates for local and national office to appear in photo ops and campaign ads in schools with precocious schoolchildren in the background, but we don't follow up by holding them accountable when school money is wasted and student performance lags. We let the politicians declare themselves "pro-education" and allow them to talk about doing right by our kids, yet we seldom hold them accountable when they fail to get the job done after the votes are counted.

At the same time, special interests representing the adults within the system (primarily the teachers unions) are more than willing to hold elected officials accountable for fulfilling their own wishes. When the needs of employee unions aren't met, for example, the politicians they helped elect hear about it. If it is a continuing problem, the special interests work to remove the politician from office and support someone who will get the job done for them.

Politicians almost always claim that education is their "top priority" but it becomes mere lip service when all is said and done because it's much easier to not rock the vote, notes former Washington, D.C., councilman Kevin Chavous, who chaired that city's Education, Libraries, and Recreation Committee. Many political advisors, he says, recommend that their clients not touch education with a ten-foot pole because it tends to be a "political black hole" due to the hardball special interest politics. "Nearly every public official or politician who runs for office claims that education is his or her top priority, but in every legislature in the country, just a handful of lawmakers are really involved in this issue," Chavous writes.[4] "This translates into reality in a negative way and, in a practical sense, makes education reform something less than a priority."

In some ways it's hard to blame the politicians; they are simply responding to what voters demand. On a visit to Paul Revere Elementary School in Cleveland, Ohio, in 1998, I noticed that the clock in principal Robert Walters' office was stuck on 2:40 for the entire school day. The paint was peeling and many windows were broken. "For a long time, the city aimed its resources at preserving jobs and accommodating industry and professional sports teams,"

Walters told me. "Schools weren't always high on the agenda."[5] Often, public school officials don't act with a greater sense of urgency because the public isn't demanding it of them. Indeed, the same week I visited Paul Revere, Cleveland's city government was riveted by more pressing issues—a controversial public hearing on what color the seats should be in the projected stadium for the Cleveland Browns football team. (Taxpayers made their voices heard and the tough political decision was made: the seats would be orange.)

Politicians respond to issues that interest voters, and voters haven't made clear that they are terribly interested in truly revolutionizing what happens in schools. It is important here to note the distinction between voters and parents. Voters tend to claim they are interested in education when pollsters call them, but it seldom becomes an issue that will get them out of the house on a cold day to hold a vigil or a rally. Parents are hugely interested in the topic; so much so, they can't afford to wait for the political process to take care of them before they take action. Parents of means who aren't satisfied with what they are getting from the school system don't bother waiting around for politicians to take on the special interests who got them elected. They do what government fails to do: they put their kids first, either by sending them to private schools or exercising a form of school choice known as moving to the suburbs. The result is that many urban school districts end up with a disproportionate number of discontented families, who are so beaten down by the unresponsive system that they just throw their hands up in despair and abandon any attempts to improve the system in a way that benefits their kids. Those without children in the system may tell a pollster that they think reforming education is important, but reform doesn't have the same sense of urgency as when their own children were the victims. As retired Berkeley law professor and author John E. Coons (a liberal who has spent much of his career analyzing school equity issues) sums it up: "The rich choose; the poor get conscripted."[6]

Because so much money is at stake in public education—New York City's operating budget for schools is nearly $13 billion per year—the system has politics oozing from every corner as unions, textbook companies, consultants, vendors, and others fight over their share. Many of these groups are wise enough to enlist parents and politicians to help them in their battles when it suits their needs; they are equally wise (and willing) to leave everyone else in the dust when the needs of students interfere with their own.

San Diego Education Association president Terry Pesta explained to his members the political nature of their school jobs in October 2002, just before a highly contested and expensive school board election:

You are involved in politics. If you are a teacher, a counselor, a librarian, or any school employee, you are involved in politics. Whether you like it or not, you are involved in politics. Politicians control everything you do every day at your school site or program. Your class size, your caseload, your curriculum, your hours of employment, your wages, and your benefits, everything is determined by either national, state, or local politicians. Why am I telling you this? It's very simple. Since politicians determine everything that you do, it's important that you do your part to make sure that the correct politicians are the ones that make the decisions.[7]

The true fault for the sorry state of education in cities across the nation and the way those conditions impact students lies not with the unions and other constituencies for trying to elect supporters—their purpose, after all, is to protect adults, not students—but with voters who fail to hold elected officials accountable. Strangely, unlike services like snowplowing, trash pickup, and crime, the inability of public education systems to meet the needs of the students seldom, if ever, dominates elections.

Just as the unions have an obligation to oppose education reforms that adversely affect their adult dues-paying members, voters in a healthy democracy have an obligation to recognize that good schools are as important as working sewers and regular trash pickup, and an obligation to act on it at the polls. Public education systems themselves are structured to protect just about everyone working in the system from ever being held accountable to voters, much less to parents. Even if we wanted to "throw the bums out," we never know who to vote against. School boards engage in important policy discussions, yet even they seem far removed and not in control of the bureaucracy that runs things. Local, state, and national officials all seem to be talking about the wonderful things they would do for education, or their ambitious plans for reform, but they don't actually seem to be in charge either.

Another reason voters don't make the connection between good schools and good government is that the demands and pressures often get dissipated by the amorphous character of the education system. School systems that do not have clear lines of authority create a situation in which people complain about the schools in the abstract but are virtually powerless to do anything about them at the polls. A school board president, a mayor, or a governor may ask to be held accountable for schools while running for office, but it often seems silly to blame them personally when your kid's second grade math teacher is incompetent. True accountability requires that we start thinking that way, however. The obvious drawback is that the nature of the political system with regard to education issues (described in chapter 7) often means that, even if we want to punish a politician based on the condition of the schools, seldom does a candidate emerge with a better plan. Neither Democrats nor Republicans seem capable of supporting anyone who can get the job done.

Another reason that parental frustration over the poor quality of schools doesn't always translate into votes is that parents of means simply don't wait around for someone else to come along and make things better for their kids. If election day is in November and things are disastrous in their child's school in February, these parents don't sit patiently until they can vote for a solution. More likely, parents of means who have any inkling that things aren't working well in their local public school system tend to exercise school choice by a realtor—that is, they move to a community with better schools before it becomes an issue. Or else, they work the system, pulling whatever political favors they can from those in power to get their kids into better schools. The end result is the education system that exists today, in which the quality of one's education strongly corresponds with one's address and/or political connections of their families.

Far too many people view education as an issue that only matters politically if you are a parent or a school employee. They vastly underestimate the importance of the public education system in a larger democracy and ignore the incredible price tag of the system that is shouldered by all taxpayers. Voters are far more likely to use education as a way to round out their overall impressions of a candidate than as an electoral wedge issue—or as an issue that trumps all others in a race, the way issues like abortion or gay marriage sometimes do. Even when education issues do emerge in elections, they tend to involve the kinds of nibbles (demands for smaller class sizes and higher teacher salaries) that are often seen as pandering to the powerful teachers unions but do nothing to change the culture of a system that isn't serving kids effectively. Indeed, political endorsements from the school unions are highly sought after because unions, particularly for teachers, are effective at getting out the vote and generating cash and campaign infrastructure.

The recent trend toward giving mayors greater control over the management of schools—in exchange for voters holding them accountable at the polls—offers a test case to see if voters will take advantage of the opportunity to cast a ballot based on a mayor's leadership on education. This control has its own set of advantages and pitfalls, as we will see later, but the trend offers a clear opportunity for voters to speak directly to politicians on the state of their schools, and provides a specific person who can actually lead the school system out of its organizational paralysis.

If we've learned anything in the years since the federal government produced *A Nation at Risk*, a call to arms about the need to radically alter the
way we deliver education in America, it's that things don't change in our
school systems unless strong—and sometimes unpopular—leaders make
them change. Even then, it is hard to name many school systems that have
managed to change the culture of the system. Few have been able to free
themselves from the notion that public school systems operate as somewhat
collaborative efforts.

San Diego superintendent Alan Bersin explains:

> It is implicit in the "collaborative" nature of the enterprise that each major
> stakeholder retains a pocket veto power over any of the agreements to be
> reached. If there is no willingness on the part of a stakeholder to proceed,
> it is assumed that the status quo is maintained. This is a perversion of con-
> cepts of consultation, collaboration, and cooperation, and it tends to drive
> agreements to a consensus level reached at the lowest common denomina-
> tor. Practiced over time, for decades in fact, it has introduced two major
> debilitating features to public education: (1) central matters affecting chil-
> dren's learning tend to fall out of the agenda and off the table as a premium
> is placed on adults (who remain in the system) getting along rather than
> children (who will be gone) getting ahead educationally; and (2) the
> process tends to drive quality from the system inasmuch as everything is
> negotiated down to where all corners are smoothed out so the largest num-
> ber of people can agree.[8]

In New York City, for example, Mayor Michael Bloomberg and his
hand-picked chancellor, Joel Klein, have made it clear they have a job to do,
and that constantly being forced to reach a consensus in a city as large and
diverse as New York would weaken their efforts to radically transform the
system. But such accountability works only if voters avail themselves of the
opportunity every four years to vote for or against the mayor based on the
condition of the schools.

It's still not clear whether voters have the interest or the attention span
to provide such electoral accountability in New York. Meantime, unsatisfied
customers of the system who can afford to will exercise consumer choice by
either sending their kids to private schools or moving someplace where the
schools are better. Those who can't afford either option must ride it out and
hope that the mayor improves the schools before it's too late.

On the issue of whether or not it is fair to expect both strong leadership at the top and grassroots consensus building in the school system,
there are strong signs of hope in the growing movement toward a "system

of schools," replacing a "school system." Under this scenario, acts of democracy play themselves out at the school level, particularly in the form of parents exercising their choices at schools they find appealing for their children. Rather than forcing parents to weigh in on everything from curriculum to dress codes to whether creationism should be taught in schools, such a democratic process would allow parents to choose for themselves which approach works best by selecting what they consider to be the most appropriate learning environment for their child.

## MAYORAL CONTROL IN GOTHAM

If you go by the day established in the state law, New York City mayor Michael Bloomberg was given control of the city's 1.1 million student public school system on July 1, 2002. But in a sense, he didn't really take control in a profoundly meaningful way until a Friday morning in December 2003. The holidays were fast approaching and reports of violence inside several high schools had been plastered all over the local press for weeks. And it wasn't just the tabloids. Even the *New York Times* was on the story. For nearly 18 months, New Yorkers had witnessed a series of changes in the school system under the mayor's newfound powers but still hadn't seen what mayoral control could really offer in terms of accountability.

This particular week, readers of the city's dailies were treated to a host of stories about out-of-control students caught brandishing weapons, a teacher and a student taken away on stretchers after a fight at a school in the Bronx, and students assaulting school safety officers. School officials at the time downplayed the incidents, even suggesting that the teachers union was playing games with the crime numbers and hyping the crime reports. But the report that caught the mayor's eye came in the form of a front-page story by David Herszenhorn and Elissa Gootman in the *New York Times* on Friday, December 12, 2003.

Under the headline "City's New System Delays Suspensions of Violent Students," Herszenhorn and Gootman pinned the blame for the recent surge in school crimes on Bloomberg's own sloppy reorganization efforts. In the process of eliminating the city's 32 bloated community school district offices and centralizing authority, school leaders had failed to devise a new method for conducting suspension hearings for violent and unruly students. In the past, the individual districts conducted the hearings and were able to determine within about 48 hours whether or not a student could be suspended. Those districts had been eliminated in the massive system reorganization.

Still, city regulations required that students receive a suspension hearing within five days of their misdeeds or they must be returned to class. The new, centralized process couldn't keep up with the demands for hearings, and the end result saw violent students often being sent back to their schools to reclaim their seats alongside their victims within a couple of days of their infractions. The message to students was clear: There are no more consequences for violent and dangerous behavior under Mayor Bloomberg's new order.

Suddenly, this wasn't just a school crime issue. It was a hot political issue for the mayor who had dared New Yorkers to hold him accountable in his reelection effort for his ability to improve the schools. In a city where for years the schools' organizational structure itself had been designed to protect anyone from ever having to take the blame for failure (with its chancellor, board of education, and 32 superintendents and their elected school boards seemingly pointing their fingers at each other all the time), Bloomberg responded in a way New Yorkers had never really seen before: he accepted the blame and pledged to fix it. "We have done a lousy job," Bloomberg said in a stunning mea culpa on his weekly radio show hours after the *Times* story hit the streets. "You cannot blame anybody else . . . I wanted control [of schools], and I got control. And I am going to do something about it."

Bloomberg quickly announced that the city would open up five new suspension centers for students. That same evening, Bloomberg called Chancellor Klein and teachers union president Randi Weingarten to City Hall for a summit with deputy mayor Dennis Walcott on what to do about the problem. There would be many more meetings of city officials and labor leaders over the next few weeks before the holidays. When students returned from Christmas break in January, Bloomberg announced an ambitious plan to flood the city's roughest schools with 150 police officers, who would take a "broken windows" approach by enforcing even minor violations. The theory was that by concentrating on eliminating things like minor fights and sweeping the hallways of straggling students once the class bell rang, it would restore a sense of order and serve to prevent more serious school crimes like stabbings and rapes.

Several participants in those meetings described a situation in which Deputy Mayor Walcott essentially took control of the situation on behalf of the mayor. They sensed that Bloomberg had decided the Department of Education on its own wasn't taking the school problem seriously enough, and that the city's highest office needed to be directly involved. Rather than have school officials handle the important school safety issue, Bloomberg and Walcott turned it over to the city's police commissioner, Ray Kelly. Conditions were still far from perfect, but this was the kind of leadership people had in mind when they suggested that mayoral control would bring some heavy doses of accountability to the school system. Mayor Bloomberg understood that what happened in the schools reflected his leadership, and he did what he felt was necessary to stop a rapidly escalating problem.

Throughout the spring, teams of police officers and administrators visited scores of schools and conducted safety assessments—tours that attempted to determine whether individual school layouts or policies (such as the length of time between classes, the level of supervision in stairways, etc.) created safety problems requiring solutions unique to that particular school. Bloomberg demanded weekly reports from school and police officials to monitor the progress.

On the day the next school year started in September 2004, Bloomberg announced that 50 more cops would be added to the school safety task force and pledged that the biggest difference in the schools that year would be attitudinal. "You can't use the back of the classroom as your personal coffeeklatsch," the billionaire Bloomberg warned students, using a phrase most had probably never heard before. Nine months after flooding the most violent schools in the city with armed cops, Bloomberg wanted to make it clear that he expected classrooms to be used for something resembling education—a foreign concept in many of the city's high schools.

Bloomberg's control over the nation's largest public school system was years in the making, with a supporting cast that included previous mayors, chancellors, business leaders, and parents who had concluded things were so bad that major changes were needed. An attempt to rid the system of its overly politicized leadership itself became a complicated set of political moves involving two mayors.

Back on the evening of November 8, 1995, about 900 people, most of them parents, were packed into Theodore Roosevelt High School in the Bronx to hear how everything was finally going to be fixed by newly selected schools chancellor Rudy Crew. It was the first of a series of listening sessions that the new chancellor held in all five boroughs. Over the course of two hours, Crew described his vision for the 1.1 million student school system and was peppered with questions from frantic parents who had concerns about the usual problems plaguing the city's schools: the schools were too crowded; there was too much back-room politicking; there was too much corruption on the community school boards.

"Politics have taken over our schools," said Nayda Franco, president of the Community School District 7 parents association.[9] She proceeded to tell Crew that local school board members were making deals to fix up family members with good jobs in the schools, a frequent complaint in a system that didn't even pretend to exist to educate children. At one point in the late 1980s in New York City, 11 of the city's 32 elected community school boards had been under investigation in separate corruption probes.

Crew, who had come to the city after leading schools in Tacoma, Washington, explained to the crowd that while they might not always agree with him, he was sure that if they looked inside his heart, the parents would agree with what he was about. He vowed that his tenure would be "about children first, foremost, finally and forever."[10]

The Board of Education at the time had seven members, one appointed by each of the five borough presidents and two appointed by the mayor. The board voted on broad school policies and vendor contracts, hired the chancellor, and approved a multibillion school construction plan every five years. Each of the 32 school districts had its own elected board that oversaw district policies and had a major role in the hiring of the district superintendent. The central Board of Education, set up to provide equal representation to each borough, did just that: carving up the education pie so that each borough got its fair share of school money. If crowding was greatest in Queens (which it was), fairness dictated that Staten Island (which actually had room to spare) should get a new school built in the capital budget even if the compromise still left Queens schools overcrowded. Essentially, the appointees on the board were charged with looking after the needs of the borough presidents, not the needs of New York City schoolchildren.

The central board itself cost taxpayers a fortune. While board members were only paid $15,000 per year, the city spent an average of $580,000 on each of its seven representatives and their staffs, which included secretaries, legislative assistants, and cars and drivers/bodyguards.[11] (In contrast, several volunteer members of the body that eventually replaced the Board of Education in 2002, the Panel for Educational Policy, used personal Metrocards to ride the subway to their first formal meeting in the Bronx.)

Around the same time that Crew was hearing about how overly politicized the school system had become by 1995, another Rudy, mayor Rudy Giuliani began complaining that the only way to fix the schools would be to have complete control given to the mayor. Giuliani had already grabbed national attention for reducing crime through strong and smart management of the police force, and he was essentially proposing to try to do the same with the city's struggling school system. Giuliani was backed in his quest by the governor, George Pataki, and the State Senate majority leader Joe

Bruno, both Republicans. The plans went nowhere, however, because they were opposed by the Assembly speaker Sheldon Silver, who was so widely viewed as a pawn of the teacher's union that the *New York Post* sometimes referred to him as one of union president Randi Weingarten's "Albany toys." The union for years opposed Giuliani's calls for mayoral control, because it would involve giving up the power the union was able to exercise over the central board and its administrators.

Giuliani frequently used his daily press briefings to rail against the Board of Education whenever there were problems in the schools. "This is why control of the schools should be given to the mayor," Giuliani would say, whenever he was asked about a growing scandal or report of incompetence. In a 1999 budget speech, Giuliani even said, "The whole system should be blown up." For his part, Silver would counter that if Giuliani really cared about improving the schools, he should pay teachers more.

At the time, several cities—notably Cleveland, Chicago, and Boston—had changed their school governance structures to give more control to mayors in the hope that, if they could tame their out-of-control and corrupt bureaucracies, it might lead to better educational outcomes for kids. At the same time, Baltimore moved to take power away from the mayor and put it in the hands of the state for the same reasons, suggesting that the cure wasn't the specific structure per se, but a change in structure to solve the individual problems each city faced. In New York City, Giuliani and others argued that there were too many forces tugging at the system and representing only their own interests, and that no one was looking after the needs of schoolchildren and their parents in the final analysis. Even more, they claimed that because the lines of accountability were so blurred, there was no one to hold responsible when children's needs weren't met.

Business leaders in the New York City Partnership, which long supported the idea of placing the schools under the mayor's watchful eye, urged Silver to soften his stance on the issue and at least give it a look. Sources at the time said then chancellor Harold Levy even made a pitch to Silver to consider streamlining the lines of authority in the school system, although Levy claimed not to have lobbied Silver on the issue.

In what was a huge development in Giuliani's quest for control of the schools, the United Federation of Teachers studied the issue for a year and in June 2001 unveiled a proposal to increase the number of representatives on the Board of Education from 7 to 11, with the mayor appointing a majority of the members. It wouldn't have eliminated the Board of Education, but it would have given de facto control of the schools to the mayor. The proposal, widely viewed as a major opening for significant structural changes, was nonetheless met with a slap from Giuliani, who demanded during teacher contract negotiations that the union use its considerable influence over Silver and other Albany Democrats to change state law so that the mayor could hire and fire the school's chancellor.

"What they're proposing makes matters worse, not better," Giuliani said at the time. "I don't know what good we'd do in having more and more and more board members. We end up reducing accountability even more."[12] For Giuliani, and later for Bloomberg, mayoral control was a solution to the problem of accountability—no one was ultimately responsible for whether or not the schools were any good.

The pressure continued to mount for a major governance change and two months later, when it looked like a sure thing that a Democrat would replace Mayor Rudy Giuliani in the November election, Silver announced he was appointing a 15-member panel to examine possible alternatives to the Board of Education. It was widely understood that one possibility that would be considered would be giving control of the schools to the city's mayor. The panel included politicians, business people, activists, and union leaders, including Weingarten. In the mayoral race that summer, the United Federation of Teachers ended up endorsing just about everyone running except Bloomberg, who was considered a long shot.

Within weeks, the World Trade Center was attacked by terrorists in the most significant attack against the United States on our soil, and the political dynamic changed forever. On the morning of September 11, voters were on their way to the polls for the party primaries; many observers believed whoever won the Democratic race would be a shoo-in to replace Giuliani, who had to step down due to term limits. The primary election was postponed for obvious reasons. New Yorkers, who had grown weary of Giuliani in his final year in office, came to embrace and rely on his leadership in the weeks and months following the attack. Suddenly, Giuliani's endorsement of Bloomberg, who had switched parties to avoid a party primary, meant something tangible. Combined with the perception that Bloomberg was a strong manager who could help the city rebuild its post-9/11 economy, the endorsement helped Bloomberg win his way into City Hall. In a city where registered Democrats outnumbered Republicans 5 to 1, Bloomberg beat Democratic challenger Mark Green in one of the closest races in city history.

During his campaign, however, Bloomberg didn't stand out as a candidate with education plans, and most of the Democrats in the running also supported abolishing the central Board of Education. Bloomberg called, for example, for voice-mail in schools in cases of an emergency and mentioned his support for school uniforms. But with the momentum already having gathered for a switch to mayoral control, he quietly assumed the role of carrying the torch from Giuliani, who continued to trash the Board of Education in his final days in office. In an exit interview, Giuliani accused the bureaucracy of only looking out for itself. "And until that is changed, we are basically just fooling ourselves that we care about kids," he said. "What we care about is job protection for people in the system."[13]

In addition to Giuliani, the editorial boards of the city's dailies pretty much dared Bloomberg to take on the issue of mayoral control of the schools. My newspaper, the *New York Daily News*, in an editorial challenging Silver to stick to his pledge to study the issue now that a Republican had been elected, called the system in place at the time a "five-borough, seven-headed hydra" that needed to be scrapped once and for all. Reporters in the city began calling Silver's office to ask if he now planned to change his mind about the study as a result of the election.

## BLOOMBERG TAKES UP THE CAUSE

The abolition of the Board of Education and restructuring of the city's 1.1 million student school system became the cornerstone of Bloomberg's first state of the city address in January 2002 and set the tone for his entire first term in office. "We have waited too long for change," Bloomberg said. "It is time to act."

Wresting control of the schools and restructuring them in a way that put children first would be two different battles. For starters, he stepped up his own attacks on the dysfunctional Board of Education, calling it a "rinky-dink candy store,"[14] and likening it to a ship that couldn't steer itself. Bloomberg also scrapped plans to relocate the Museum of the City of New York downtown to the refurbished Tweed Courthouse and announced, instead, his intention to move the schools administrative office from its famed 110 Livingston Street address in Brooklyn. The move to the courthouse, located directly behind City Hall, was symbolic and practical: The mayor need only walk a few yards to take his chancellor to the proverbial woodshed if it became necessary.

The deal in the state legislature in the spring of 2002 that gave control of the city schools to the mayor was cleverly tied to negotiations with the city's teachers that eventually resulted in pay increases of between 16 and 22 percent over two and a half years, depending on a teacher's longevity in the system.

The union expressed cautious support for some kind of mayoral control, hoping it would force future mayors to get more involved in fighting for more funding for the schools, but it was clear at the time that the union also wanted to deliver to its members a hefty raise. Bloomberg, in March of 2002 on his weekly radio show, declared that a settlement with the teachers union would not be reached until the Board of Education was eliminated and control placed firmly under the mayor. Bloomberg, who understood that the tremendous power of the teachers would be needed to make the governance change a reality, also threatened to seek new demands from the union if he didn't get that control. The tactic was widely viewed as a way to prod two powerful local Democratic assemblymen (speaker Sheldon Silver and Education Committee chairman Steve Sanders) to action on negotiating the change with the Republican senate and governor. Both men, widely viewed as being in the pocket of the teachers union, appeared reluctant to restructure the school system's governance because it had served the local party apparatus well over the years as a source of jobs for campaign workers.

For his part, Silver in April 2002 threatened that he wouldn't give Bloomberg control of the schools unless the teachers union was well taken care of. "All the mayor can talk about is getting control of the schools," Silver said. "But I cannot in good conscience move forward with a schools plan . . . unless this city's teachers get the contract and the pay raise they deserve."[15]

Weingarten, more used to steering the debate over contract issues than reacting to them, was not pleased with the way the contract was positioned and lashed out at Bloomberg, comparing him to his predecessor Rudy Giuliani. "He's saying, 'Until I get exactly what I want in terms of control, you aren't getting a raise," Weingarten said.[16] Complicating the negotiations in Albany was the fact that chancellor Harold Levy's contract was due to expire in June and the seemingly lame duck Board of Education had no idea how to proceed. At Bloomberg's request, the board president, Ninfa Segarra, convinced the board to hold off making any long-term decisions until after the governance issue was resolved. There were two main scenarios in play in the negotiations: expanding the number of Board of Education representatives from seven to eleven while giving the mayor the right to select a majority—as proposed by the union's study in 2001— and taking power away from the city's five borough presidents and allowing all representatives to be appointed by the mayor, controller, and public advocate, all of whom are elected citywide.

"I commit to you today, I will make the schools better," Bloomberg said when he was formally given control of the schools by the Legislature in June

2002. "I want to be held accountable for the results, and I will be." New Yorkers were sold on the notion that with one person in charge, they could better determine the fate of their schools by voting for the mayor who would do the best job on education issues.

Bloomberg viewed mayoral control as a way to kick some of the cooks out of the crowded kitchen at 110 Livingston Street. Upon gaining control, he ripped up the entire kitchen, moved it across the river and next to City Hall, and gave the keys to his own hand-picked celebrity chef. He set out to change a system in which everyone offered input but no one took responsibility. He called for "clear lines of accountability" with the mayor ultimately responsible for what happens in schools.

In many ways, the legislation seemed to be tailor-made for Bloomberg. As a Republican who had only months before been a Democrat, Bloomberg was seen as being above partisanship—exactly the type of independence that would be required to make mayoral control of the $13 billion school enterprise a success. "As a billionaire, he was seen as uncorruptable," said education historian Diane Ravitch.[17]

The deal reached between Bloomberg and the Legislature allowed the mayor to select and fire the chancellor, as well as appoint 8 of 13 members of the Panel for Educational Policy that replaced the Board of Education. The panel was weakened and usually would serve as little more than a rubber-stamp for Klein's policies, but it was expected to approve major education initiatives and the school budgets. The legislation sunsets on June 30, 2009, which will either mark the end of Bloomberg's second term or the end of a potential challenger's first term, depending on what happens in the 2005 elections.

Bloomberg understood that the clock was ticking the moment he was given control of the school system. One of his first moves was to hire former antitrust lawyer Joel Klein to serve as his chancellor. Born and raised in the city and a graduate of its public schools, Klein frequently told people he viewed saving the city's public school system as the unfinished business of the civil rights era.

Because Klein did not have education experience, the city hired a controversial educator named Diana Lam as the top deputy in charge of academics, paying her the same $250,000 salary as Klein. The two-person, CEO-educator structure paralleled what San Diego superintendent Alan Bersin, another former federal prosecutor with no education experience, created when he hired former New York City educator Anthony Alvarado as his top instructional person. (Hiring Lam, who was serving as superintendent of the Providence, Rhode Island, schools at the time, would turn out to be one of the biggest missteps in Klein's early tenure. Her eventual ouster 18 months later set the stage for the promotion of a popular local educator, Carmen Farina, to the number two spot.)

Bloomberg and Klein quickly set in motion a series of structural changes. They eliminated the city's 32 community school districts and replaced them with ten regions. They were quick to refer to their critics as members of the "status quo crowd" who desperately wanted to cling to the past.

Using $3.75 million in private contributions, Klein created a taciturn nonprofit policy machine called Children First, to study the school system and develop the plans for its top-to-bottom overhaul. There was a tremendous amount of goodwill in the schools in the fall of 2002, particularly among the teachers who had just won their major pay raise. A story I wrote for the September 3, 2002, *New York Daily News* began: "For the first time in years, there is a sense of hope—or at least cautious optimism—as 1.1 million city public school students prepare to return to class this week."[18] But discontent soon began to spread among parent and employee groups due to the secrecy with which Klein and Bloomberg chose to operate. For example, when Bloomberg named his representatives to the Panel for Educational Policy he remarked that he would remove any of them who were ever quoted in the press. And even though the policies that were being designed in the Children First committees were public in the sense that they would impact the public education system, the fact that they were privately funded meant the usual public disclosure of discussions and open records rules did not apply. Essentially, the public school system was being run as a private enterprise all in the name of mayoral accountability. If the public didn't like what they were doing behind closed doors, they could vote for someone else in 2005, the thinking went.

Klein and his team were very mindful that they would never get the system in the direction it needed to go if they had to put everything they did up for a vote. The idea of mayoral control meant that voters would eventually get their say, but in order to be fairly held accountable at reelection time, Klein and Bloomberg felt they needed to be allowed to make major decisions without outside interference. At the same time, however, the top levels of the system operated in the first two years of mayoral control with an open disdain for transparency—a tactical decision that bit them in the rear as they continued to lose supporters who had initially backed them. They held data close to their vests and dragged their feet on making records available to members of the public who asked under state freedom of information laws.

The September feeling of goodwill when schools opened under mayoral control was quickly squandered when the public began to feel like outsiders in their public schools.

## ENDING SOCIAL PROMOTION

Two years after demanding control of the city schools in his annual state of the city address, in January 2004 Bloomberg announced in the middle of the school year, that, starting that school year, any third grader who did not score above the bottom level in math and science on upcoming exams would not be allowed to advance to the next grade. It was a perfect example of a controversial decision that would have been impossible to pull off with an elected school board.

Bloomberg was pressured behind the scenes to launch the retention plan by former mayor Ed Koch, and Herman Badillo, the former chairman of the City University of New York, who had publicly criticized the mayor a month earlier for failing to do more to deal with the social promotion problem in city schools. Appeasing his critics created a new level of headaches for Bloomberg. Even many of the mayor's supporters demanded that he and Chancellor Klein go back to the drawing board and come up with a more reasoned plan that better prepared students starting with pre-kindergarten and kindergarten. Education historian Diane Ravitch, known for criticizing any education reform that weakens academic standards, called Bloomberg's original plan "draconian" because it punished kids for the failure of the adults to provide them with the basic skills they needed to pass the tests.[19] As an educational debate, the issue of whether it is better to hold kids back or socially promote them has been around for years, with researchers on both sides able to point to studies and data to prove their point.

The controversial plan itself reached a boiling point in March when Bloomberg realized some of his own administrators and appointees to the Panel for Educational Policy were opposed to the plan the way it was presented to them. Although the Panel for Educational Policy was stacked with his own appointees, hours before a vote on the plan Bloomberg realized he simply didn't have enough votes. In a stunning move to regain control, he fired two dissenting appointees and got the Staten Island borough president to fire his dissenting appointee. All three were replaced by people who voted to support the plan. Since Bloomberg's appointees to the policymaking panel serve at his pleasure, he was technically within his rights to remove them if they disagreed with him. Nonetheless, the move underscored some of the pitfalls that come when power over important education decisions is concentrated in the hands of one individual. The move, which became known as the Monday Night Massacre in the press, was not popular with the public.

It became an interesting lesson about how tricky it can be to make important school policy, even when you are the mayor and have control of the school system. On the one hand, when we give a mayor control of the schools, we do it with the expectation that he or she will make the tough decisions that need to be made, regardless of the short-term political implications. We often forget that we have traded instant democracy for a more drawn-out form that gives the mayor room to operate over the course of his term in office, reserving time for accountability only once every four years.

Basically, if the mayor is asking—even begging—to be held accountable at reelection time he or she should be allowed to operate with some breathing room, Bloomberg's staff argued. A good bargain in terms of public policy would be to allow the mayor to have the wiggle room to make the tough decisions over the long term, while giving parents and students some wiggle room of their own in the short term. If parents don't like the direction the mayor is headed, for example, they should be allowed to get their money back and enroll their kids someplace else where their needs come first.

The public must insist on total transparency from public school leaders so that we can judge their work and their decisions accurately. This is a major problem in Mayor Bloomberg's public schools; the public is not welcome in school buildings and there is little regard for public oversight. It can take over a year—sometimes much longer—for the public to obtain documents and basic statistics from the city Department of Education through the Freedom of Information Law.

The flaw in Bloomberg and Klein's transformation of the schools is that it provides no relief for parents who are not satisfied with what their children are getting. Basically, power was transferred from one group of bureaucrats to another. Parent-consumers are still powerless. The "haves" still control the system, and the "have-nots" are once again forced to settle for a second-rate education. There is discomfort felt in the schools, and it more often than not is felt by the students rather than the high-priced bureaucrats who continue to hold all the cards.

Throughout the spring of 2004, critics (including some within the top ranks of the Department of Education) lashed out at school leaders as it became apparent that the plan to help the third grade kids was being made up as they went along. But a remarkable thing happened. Despite dismissing the critics publicly and making them look as if they didn't care about kids, Klein acknowledged several times that his team had quietly made numerous adjustments to their plans based on some of the more thoughtful criticism from the community. It was like a dictatorship where the dictator keeps his ears open for better ideas along the way. It didn't look pretty, but it seemed to work, to an extent. Bloomberg even testified before a state panel in the fall of 2004 that he believed the public was holding him accountable, in part, through their reactions when he was marching in parades. That is, that he and Klein care so much about what the public thinks of them that the noise they hear sometimes influences them.

The $32 million Summer Success Academy for third graders who had flunked their exams in the spring appeared to be a success, even if the number of kids who were being held back hadn't actually changed much from the previous year, mainly because English language learners and special education students weren't held to the new promotional standards. By the end of the summer program, 41 percent of students who flunked the tests in the spring had managed to pass—more than double the 19 percent who had done so the previous summer.

Giving the Summer Success Academy program a rosy name proved to be a stroke of genius, as it helped the administration make the case that it was a completely new program and not the same old summer school. Under the teachers' contract, if it was considered a new program, then administrators were allowed to hire summer school teachers based on their ability, not based on their seniority as with the old summer school. That hiring ability was listed by administrators as one of the keys behind the program's success.

Weeks later, as the regular school year was about to begin, Bloomberg announced that for the 2004–05 school year, the new promotional standards would be applied to fifth graders as well as to third graders. Educators hoped this would improve the city's struggling middle schools by assuring that basic skills had been learned in elementary schools before allowing students to move on. Proving again that they had learned from some of their critics, Bloomberg and Klein appeared to actually have a plan this time. Teachers, in particular, seemed happy to know about the policy change at the start of the school year, rather than in the middle of January. This time, in contrast to the Monday Night Massacre of the previous March, the fifth grade proposal was approved by the Panel for Educational Policy by a 12 to 0 vote, with one abstention.

## MAYORAL POLITICS START EARLY

New York City's reforms under Bloomberg have been hailed as the biggest changes to the school system in a generation. Education historian Diane Ravitch believes even that claim understates the importance of what has happened since 2002. "We've never seen the kind of reorganization that we've seen in the last few years," Ravitch said.[20] She estimates that the reorganization was bigger than anything the city schools had experienced since the 1840s.

Because the revised promotion policy was eventually such a major part of Bloomberg's policy platform for the city, it set the stage for a battle between Bloomberg and some of those lining up to run against him in 2005. By May, Council Speaker Gifford Miller, a likely candidate in the Democratic primary for mayor, joined a lawsuit seeking to discard the results of the third grade test used to determine a child's promotion, because of a long list of snafus involving the administration of the tests.[21] Manhattan borough president C. Virginia Fields and former Bronx borough president Fernando Ferrer also both criticized the third grade plan as they contemplated a run against Bloomberg.

Mayoral control brings a new kind of politics to the forefront. City comptroller William C. Thompson Jr. went after Bloomberg for a questionable deal his staff inked with Snapple to make it the exclusive beverage of the city's 1,300 schools. Yet he said very little about stacks of questionable no-bid contracts in Bloomberg's school system in its first two years. Miller went so far as to hire Joel Klein's former press secretary, David Chai, to serve in the same capacity in his office as Miller prepared his own run for mayor.

The obvious downside is that mayoral control, with the high-stakes final exam being the mayor's own reelection campaign against challengers who have four years to attack, requires school leaders to be as interested in public relations and spin as they are in actually teaching kids to read and do math. "The chancellor becomes directly involved in the mayor's reelection campaign," Ravitch said. "Everything is declared a success on the day it is announced, even though there are no results yet."[22] In the spring of 2004, for example, Klein got caught shelling out a whopping $33,000 per month to a boutique public relations firm for advice—just about the annual salary for a new teacher. The firm's advice was in addition to the arsenal of highly paid public relations people on Klein's own staff.[23]

New York City has a chance to judge its future mayors based on school performance, but it is unclear whether voters will avail themselves of the opportunity over the long haul. The arrangement is far from perfect. Mayoral control is essentially a management tool that allows strong school leaders to instill some structural discipline over the bureaucracy. It shouldn't be confused with democratic accountability, however. The notion that voters will hold mayors responsible for their handling of the schools ignores the simple reality that big city mayors must deal with a host of other major issues that affect people's lives, such as whether people are allowed to smoke in city restaurants or whether taxpayers will subsidize the construction of professional football stadiums. Voters can't be expected to turn a blind eye to other issues to make education a single-issue accountability measure. Voters simply aren't used to casting ballots based on the condition of their schools, even though many will easily use education to round out their overall impressions of candidates. Ultimately, many other factors will likely drive voters to pull one lever over another at the voting machines.

One of the biggest drawbacks with accountability through mayoral elections, however, involves the emergence of the same political forces that influence education elsewhere in the electoral process. In order to beat a Republican mayor like Bloomberg, for example, a likely challenger would probably need the unequivocal support of the Democratic Party and, by extension, the teachers unions. A vote, then, for the challenger would likely allow school labor groups to have a tremendous impact on management, which is far from desirable if we want to put the needs of kids before the needs of adults.

# 11

## KIDS CAN COME FIRST

On a warm June day in 1999 along the shores of Lake Michigan in downtown Milwaukee, the city's school superintendent Spence Korte gave a Kiwanis Club luncheon speech that was considered blasphemy to many public educators in America. Speaking a year after the Wisconsin Supreme Court ruled as constitutional a plan to allow dissatisfied low-income families to send their children to private schools at taxpayer expense, Korte explained that he had a moral obligation to question whether some students would be better served than they then were in his Milwaukee Public Schools. He said that school choice—including private and religious schools—just might offer that opportunity. "I know I'm supposed to be the opponent of choice and charter schools, but I'm here to say I can't do that," Korte said. "It's about children."[1]

Earlier that same day, Korte met publicly with Roman Catholic Archbishop Rembert Weakland inside Hi-Mount Elementary School on the city's north side to discuss how they could work together to improve the city's public and religious schools. The message from the leader of Wisconsin's largest school district was clear: public education means taking responsibility for the learning of all students in the city, regardless of where their parents decided to enroll them. It was time to put kids first.

Within days, readers of the *Milwaukee Journal Sentinel* Web page posted comments on how strangely refreshing it was to hear a public school administrator talk about children for once, rather than defending a public school system that clearly wasn't serving the kids who needed it most.

Over the course of the 365 days between the state supreme court's decision in favor of the Milwaukee Parental Choice Program and the meeting between Weakland and Korte that morning, an entrenched school board dominated by the teachers union had been thrown out of office by voters in grand fashion, an anti-establishment superintendent was seated, several foot-dragging school administrators were forced to look for new jobs, and the unconventional notion that parents are uniquely qualified to make the best educational decisions for their children began to take root. Milwaukee's experiment with parental choice was living up to its billing as one of the most radical experiments in the history of public education.

Although the introduction of private school choice and charter schools was not the sole catalyst for what happened after the supreme court ruling, the imprint of these customer-driven reforms was unmistakable because people all over the community were talking about the importance of choosing good schools. One year after the court ruling in favor of parents in their battle against an unresponsive school system, the status quo in Milwaukee was turned on its head.

Korte, who had been a maverick school principal in the system, was the sole choice of seven of a nine-member board who gained power in high-profile elections that preceding April. In an election that the winners hailed as the rightful return of public education to the public, all five candidates endorsed by the local teachers union, including three incumbents, went down in flames.

The winning candidates differed in their degrees of support for school choice, but each was able to tap into a grass-roots political network that formed years before in Milwaukee to push for bold changes in the public school system. It was the efforts of these grass-roots community activists and parent groups that were legitimized—and energized—when the Wisconsin Supreme Court issued its decision in the school choice case. After the 1998 ruling clear signs emerged that it may be possible to return children to their rightful position as the primary focus of the public education system: It requires a kind of boldness that most modern politicians simply don't have, not to mention having all the other necessary players do their part to make it a reality.

While many Americans have been led to view vouchers as a right-wing concept advanced by free marketeers like Milton Friedman, Milwaukee's story is a bit more complicated—and far more interesting—in large part because it had deep roots in the black power movement. The systemic revolution involved nearly everything we've discussed so far in this book: uncaring bureaucrats and an arrogant teachers union whose shameful actions reminded the city why regime change was necessary; an impatient business community that understood the need for radical change and made it the top priority; philanthropists with deep pockets willing to invest in strategies to give power to the people; Democrats who were willing to break ranks with their party to put the needs of kids ahead of special interests; Republicans who matched their rhetoric with action; and frustrated parents who were mad as hell and weren't going to take it anymore.

In short, everyone lived up to their part of the bargain in this story. Any one of these groups alone could not have gotten the job done. Together, they packed a punch that knocked out cold the education establishment as Milwaukee knew it. Every community seems to have a cast of characters like the ones who made parent choice a reality in Milwaukee, but no other city in modern history has pooled the collective talents of the group in such a politically powerful way.

What happened in Milwaukee shows that parents can prevail; it is also a cautionary tale that shows how difficult it is to make reforms happen—and how fragile any reforms are that require reluctant employee and vendor interests within the public school system to cede their power. Even with a growing list of victories over more than a decade, parental choice supporters in Milwaukee remained just a few votes short of seeing the teachers union block the rights of parents to select schools for their children. Fourteen years after low-income Milwaukee students won the right to choose their schools, the parental choice program continued to have a bull's-eye on its back, as teachers unions and their backers in the Wisconsin state legislature engaged in annual attempts to undermine choice or kill it once and for all. Activists who have been working on the choice issue for years have come to realize (with ample justification) that they will never be able to put their guard down because their opponents are willing to wait as many years as necessary to restore student assignment power and education dollars to the bureaucrats.

The key to Milwaukee's transformation rested with the convergence of unlikely forces: parents and business leaders, left-wing radicals and right-wing free marketeers. In Milwaukee, as in perhaps no other city in the country, those usually polar opposite groups pooled their resources, talents, and passions to create a new political force with considerable power. While this coalition fought for alternatives to the public school system, they did so with a sharp eye toward forcing improvement in the same system. In the short term, students whose needs had been ignored by the system would find relief in a new school placement outside of the traditional school system. In the long term, they hoped the exit strategy for parents would provide a necessary jolt to the system, an incentive to improve. School choice supporters played a tremendous role in changing the public mindset in Milwaukee with regard to the concept of public education. In short, they decided together that public education meant giving every member of the public a shot at a decent education financed by the taxpayers.

"A strong coalition was everything," said Susan Mitchell, who at the time of our discussion in 2001 was president of the Milwaukee-based American Education Reform Council, which shared the Milwaukee story with reform advocates throughout the nation. "The people [primarily the teachers unions and their allies] we were up against were too powerful to fight with anything less than a unified effort," she said. In many ways, the story of Milwaukee's education transformation depended on a disciplined adherence to the central strategy developed by the coalition. Susan Mitchell and her researcher and husband, George Mitchell, were the glue that kept everyone together.

To be sure, there were many issues on which individuals within the coalition disagreed, but the central concept that drove the diverse movement was parental choice. I once got caught in the middle of an argument between a right-leaning school choice supporter who loved phonics as a method for teaching reading and a left-leaning (public school supporter?) who loved the less-structured whole language approach. Their philosophies couldn't have been more different, yet they were united by their joint appreciation that parents should be able to choose the kind of school was best for their children. Most everyone involved in the coalition understood correctly that the vast majority of students in the city would continue to be educated in public schools, and that the hard-fought choices for parents would be meaningless if they didn't in turn have good choices. The cooperative spirit helped protect and enlarge the voucher system, and it provided the backing for the state's charter school laws in 1995 and 1997. Republican business types understood that true parental choice would force better customer service from the school system; parent activists understood that with help from powerful friends in the business and philanthropic sector they could form a strong political voting bloc that put their kids first.

All parents in Milwaukee are able to select schools for their children from among specialty public school programs all over the city, as well as open enrollment options in suburban schools, and public charter schools that have sprouted across the city's landscape after the advent of expanded school choice. What makes Milwaukee most unique, however, is the ability of low-income families to do what families of means have always been able to do: yank their kids out of public schools and enroll them in private schools if they feel this is best. The concept of customer-driven choice ushered in a new era in Milwaukee's education scene.

The emergence of new charter schools and stronger private schools in the wake of vouchers has helped stimulate the additional investment of millions of new education dollars from businesses, foundations, and individuals who wanted to be a part of what former school superintendent Howard Fuller called the transformation from a school system to a true "system of schools." In many instances, this investment took place in Milwaukee's poorest neighborhoods, helping establish these newly won school options as a part of the community's social fabric. If anything, school choice in Milwaukee served to make public education bigger, not smaller. The public's attention became more focused than ever on addressing the needs of students—no matter what entity issues the paychecks for the adults who are doing the teaching. What had once been a debate about whether private schools were better than public schools evolved over time in Milwaukee to a more important question: Who is best poised to decide what is truly appropriate for each individual child—the parent or the bureaucrat?

To understand and appreciate how Milwaukee became ground zero for modern school reform, as *Education Week* called it,[2] you need to meet the dynamic individuals who brought their unique perspectives to the table in the early debate over parent power and schools. Each had a different motivation for being there, but all were committed to a simple concept: that in order for anything to really change in the city's failing education system, the consumers needed to steal the power away from the bureaucrats and special interests. It would be impossible to summarize the contributions of all of these reformers in a single chapter, or even a single book, but some individuals stand out and deserve to be mentioned.

## "POLLY"

While Milwaukee's school reform movement was much larger than any single individual, there were a handful of dynamic characters whose leadership inspired others within the movement and helped the community make sense of what was happening. If there is any one person who came to personify the movement in its early years, it was a feisty black Democrat from Milwaukee's north side named Annette "Polly" Williams. A former Black Panther, Williams had twice run Jesse Jackson's statewide campaigns for president in Wisconsin.

Milwaukee grabbed national headlines in 1990 when Williams, a state representative, and Republican governor Tommy Thompson joined forces to successfully persuade the Democrat-controlled legislature to enact what became known as the Milwaukee Parental Choice Program. This program originally allowed low-income students in the city to use a taxpayer-funded voucher to attend the secular private school of their choice. Commentators at the time hailed it as a big deal, but it wasn't exactly the kind of thing that could possibly revolutionize the education system. It couldn't even come close to helping meet the needs of more than a handful of low-income families with kids stuck in failing schools. In the original legislation, participation was limited to a maximum of 1 percent of enrollment in the Milwaukee Public Schools, or about 1,000 children.

The fight for school choice in Milwaukee had begun in the late 1960s, led by community activists who were tired of seeing the city's public schools fail their African American students. These activists were looking for financial support—especially for a small group of community-based private schools that served the predominantly poor, minority student population in the central city and that struggled year after year to make ends meet. It was schools like Harambee Community School and Urban Day Academy, both independent schools in the inner city that were run by African Americans and catered to black students, that Williams had in mind when she championed the original school choice legislation. If public money could cover some of the cost for the poorest students, then the constant financial crises faced by these mission-driven schools would ease and more needy students would have access to them. Grass-roots activists had tried for many years to access government funds for these schools, but it wasn't until Williams took the lead and teamed up with the Republican governor that these efforts were successful.

Born in Betzoni, Mississippi, Polly and her family moved to Milwaukee when she was ten. She attended the city's public school system and sent her own children to Urban Day Academy, a private school that used to allow parents to volunteer their time in lieu of some of the tuition.

In the 1970s, a then admittedly soft-spoken Williams was elected to the parent council at Urban Day—her first elective office. "I had a hard time walking into a room filled with people back then," Williams once told me. "People who knew me back then can't believe it when they see me now." In the early 1970s, she divorced, and her family income was slashed so dramatically she had to go on public assistance for a time, but she put herself through college at night and began building a political future for herself. Williams was first elected to the legislature in 1980 and quickly became known as a fierce fighter for the people in her district, many of whom were below the poverty line.

As an elected state representative, she was known for bluntly calling things as she saw them, whether they made people (usually white people) uncomfortable or not. She once referred to one of her Democratic colleagues in the legislature as a "white, do-gooder liberal" who wouldn't understand school choice if it hit her on the head. Many of Williams's policies could be considered hardcore liberal, but she had an unveiled disdain for white liberals who assuaged their guilt about race by treating blacks as pawns for big government or "trophies of white social engineers." For reporters, Williams was a walking quote machine. Recalling when she first met Michael Joyce, who allocated millions of dollars for school choice on behalf of Milwaukee's Lynde and Harry Bradley Foundation, she said, "Mike, for a white man, you're a really nice guy."[3] When the teachers union opposed her plans to create the original school choice program, she shot back: "Their meal ticket is escaping, and that is what is shaking them up."[4] On the afternoon in 1998 when the Wisconsin Supreme Court upheld the constitutionality of school choice, Williams rejoiced: "They wanted smaller classes, well, we just took 15,000 students off their backs!"

If there was anything that consistently galled Polly Williams from her days as a parent through her days in the legislature it was the way black children and their families were treated by the Milwaukee public school system. Journalist Mikel Holt, who was a friend of Williams noted in his book *Not Yet Free at Last: The Unfinished Business of the Civil Rights Movement* that many administrators in the school system back then treated black students as if they were unable to tell the difference between a urinal and a water fountain.[5] That is to say that the people in the system treated black kids like savages, Williams and many other black parents believed. Her complaint in the 1970s when court-ordered busing for desegregation took root was the same complaint she had two decades later: Black children were shouldering all of the burden of integration by being the ones uprooted from their neighborhoods to be transported to other schools across town, where they were often treated like outsiders and otherwise disenfranchised from the cultural and civic fabric of the school.

She resented the fact that magnet schools in the inner city forced black children out of their neighborhoods in the name of integration, allowing white kids to assume their seats in good schools that were better funded and staffed than their original neighborhood schools from which they were displaced.[6] Kids in a single predominantly black attendance area were being bused away from their homes to any of 100 different schools under the city's integration plan—a practice that drove Williams and her longtime legislative aide, Larry Harwell, up the wall. Polly would get fired up talking about how she had seen black children written off as "unable to be educated" in the school system, who went on to thrive in the black-run community schools. Originally intended to be a way to improve educational options for black students, busing in Milwaukee made the situation worse for many black families whose children were whisked away to other neighborhoods. Busing treated students as a number in a constant attempt by school officials to show to the court that schools were "racially balanced." The focus of the system was on achieving the racial balance, not on educating all the children in the city.

When she talked about a culture clash between white teachers and black students, Polly insisted she wasn't suggesting that white teachers couldn't get the job done, but that black parents were better positioned to make important decisions regarding their children's education. "The culture clash is really about control over the learning environment and the governance of the schools our children will attend. It was and is my intent to put both in the hands of the people who care about these kids the most—their parents," Williams said.[7]

Williams's persistent complaints about the way black children were treated got some evidentiary reinforcement in the form of a 1985 study commissioned by then governor Anthony Earl and chaired by George Mitchell. Despite the rosy picture of academic success that Milwaukee's school leaders long publicized (claiming that students were "at or above average" when they scored as low as the twenty-third percentile on standardized tests), the commission's report found an unacceptable gap in both educational opportunity and achievement between black and white students in the district, despite nearly a decade of desegregation attempts. For years, the superintendent and top administrators had fiercely resisted disaggregating performance school data by race and income, leaving the larger public in the dark about how poorly many students were faring.

In 1987, Williams and activist Howard Fuller, both North Division High School graduates, pushed for state legislation creating an all-black school district that would be carved out of the Milwaukee Public Schools on the city's north side, and would be called the North Division School District. The plan grew out of years of grass-roots frustration that black kids weren't getting a good education in the Milwaukee public schools. "These children were neglected," Williams said at the time, referring to the school system's unwillingness to get the job of educating black students done. "They (school leaders) just abandoned them."[8] It would also have allowed the students in the inner city to attend schools in their own neighborhoods rather than being bused across town.

Critics argued it would be a movement away from integration. Grover Hankins, an attorney for the national NAACP, said the plan would go back to "separate but unequal."[9] The data Williams and her group put out proved otherwise. The proposal would have created a mini-district of ten schools: North Division High School; Malcolm X Academy and Parkman Middle School; and seven elementary schools—Auer, Clarke, Franklin, Hopkins, Keefe, Lee, and Wheatley. Nearly all 6,500 students who were already enrolled in those schools were black, making the resegregation issue a moot point, they argued. "These schools are 99 percent black whether they are separate or not," Williams said.[10]

The mini-district advocates even tried to introduce parental choice into that plan: parents would be able to choose from either the North Division School District or the Milwaukee Public Schools. If parents were content with what the Milwaukee Public Schools was giving them, no one was going to hold a gun to their heads to make them change schools. This was about personal choice, especially for those blacks in the area who were miserable with their schools and who felt powerless to do anything about it.

Governor Tommy Thompson was asked by Howard Fuller, who at the time was dean of Milwaukee Area Technical College, and George Mitchell to support the North Division plan, but the governor rejected the idea because of concerns that it was unaffordable given the area's low property tax base. "In my view, it wasn't going to change the system," Thompson later wrote of the meeting. "I wanted to try something new."[11] There were so many forces advocating for school choice in Milwaukee that it is difficult to say for sure when the movement was truly born. From Thompson's perspective, the seeds for choice were planted in his office that day.

The controversial North Division plan died in 1988 because Williams couldn't gather enough support from her colleagues in the state senate. The NAACP's Hankins dismissed Williams's movement as a "whim raised by a few dissident people." Despite her intentions, the Milwaukee Public Schools would retain its monopoly over black kids. The monopoly would not last for long, however. Within months, this "whim raised by a few dissident people" would turn into one of the most radical education experiments in American history.

Working on his own, Governor Thompson in 1988 floated a small voucher plan as a part of his executive budget. Vouchers were worth $2,400, the same amount of state aid that was going to the Milwaukee Public Schools for each child at the time. Religious schools were included in the plan. The budget item died quickly, mainly because the Republican governor hadn't included the grass-roots community groups that were poised to fight for it. Thompson said he learned from the experience that white Republicans couldn't implement programs affecting inner city schools on their own, yet, he surmised they could help black Democrats meet the needs of their constituents if they worked together.

The unlikely pair of Williams and Thompson soon began doing exactly that. They worked together to craft a new budget proposal, which was introduced in January 1989 and did not include religious schools. The measure was soon stripped from the budget, however, by the legislature's powerful Joint Finance Committee. Williams also simultaneously introduced actual legislation for the choice program which passed in the assembly (while a large crowd of supportive parents from the inner city watched from the gallery), but was later doomed in the state senate after Democrats refused to take it up. To get her own bill passed in the assembly, Williams had to badger her Democratic colleagues just to hold a hearing, which took place at the Milwaukee Public Schools administration building and was attended by hundreds of parents. The fact that so many largely minority constituents were present was widely viewed as having flipped some votes among Democrats in the assembly, who helped pass the bill there.

Just when it looked like the groundbreaking school choice plan was heading for the trash heap, it snuck its way back into the state budget bill thanks to an amendment by Gary George, a powerful Democratic senator from Milwaukee who chaired the joint finance committee. George happened to be the only black member of the state senate at the time. Several school choice supporters later recalled that Williams had privately threatened to either run against George or find another strong candidate to do so. "That was when the grass-roots effort paid off," said former mayor John O. Norquist, another Democrat who supported school choice. "Gary had been very much against school choice and then suddenly he was for it because of the grass-roots pressure."[12]

The original school choice law left much to be desired in terms of revolutionizing the education system. There was a cap, for example, on participating private schools which prevented them from enrolling more than 49 percent of their students using vouchers. Because most of the city's private schools were religious and the original law applied only to secular schools, there was quickly a supply and demand problem in the choice program: lots of kids vying for a very limited number of available seats.

Those problems aside, the 1990 school choice law clearly paved the way for more significant changes that would come a few years later, including the inclusion of religious schools in the program, the creation of public charter schools, and the emergence of parental choice supporters as an important political constituency to effectively battle the teachers unions on behalf of their kids.

In 1997, Williams was named by the *New York Times* as one of 13 "of the century's innovators and doers who forged the path" that brought America to regard education as its number-one priority. In the article, Williams was listed together with such people as philanthropist Andrew Carnegie, teachers union leader Albert Shanker, educator Maria Montessori and president Franklin D. Roosevelt. The *Times* quoted her as saying: "People with money have always been able to choose schools for their children. They can afford to send their children to private schools, or they can buy expensive houses in communities that have good schools. What this law does is put power in the hands of poor people. Now they can choose."[13]

Williams has often been credited with productively channeling the anger of frustrated parents into political action, through prayer vigils, protests, and general parental hell-raising. Under her watch, busloads of choice-hungry parents began making regular trips west along Interstate 94 from Milwaukee to Madison to demand parent power before the legislature and the Wisconsin Supreme Court. In one episode that has become legendary for its symbolism, the buses filled with parents and students were late rolling into the capital during oral arguments in a case challenging the constitutionality of the original school choice program. By the time the Milwaukeeans arrived, all of the seats in the supreme court chambers were taken by leaders and lobbyists of the teachers union and the education establishment. The students and their parents were forced to peek in on the proceedings from the door, in what became the ultimate symbol for the battle they were trying to fight. They were sick of being on the outside and looking in.

For Williams and other parents of limited means at Urban Day back in the 1970s, the idea of school choice was a direct response to a school system that they felt was consistently hurting their kids. She laughed at the idea that conservatives like Milton Friedman are considered the originators of school choice. "School Choice didn't start with Tommy Thompson," Williams said. "Black parents were talking about it way back then."

## OWUSU SADAUKAI

Howard Fuller has "power to the people" running through his blood. This was a man whose entire life had been about helping the powerless figure out how to obtain power to make their lives better. He led an AFSCME union of nonacademic employees at Duke University in the 1960s and once led an organizing drive at Duke's medical center. In the summer months back in the '60s, he trained students to be organizers. As a leader in the African Liberation Support Committee, Fuller went by the Swahili name Owusu Sadaukai. (Owusu means "One who clears the way for others." Sadaukai means "One who gathers strength from his ancestors to lead his people.") The committee worked to increase support in the United States for the liberation movement in Africa and organized the first African Liberation Day march on Washington in 1972. Back then Fuller was a leading black militant in North Carolina, a Pan-Africanist, and a Marxist. He founded Malcolm X Liberation University and in 1971 marched through war-torn Mozambique for a month with Frelimo guerillas as they attempted to unseat the Portuguese colonial government. "My aim has always been to give lower-income families and black people more control over their lives," Fuller said.[14]

His activism turned toward American public education in 1977, when his former high school, Milwaukee's North Division High, was in danger of being closed and converted to a magnet school intended to attract white kids to the mostly black neighborhood. Joining with Polly Williams, a classmate of his at North Division, they led an old-fashioned protest march that caused the school board to blink and withdraw the plan. The experience in saving the school, he later said, got him thinking about how black power could be better used to improve educational opportunities for minority students in a system that seemed to be constantly going out of its way to appease whites.

Fuller decided to go to graduate school, and in 1985 he earned a Ph.D. from Marquette University. His doctoral thesis was tied directly to his experience in fighting to save North Division: the Milwaukee Public Schools' desegregation and busing policies. Like Polly Williams, Fuller was convinced that the system was rigged to benefit white kids at the expense of black kids. It was Fuller who convinced governor Tony Earl to create the study commission that eventually blew the lid off the baseless claims from administrators that all was well within the public schools.

Two years later, he was working with Williams on the plans for an entirely separate school district in the North Division area. A report drafted by Fuller and another activist, Mike Smith, titled "Manifesto for New Directions in the Education of Black Children," set the framework for the legislation that Williams ultimately proposed. It was the failure of this plan that, Fuller says, led to the idea of real educational choice for poor parents in

Milwaukee. "Our thinking was that if the legislature was not going to let us create a separate district to educate the kids, then you should set us free and not confine us. However, the evolution toward vouchers was much more a product of our struggle than of anyone sitting down in the basement reading Milton Friedman," Fuller said.[15]

In 1991, Fuller became one of the nation's first nontraditional school superintendents, leading the 100,000-student Milwaukee Public Schools system. At the explicit direction of the school board, he kept his distance from vouchers publicly, but he set out to create what he described at the time as "a system of schools," which would one day replace the "school system" that had proven to be ineffective. Decentralization of power was the watchword in Fuller's four years at the helm of the district.

Perhaps his greatest strength as superintendent was his ability to effectively communicate simultaneously with parents in the inner city and with Milwaukee's business leaders, who were strong backers of his reforms. Unlike his predecessors, Fuller made it a point to speak bluntly about the problem the city had on its hands, about the school system's inability to effectively educate the kids who most needed an education. He asked for power to close failing schools and was fought tooth and nail by the teachers union, who tied up those plans in court for several years. He fought to fire incompetent teachers, and the union put a bull's-eye on his back, making it clear it wanted Fuller out of the picture.

The Milwaukee Teachers Education Association sought to remove Fuller at the polls in traditionally low-turnout school board elections. Their plan worked. In 1995, after hard-fought campaigns in several races, the union took over the management of the Milwaukee Public Schools, and Fuller resigned, saying he didn't "want to die a death of a thousand cuts." With the freedom to talk about private school choice again, it's very likely that he was able to do more to change Milwaukee's education from the outside in the years since, than he ever could have done by trying to steer the massive school bureaucracy from the inside.

In front of a group of black parents, Fuller sounded more like a preacher than a school leader. His calls for moms and dads to become "those crazy parents" who constantly stick their faces in the schools always drew smiles with the right crowd. His insistence that the public money spent on education belongs to students and not to bureaucrats almost always stirred parents to action. "The people in the system are talking about how they'll lose money if parents have choice," Fuller would say. "But the money doesn't belong to them, it belongs to our kids."[16]

As someone who had closely studied how power is obtained and used, Fuller believed that the key to changing education's power dynamic was controlling the money. When parents had the ability to yank their kids out of a school and take their money with them, they had real power, he would say. When those same parents were welcomed with open arms at a school that wanted the money, their children were being looked at a whole lot differently than under the old system. Later, Fuller founded the Black Alliance for Educational Options, a national group of black school choice supporters, and was a key player in the national charter school movement, bringing his lifelong message of power to the people to education reformers across the country.

Like Williams, Fuller took some hits in the black community for agreeing to work side by side with business leaders and conservative foundations that supported school choice, but he never let it stop him from fighting for the same kind of power that he had sought for poor black families since the 1960s. "I've been called a sell-out, an Uncle Tom, a right-wing opportunist, the white man's dupe, all kinds of names," Fuller said. "But you have a responsibility to stand up and fight for what you believe. And if you are not willing to take the weight, you can't exercise leadership."[17]

## TOMMY

While there is room for debate about who first came up with idea for school choice in Milwaukee, there is hardly anyone who debates how important governor Tommy Thompson's leadership was in terms of advancing the program and, later, protecting it from near-constant attempts by the teachers unions to dismantle it. In his 1996 autobiography Thompson credits himself with coming up with the idea, but he concedes one reason he believed he could win in the legislature was the growing political climate for radical change in the schools. "There was a coalition developing," he wrote. "There was support for fundamental reform among real people who were fed up with how the public school monopoly was treating them and their children."[18]

More important than whether or not Thompson originated the idea, this white Republican from rural Elroy, Wisconsin, felt his own legacy was at stake in protecting Milwaukee's school choice program and the participating families. His resolve to improve the original program was strengthened in 1994 when he was approached by key leaders from Milwaukee's business community during a campaign stop. The corporate titans, who had not been a factor in the creation of the original 1990 choice program, told Thompson that they had come to realize that expanding the program—in terms of both the number of students who were allowed to participate and the inclusion of religious schools in the mix—was their number one priority in the next budget. The Milwaukee business community placed the right of low-income parents to select their schools as its highest legislative priority, as important as any corporate tax break or any of the other of the favors that businesses usually seek from government. "Business people saw choice as a way to improve their future," Thompson wrote, given their difficulty in hiring workers with basic literacy and math skills. "They argued strongly that religious schools had to be included—without them there would be no capacity to expand."[19]

In early 1995, Governor Thompson publicly expressed his support for expansion of the voucher program in his state of the state address. By then, a coalition of parents, business leaders, philanthropists, and community activists was working at full speed to solidify grass-roots and political support. Individual business leaders had been encouraged to twist legislators' arms to ask for their support. Parents were organized to visit legislators too, to talk about their hopes for their children. These combined efforts paid off. In 1995, the legislature voted to expand the Milwaukee voucher program to serve more low-income students—up to 15 percent of the public school enrollment—and to allow religious schools to participate.

Thompson remained the choice program's guardian angel until he left office in 2001 to serve as secretary of Health and Human Services under George W. Bush. In case there were any doubts how important Thompson's role had been in protecting the program from relentless attacks from the Wisconsin Education Association Council, they were answered by the sudden vulnerability many school choice supporters felt after Thompson departed for Washington. Thompson frequently used his bully pulpit as governor to swat at obstructionists in the state's Department of Public Instruction, which was tasked with administering the choice program it had fought against for so many years. After news broke in Cleveland, Ohio, in the late 1990s that the state was forced to pay for taxis to transport students to their voucher schools because someone in the school system refused to let their buses roll, one Milwaukee voucher supporter told me: "If that had happened in Milwaukee, Tommy would have made life so miserable for whoever was standing in the way of those kids that they wouldn't know what hit them." Thompson exercised his power by playing hardball with his opponents.

The governor, along with Republican assembly speaker Scott Jensen, had been able to use the weight and power of his political machinery to ward off attempts to remove funds from or otherwise eliminate the choice program through budget amendments and other legislative proposals. While he was in office, there was little chance anyone was going to pull the rug out from under the feet of Milwaukee schoolchildren who were using vouchers to attend religious schools. His departure for Washington, however, served as a reminder for many within the school choice movement that they needed to constantly work to make sure that they had a political base that was bigger than any one politician.[20] Thompson had hardly left the state before Senate Democrats in 2001 and 2002 approved plans to virtually gut the school choice and charter school programs. Representatives John Gard and Scott Jensen, both Republicans, led the fight to save the programs.

## JOHN O. NORQUIST

If Polly Williams was focused on meeting the specific needs of poor parents in her assembly district, Milwaukee mayor John O. Norquist believed he had an entire city to save. Norquist's own personal politics were rather complicated. One of several New Democrat mayors who dominated urban policies during the Clinton administration, Norquist was described sometimes as an old-style socialist and other times as a closet neoconservative. A hardcore new urbanist, Norquist believed that industrial cities like Milwaukee could not possibly revive themselves if the quality of the public education system was perceived as being so poor that it was considered a liability for city living. Norquist was an early believer in the idea of breaking up what Marquette University professor Quentin Quade called the "education finance monopoly" through parental choice.[21]

"I was even one of the few Democrats to support home-schooling when I was in the legislature," said Norquist, who was elected mayor in 1988. "I just identified with this idea that parents were being trapped in situations they didn't want to be in and I didn't like the idea that they had to leave town in order to get their kids an education."[22]

Norquist said he was somewhat open to the idea of vouchers for Milwaukee, but that it was the urging of Polly Williams that put him over the top. "She was very persuasive and made a clear argument that this would give power to people who felt they hadn't been treated well by the monopoly," Norquist said. Having the full support of the Democratic mayor of the city helped to round out the Republican governor's support in the statehouse and allowed school choice supporters to point to the bipartisan effort to help parents find better schools for their kids.

But Norquist early on felt the original voucher law, which didn't include religious schools, was not enough to make much of a systemic or citywide difference. "I understood that the only way to get the capacity to have real choice was to get the Catholic and Lutheran schools involved in the mix," Norquist said. The mayor said many of the political players, including Thompson himself, were afraid of the possible constitutional problem of giving money to parents to use at religious schools. "But to the governor's credit, he put it out there and got it done," Norquist said.[23]

Once the program was up and running, Norquist used the mayor's office to bully pulpit, and lashed out at the critics of school choice for standing in the way of a better education for students. His support for vouchers, and later for charter schools, put him on the teachers unions' bad boy list, but Norquist notes that the union was never particularly thrilled with his independent voting streak in the Legislature.

The highlight of his mayoral involvement in school issues was in April 1999, when a slate of five school board candidates who were backed by Norquist's own political machine swept the election, knocking out all but two of the teachers union-backed representatives on the nine-member school board.[24]

## GEORGE AND SUSAN

If Milwaukee's school choice groupies were a coalition of strange bedfellows then Susan Mitchell and her husband, George, were the ones who tucked everyone in each night. This couple, both of whom worked in Wisconsin state government in the 1970s and in journalism (for the *Wall Street Journal*), got so wrapped up in fighting for more educational choices for parents that it eventually became their full-time jobs.

The Mitchells got sucked into the education issue the way most people do, that is, as parents. When the couple moved from the state capital in Madison to Milwaukee in 1982, they started investigating public schools where they could send one of their daughters. What they quickly discovered was an obnoxious system that appeared, on first glance, to be rigged against minority students. The Mitchells are white, but they had two adopted daughters who were not. One of the schools they visited, a popular public magnet school, seemed as if it was a good fit, and their odds of getting their oldest daughter enrolled seemed good, until the school learned that the girl had the wrong skin color. The racial quotas in place to achieve racial balance in the school were working against them, just as they worked against thousands of black Milwaukee parents every year. In the quest to meet the court's definitions of racially balanced, the limited number of white students in the city were generally able to select the school of their choice, while caps were placed on the number of nonwhite students who could attend any one school, so as not to surpass a tipping point that would indicate the school was racially segregated. Intended originally to help black students integrate the best schools in the city, it eventually had the effect of shutting them out of the city's most popular schools as demographics changed and black students made up an increasingly larger percentage of the school system. One black Milwaukee leader told me years later: "George and Susan were unique in that they were part of the white establishment, but after their own experience trying to enroll their daughter, they didn't need to be convinced that our [black] children were getting a raw deal from this school system."

Two years after moving to Milwaukee, George Mitchell was named chair of governor Tony Earl's Study Commission on the Quality of Education in the Metropolitan Milwaukee Schools, which issued a series of ten reports that shattered the myth created by educrats in the system's Vliet Street headquarters that the city's minority students were performing well.

In 1991, after Howard Fuller was named superintendent of the schools, Susan Mitchell began working for him as a consultant (whose bill was paid by the Metropolitan Milwaukee Association of Commerce) to help reorganize the management structure of the school system. Her insider's view of the system helped form the basis for a groundbreaking report she wrote in 1994 titled *Why MPS (Milwaukee Public Schools) Doesn't Work.* The report, which detailed the unresponsive bureaucracy and the many barriers to meaningful reform in the city's public school system, was widely circulated among business and civic leaders and helped lay the groundwork for the support the school choice movement would eventually receive from business leaders and philanthropists.

The role of the private sector in Milwaukee's reforms has already been discussed in earlier sections. Its contributions didn't just happen in a vacuum, however, and careful coordination with the rest of the choice movement was crucial in harnessing its ultimate power. The opponents of school choice (mainly the teachers unions) widely assumed there was a vast right-wing conspiracy at work. They were half right. What happened certainly was a conspiracy in the form of careful coordination of all of these diverse players and groups. Much of this coordination was handled by Susan Mitchell.

Susan Mitchell and members of the coalition worked quietly behind the scenes for an entire year before their plans to expand school choice to religious schools in 1995 ever became public.[25] There were many groups working at the same time to make school choice a reality, and their organizational discipline was an important part of the coalition's strength. The scholarship group Partners Advancing Values in Education (PAVE), the parents group Parents for School Choice, the principals and parents at the city's private and alternative schools, local politicians, and business and philanthropic leaders all contributed to the coalition's efforts. In 1994, for example, before the group went public with their calls for an expansion of the school choice program to religious schools, organizers gathered the names of 4,000 parents to advocate for the cause. The October 1994 rally at Milwaukee Area Technical College where parents urged Thompson to back the plan had 750 parents in attendance.

As the program grew, Susan Mitchell continued to keep the coalition focused, on both the city's voucher program and the budding charter school movement. George Mitchell scoured the research and challenged reporters and editorial writers any time there was even the slightest inaccuracy or un-backed assertion that cast parental choice in a bad light. Later, after school choice had made it past the Wisconsin Supreme Court, George Mitchell organized the Fund for Choices in Education to raise money for Democratic and Republican candidates for state and local office who support parental choice, highlighting the importance of maintaining a political movement that could withstand the test of time, even as its original guardians, like Thompson and Norquist, moved on to other things.

As impressive as the Mitchells' work has been in Milwaukee, that they were still fighting legislative and public battles to cap the number of participants and/or eliminate funding for the program in 2004—14 years after the first tuition vouchers were used in Milwaukee—is a reminder that when your war is against the public education cartel, you can win many battles but there is never an end in sight. The teachers unions—who make no bones about the fact that they consider school choice to be their "Roe vs. Wade" issue because they believe at their core that public school money should be spent only in public school buildings—appeared perfectly willing to outlast reformers like the Mitchells, and everyone else in Milwaukee if they must, in order to kill the program.

## UNIONS AND THE BLOB

No list of people or groups who are responsible for making vouchers a success in Milwaukee would be complete without two of the most important groups: the teachers unions and the bureaucrats. The Milwaukee Teachers Education Association (MTEA) and the Wisconsin Education Association

Council (WEAC) joined school administrators in playing the perfect part of obstructionists, proving day in and day out that they had little regard for the well-being of Milwaukee's schoolchildren. The MTEA "alienated a good deal of the community" when the union was run by Donald Ernest between 1989 and 1994, the labor friendly *Milwaukee Journal* opined when he retired. "Ernest's brand of unionism was breathtaking for its rigidity, and at a time when the school administration was seeking flexibility to effectuate desperately needed reforms. . . . Thus the union has been one of the biggest stumbling blocks to the rescue of the Milwaukee Public Schools."[26]

As choice supporters like Polly Williams and Howard Fuller struggled to get their message out to the grass-roots, the unions and educrats did their part by reminding the public why choice was so necessary in the first place, blocking proposal after proposal designed to improve the school system, whether it involved contracting with organizations to teach at-risk students, closing failing schools, or creating new charter schools.

The tight grip the union leaders had on all aspects of the education system helped choice advocates to convince minority parents that the public education deck was stacked against them and their children. Former University of Wisconsin- Milwaukee professor Alex Molnar, a strong opponent of school choice, in 1995 suggested that the law was initially created as Polly Williams "was casting about for a way to slap the arrogant and ignorant bureaucracy of the Milwaukee public schools and a racist, backward-looking teachers union."[27]

Had the education establishment not gone out of its way to actively disenfranchise so many low-income parents, vouchers likely never would have materialized in Milwaukee. One of the groups that ultimately joined in the school choice coalition in the early 1990s were the left-wing types who ran alternative schools for dropouts and other at-risk kids. They saw their cause deflated by the teachers unions to snuff out any semblance of school choice. "If Polly Williams was the mother of school choice, then Morris Andrews was the father," one alternative school operator told me in the late 1990s. Andrews had long been the powerful head of WEAC, the state teacher's union which dominated all education policy in the 1980s before Thompson's election as governor.

In 1995, Andrews (who had retired three years earlier) visited the *Wisconsin State Journal* newsroom to argue against the plan to expand school choice. His defense served as a reminder for why so many people wanted vouchers to be made eligible for use in religious schools. "I won't defend the Milwaukee school system. It's a bureaucratic mess," the newspaper quoted him as "growling." "There's no question the Milwaukee public schools right now aren't doing the fundamental job of educating children."[28]

But it had been the opposition of Andrews and WEAC to legislation in the mid-1980s to provide more options for at-risk students that drove many left-leaning reformers into the school choice camp. In the late 1980s, when MPS Superintendent Robert Peterkin attempted to establish "partnerships" or arrangements with community-based private schools such as Highland Community School, Bruce Guadalupe, Urban Day, and Harambee to educate at-risk kids who were having trouble in the school system, the MTEA's staunch opposition propelled many left-leaning supporters of these schools to join the original school choice constituency. This further helped the movement show itself publicly as a broad coalition. "If anything, it was the left who took advantage of the right's money and influence in order to achieve very liberal goals," a left-leaning school choice supporter told me. One very liberal school choice supporter, former school board member John Gardner, became active as a parent at the Highland Community School on the city's west side. Gardner, who espoused many socialist theories, had been a labor organizer who once worked with Cesar Chavez in the United Farm Workers union. Like Howard Fuller, his goal as an activist and as an elected school board member was to force radical change in the public school system by giving power to the people. The harder the teachers unions fought Gardner, the more opportunities he had to make his case. (In 1999, to protest political advertisements the teachers union had bought that he felt were unfair to him, Gardner held a press conference on the sidewalk in front of the union's office, so that the television crews could capture the union's logo as a visual prop over his shoulder.)

The biggest help the unions and the education establishment provided to the choice movement, however, came after the school choice expansion to religious schools passed the legislature in 1995. Hundreds of students who thought they were about to start classes in their new private schools were suddenly blocked by an injunction from the union's lawsuit challenging the constitutionality of the program. The legal move backfired on the opponents, not only because they would go on to lose before the supreme court three years later, but because the story tugged at the city's heartstrings. Many members of the public came to regard those students as the victims of a system that was working against them. Suddenly, those who opposed school choice were "standing in the schoolhouse door" preventing low-income African American and Hispanic kids from getting a decent education, the story line went. In the week following the injunction halting the program, the PAVE group raised $1.5 million in scholarship money from school choice supporters who felt sorry for the hopeful students. The unions learned that it was much better to battle school choice as a faceless concept than to take on the real life parents and students who were simply trying to get ahead by attending a better school. Michael Joyce, of the Lynde and Harry Bradley Foundation, played a crucial role by opening the foundation's checkbook to keep the school choice movement moving along. Without strong support from the foundation and from the Milwaukee Metropolitan Association of Commerce, it would have been difficult for many parents to dig their heels in for the long, drawn-out legal battle.

## CHOICE TAKES HOLD

The decision posted on the Wisconsin Supreme Court's Web site very early on June 10, 1998, granted Milwaukee's low-income parents a chance to determine their children's education. Not only did the justices decide that low-income Milwaukee students had the right to attend private and religious schools at public expense, but they established the notion that the child was the most important stakeholder in the education system—not the bureaucrats, not the unions, and not even the participating religious schools. Public education, the court ruled, meant educating the public's children, regardless of the school. Parents who had waited for years for the judicial green light for school choice broke down in tears at the news. "I have more hope than I've ever had before today," parent Val Johnson told me. The expansion drastically increased the potential impact of competition on the city's schools, enlarging the program from about 1,000 students to as many as 15,000 students, and including many more religious schools in the menu of options for city parents. At the same time, the city was opening public charter schools that didn't have income restrictions, thus increasing even more the number of parents who might act as education consumers in the city. Opponents of school choice deep within the education establishment vowed to continue the fight against vouchers. State schools superintendent John Benson even warned that day that people like Oklahoma federal building bomber Timothy McVeigh would soon start schools in Milwaukee that would get tax money—suggesting that parents weren't capable of distinguishing good schools from bad.[29]

Superintendent Alan Brown, who came to Milwaukee long after the school choice program began and never expected it to be found constitutional, was shell-shocked. At a press conference hours after the decision was released, he warned that the school system might lose as much as $100 million if parents yanked their kids out of schools.[30] Howard Fuller, who always viewed control of the money as the key to change in the schools, reminded parents gathered at the St. Joan Antida celebration that the money was theirs to spend on education, not Alan Brown's. "If the concern is you want to keep the money, you have a very clear mandate: change," Fuller told Brown.[31]

A decade after her calls to liberate the north side neighborhoods of Milwaukee from the Milwaukee system, Rep. Annette "Polly" Williams credited the grass roots for the revolution. "This is a good example of what people can do if we get together and focus on the children," Williams said.[32]

A concept that began in 1990 with only 341 students attending seven nonsectarian schools would grow to 12,950 students at more than 100 private and religious schools by the 2003–04 school year. And the longer the concept had to develop roots, the more support it got from Milwaukeeans. In 1998, shortly after the state supreme court issued its ruling, the *Milwaukee Journal Sentinel* polled city residents and found 60 percent supported the program as it existed, allowing low-income students to attend private and religious schools at taxpayer expense.[33] A year later, the newspaper's poll showed support inching slightly higher, at 62 percent community support, with the strongest support coming from African Americans (74 percent in favor of choice) and respondents with incomes below $11,000 per year (81 percent).[34]

Milwaukee school superintendent Bill Andrekopolous, who took over after Spence Korte retired in 2002, argued that pressure from the school choice issue forced the school system to improve in a number of areas—a positive reaction to the loss of its monopoly status. "That competitive nature has raised the bar for educators in Milwaukee to provide a good product or they know that parents will simply walk," said Andrekopolous, who himself helped convert Milwaukee's Fritsche Middle School to the city's first charter school when he was its principal in the late 1990s.

Some of the most widely cited changes in the Milwaukee public schools in the wake of power being transferred to the parent-consumers came in the form of major changes negotiated in the teachers' contract. The new order assured that teachers were more often chosen by site-based selection committees rather than based on longevity in the system, allowing teachers to seek out like-minded colleagues who would be a good fit in their schools. The teachers union also eased provisions in the contract for releasing teachers who aren't getting the job done. But the changes went far beyond just the contract. Full-day kindergarten programs for four-year-olds, for example, were dramatically expanded to compete with private schools that were winning the market share.[35]

Most major indicators showed that the public schools had improved in the years since competition took hold. The percentage of third graders who scored "proficient" or above on the key third grade reading exam shot up from 50 percent in 1998 to 66 percent in 2004; the drop-out rate declined from 16.2 percent in 1991 to 10.2 percent in 2003. Harvard economist Caroline Minter Hoxby in 2002 showed that since Milwaukee's program expanded to religious schools in 1998, public schools in low-income neighborhoods (the ones in danger of losing students eligible for vouchers) increased their student performance by a much higher rate than other schools in Milwaukee and Wisconsin where the threat of losing students was not as great. Hoxby's study was widely hailed as a sign that competition had some educational merit.[36]

There was certainly no magic voucher wand that suddenly made everything perfect in Milwaukee's education system, but the simple shift in power from the system to low-income parents itself assured a greater likelihood that the focus of education would be squarely on the student to whom public education dollars were attached. Clearly, many public and private schools continue to need additional improvement if Milwaukee wishes to guarantee every child a chance to get an appropriate education. Additionally, the long-term success of parental choice in Milwaukee will come down to whether or not parents themselves exercise good choices for their children, and whether they continue to fight to retain their power.

It took a tremendous effort on the part of many individuals to create the kind of political force that produced school choice in Milwaukee, and history may go on to show that its potency was short lived. The same diversity of ideology within the initial coalition that provided its tremendous power also proved problematic after several years of parental choice in Milwaukee. Polly Williams eventually grew disenchanted with others in the movement after the choice program was expanded beyond the original community schools. She criticized those who were pushing for broader choice for parents beyond means-tested vouchers. Splits developed within the choice coalition over how much public regulation there should be for private schools participating in the program, and the political movement to elect choice-friendly school board members lost the steam it had had when it was able to tap into Mayor Norquist's political machinery. Perhaps most problematic of all, the low-income parents who benefited from school choice never translated their earlier activism into anything as powerful as it could have been at the polls. Their passionate fight to get power fizzled when it came time to preserve it, and they never fully emerged as a long-term voting force that could punish elected officials who wanted to remove their power.

Meanwhile, the teachers unions, demonstrating a disciplined patience, remained sharply intent on stalling and killing the choice program—a singular focus that took on a new significance once the school choice coalition began to lose some of its punch. Democrats representing the city remained pressured by the powerful unions to oppose the program; they lessened their support for the program once it was enacted and some of the original organized parents moved on to other things. Parents who were no longer directly in battle to get the law enacted naturally were less positioned to remain a political force, making it easier for elected Democrats to return to pandering to the teachers unions. Suburban Republicans grew increasingly frustrated that they were being asked to carry the city-specific program on their shoulders as Democratic support weakened.

The teachers union and the choice coalition appear to be heading for a showdown in the fall of 2005, when, for the first time in the 15 years of vouchers, the enrollment will be expected to surpass the legislated cap of 15 percent of the city's public school enrollment. Without a raise in the cap, some parents would see their hard-fought choices once again stripped away from them. In many respects, the long-term viability of Milwaukee's voucher program will come down to whether or not parents will continue to assert their power in the political arena to protect a program they have come to cherish.

Milwaukee's experience offers some optimism—even if cautious. It remains to be seen whether these parents will continue to benefit from the kind of education decisions made by other parents who have the financial means to select schools for their children. The political nature of the process means the fight for school choice is never ending, and those battling to put children first must be in it for the long haul to ensure no backtracking. The same forces that regularly put children last in the school system would like nothing more than to return to the good old days, when all parents were a captive audience for the school system. This sobering reality needs to be considered along with Milwaukee's story, because it is a reminder of just how powerful and patient the school employee groups can be—even after they appear to be down for the count.

Parents in Milwaukee showed that the fight for power over their children's education is winnable, and that children can become the focus of a very public education system. They demonstrated the importance of partnerships with philanthropists and business leaders, and the importance of strong political leadership that is willing to consider the interests of the little guy over the special interests that typically hold all the cards in school systems. These were "crazy parents" who decided that their children deserved to have a good education and were willing to stand together to fight some of the most powerful forces in state politics. They put their feet down, made their children's education the highest priority, and in the process, turned the status quo of the Milwaukee public schools on its head.[37]

# 12

## PARENT POWER

In March 2000, a suburban Florida woman named Carol Goings complained to Seminole County school officials that a special education teacher, Kathleen Garrett, had walloped her disabled daughter on the head. The mother sent a four-page letter detailing her complaints of child abuse to the principal of Indian Trails Middle School and began openly discussing her concerns with other parents and administrators. But faster than you can say "cease and desist," Goings was forced to back off after she was threatened with legal action by the state teachers union. The union, the Florida Teaching Profession–National Education Association, decided the mother was out of bounds and the union's lawyer, Pamela Cooper, fired off a letter to Goings threatening to "consider formal legal action against you and pursue whatever damages are available to Ms. Garrett" for harming the teacher's reputation.[1]

The mother's case, which the teachers union's lawyer termed "malicious and actionable," ended up being handled the way many contemporary school officials prefer: it was quietly swept under the rug. Goings, who had been allowed to transfer her 13-year-old daughter to another classroom after the incident, withdrew her allegations because she wasn't prepared to wage a legal battle with one of the most powerful special interests in the state. In fact, the world likely would never have learned about the allegations if Garrett hadn't landed on the front pages of Florida's newspapers four years later, accused by authorities of beating and humiliating other autistic students. Authorities accused the veteran teacher of sitting on some students, knocking out one child's teeth by smashing his head into a desk, and pushing another's face into vomit. Investigators also found "adult material" on her classroom computer.

The case and the attention it gathered brought out of the woodwork a long list of parents and students who had quietly complained to school officials over the years about Garrett's actions. One student told the *Orlando Sentinel* that while working in Garrett's class as a peer tutor in 2000, he saw her grab a disabled child by the neck and throw him into a closed closet door. The disabled student had been using a walker to make his way across the classroom at the time. Another parent that same year reported that Garrett had beaten her son with a ruler until his head was bloody, but school and police officials said Garrett told them the boy had fallen. Case closed. Meanwhile, Garrett's official record with the school district was stuffed with favorable write-ups from administrators, because it's always easier to give someone a good evaluation than to risk a grievance or legal action by saying something the teacher may not like.

The chilling letter Goings had received four years earlier from union lawyer Pamela Cooper had accused Goings of impugning Garrett's reputation and undermining her credibility with other parents and her supervisors. "You have falsely made formal allegations that Ms. Garrett mistreated your child and have criticized, among many other things, Ms. Garrett's teaching abilities," Cooper wrote, saying Goings' motives were "clearly suspect and reinforce our belief that your actions are not in good faith."

The union accused Goings of slandering the teacher by making her concerns about Garrett known publicly, saying that the parent had stepped over legal boundaries, and threatening to make Goings pay for impugning Garrett's good name.

"By this letter, we are demanding that you cease and desist in making these false and malicious statements against Ms. Garrett and urge you to develop a more cooperative approach in dealing with those who are genuinely concerned about providing the best education for all students," Cooper wrote. "Rather than attacking those educators who have the students' best interests at heart, it would certainly be more productive to work together to enable all the students to meet their fullest potential. This was and remains Ms. Garrett's primary goal despite your treatment of her."

The union's lawyer ended the letter with a stern warning in all capital letters: "PLEASE GOVERN YOURSELF ACCORDINGLY."

Goings may have been fearful when she was all alone and the teachers union lawyers threatened to sue her if she followed through with her complaints back in 2000, but she never forgot how she was pressured. When the story broke about the new allegations against Garrett four years later, she let loose, releasing copies of the union's shocking letter to her to the press.[2]

As observed earlier, teachers unions have a responsibility to defend the rank-and-file who pay dues, even after they have smashed a student's skull into his desk. It is their right (and arguably their responsibility) to threaten and harass parents if they feel it will help their members' chances of keeping their jobs. And while editorial writers in Florida blamed the union for the mess, the case against Kathleen Garrett exposed a problem that goes far beyond the muscle of organized labor. Garrett's case shed light on one of the dirtiest little secrets of public education today: Parents who assert themselves in order to protect the interests of their children often are treated like the ones who are doing something wrong.

If anything is to change in public education, parents must start asserting themselves as the customers of the system, even when the forces within the system respond by kicking and screaming or attacking the customers' motives. Parents are the only special interest within the system capable of truly making the needs of their children their primary motivation. When parents and the public set the bar high and hold school leaders and politicians accountable, the education of students can become a higher priority than the sometimes vicious fights over school money and power. It is parents, for example, who have a shot at reminding the major political parties that they make up a bigger potential voting bloc than the powerful teachers unions, who have historically exercised veto power over most plans to radically alter the present system. In New York City alone, there are some 100,000 teachers union members, but more than ten times as many students and parents by extension.

Allowing parents to choose schools is the ultimate form of customer empowerment, but there are other ways that parents can assert themselves to improve their children's education. School bureaucrats and other members of the education cartel have a reason why they often treat parents the way they do—they like the current arrangement and the power it affords them. The expectations of parents are often sharply defined within the school system: buy supplies for your child's class, raise money from time to time, bake cookies for fundraisers, and keep your mouth shut—unless, of course, we need you to pressure elected officials to give us more money, at which time we'll tell you where to send your letters and what telephone number to call.

Carol Goings' case is extreme only in that the threats against her parent activism were actually put on paper, but similar situations play out all the time on all sorts of matters both more and less serious in nature. As long-time Harlem (New York City) activist and parent Babette Edwards told me:

"They make you feel like you are the problem. It's all right if you have cake sales and all that, but when you ask why the reading scores haven't gone up in three years, or God forbid about something even more serious, then you have to be shut up."

Some schools get restraining orders or take other drastic measures against parents who stand up for their kids. Virginia mom Chrystal Stevens and her daughter were banned from Asbury Elementary School in 1998 because the mother had the audacity to walk her daughter directly to her first grade classroom without a visitor's pass. The ban lasted for more than a month before a compromise was reached, but the details of the case, as described in the *Newport News Daily Press*, and the compromise itself are illustrative of how many parents are made to feel unwelcome in their children's schools.

On the day when Stevens broke the school's golden rule, her daughter refused to walk alone to class so Stevens and her daughter stopped into the school office to get the mandatory visitor's pass. A secretary in the office told her that only the principal, Joseph Tatum, could sign a visitor's pass, but that he wasn't there at the moment. In public schools, rules are rules and that's often the end of the discussion. Fearing that her daughter would be late for class, she decided to escort the girl to her classroom because the child didn't want to walk alone. Bureaucratic bells and whistles went off instantly: Intruder! Intruder! When a frantic Principal Tatum eventually caught up with Stevens, he informed her that she was trespassing on school property and ordered her out of the building.[3]

A month later, after a meeting among the mother, the educrats, and Tatum, the school agreed to allow the little girl back to class, but only after Stevens promised (cross her heart) to obtain a visitor's pass in the future. As a part of the negotiated compromise, the school agreed to allow Stevens to use a special visitor's pass that wasn't signed by the principal. Principal Tatum's comments in the press afterward declared a victory on behalf of the bureaucracy: "I think things are a lot better. We developed a plan for the child to come into school. We agreed together that the mother could come back to the grounds as long as she adhered to the policy of coming in and getting the pass."[4]

Far below the radar screen of the public's awareness, these kinds of incidents play out every day in American schools, where the message is crystal clear: Parents are welcome only if they are doing exactly what the system wants, which typically involves not rocking the boat. It's about power. The parents who aren't on task have no power.

## A WALL BETWEEN PARENTS AND SCHOOL LEADERS

In May 2003, a group of angry parents stormed into the headquarters of the San Francisco Unified School District, demanding to meet with superintendent Arlene Ackerman about their kids' assignment to what they considered to be a substandard high school. It's a supply-and-demand problem that plagues many urban school districts with more deserving students than seats in nonfailing schools. The parents that day, mostly Asian, wanted their kids to attend either George Washington or Abraham Lincoln High School, two of the most popular and sought after schools in the city.[5] At a time when school employees all over the country complain that parents aren't interested or engaged in their children's schooling, this was yet another example of parents who were more than willing to assert themselves so that their kids might have a better education.

Despite this passionate form of parent involvement, San Francisco school officials weren't impressed. Rather than taking bold steps to increase the supply of good schools, they instead built a wall, literally, between the public elevators and the superintendent's office, so that the customers would be kept at bay if there were any future confrontations. City and school officials drew up plans for a glass partition to be constructed, but the project would have required the construction of a new bathroom and a major overhaul of the entire third floor of the district offices. The plans, which were later scrapped because the cost of the project would have hit six figures, cost taxpayers $21,200.[6] Instead, a scaled-back version was designed and built. Rather than a glass partition, crews constructed a wood partition with a door framed by glass windows. Ackerman, however, went through the roof when she learned that the revised $8,000 wall project cost an additional $9,000 to design.[7] "I could have designed that wall," Ackerman told the *San Francisco Chronicle*.

The San Francisco case is rare in that the wall that is built to keep interested parents out was physical. More often, the wall is theoretical. Parents around the country continue to walk into school offices where secretaries and clerks don't even bother to look up to acknowledge their presence, much less offer their assistance; the pointed message sent is that dealing with moms and dads isn't their job. Just try getting a phone message returned at most schools and you'll understand that there is seldom any degree of respect given to parents and others who operate outside the school building. Villanova University political science professor Robert Maranto described a frustrating experience checking out public schools for his kindergarten-age son in Lower Merion, Pennsylvania, a Philadelphia suburb. "Many public schools still treat parents like mushrooms: Feed them guano and keep them in the dark,"[8] Maranto wrote in an essay published by the *Wall Street Journal*. Despite the $20,000 per child spent by the school system each year, Maranto said the principal had trouble returning three telephone messages left during regular business hours. On his fourth try, he got a real live person and inquired about tours of the school. "We don't have any visiting this year," he was told. Parents are not permitted to observe classrooms, he was told. The answer wasn't good enough for Maranto. He persisted and was eventually allowed to peek inside the public school, but it took five months, and 22 phone calls, faxes, and e-mails to the superintendent's office to make it happen.[9]

In Maranto's case, since he was merely shopping around trying to find a school for his son, the resistance he encountered from the educrats was more passive than that encountered by parents who already have kids enrolled. When they speak up on their behalf, they are many times greeted with active resistance from the system, reminding parents once again that their children come last. Situations often are twisted to make parents feel as though they, or their children, are the ones who have done something wrong. Other times, busy administrators hear the complaints from parents, promise to do something about it, and then immediately get back to their long list of tasks for the day without ever addressing the problem. History shows, however, that if there is one thing that educrats fear more than a parent who speaks up for his or her child, it is when dozens or even hundreds of parents stand up for their children at the same time. Because the structure of any public school system is too strong for most individual parents to take on alone, getting action from school leaders often requires strength in numbers—and sometimes some help from the media. Parents who make a difference often understand that confrontation is sometimes necessary. In order to get results within the system, the frustrated parents need to inflict discomfort on school leaders.

We have seen how various forces within the school bureaucracy look out for their own interests so that the educational needs of children often are trumped by the wants of adult employees. We have also seen the effect this reality has on the modern political process, as well as the role of the business and philanthropic communities in keeping the public school system humming along. As Americans have known for a long time, the status quo hasn't been serving all of our children to the extent that it should, but because the status quo works just fine for those who earn their livelihoods off public school budgets, we have seen very little change.

One of the most overlooked tools of modern school reform is the concept of power—who has it, who wants it, and who needs it. One reason so little changes in education is because the people who hold the cards are always the same, no matter what the popular reforms of the day involve. We have tried centralization of decision-making power and decentralization of decision-making power. We've raised standards and enacted zero-tolerance policies. We've beaten into the ground such catch phrases as "lifelong learners" and "capacity building." Yet, in all these reform efforts, parents have never really been allowed to be the ones who get to make the ultimate decision: choosing their child's school. Bureaucrats and politicians always seem to get the last word, even though parents have the best odds of making decisions that put their kids first. I'm not talking about letting parents *run* schools, I'm just talking about letting parents *pick* schools. In short, we seem to have tried everything in American education but allowing parents and their children to truly act as customers of the public school system.

## PARENT POWER VS. COMMUNITY CONTROL

In December 1966, a group of community activists joined in a three-day takeover of the New York City Board of Education. The whole thing started when board members refused to allow a black mother from Brooklyn's Brownsville section to speak out of turn during a meeting. At the time, there was a growing frustration in New York City's black neighborhoods that white school leaders (including the men running the teachers union) were not taking the educational needs of black students seriously enough. Activists throughout the city already were buzzing about the idea of community control, where locally elected boards would have the power to run the schools in their community, select the curriculum and hire the principals and teachers. Historian Diane Ravitch describes what happened that night in *The Great School Wars:* "Supporting shouts from the audience disrupted the meeting to the point where the Board members called an early adjournment and walked out. The leather chairs of Board members were promptly filled by several members of the audience who declared themselves the 'People's Board of Education' and designated the protester from Brownsville as the superintendent of schools. The group then continued the hearings, which consisted of attacks on the regular Board of Education."[10] Babette Edwards was one of the women who stormed the board table that heady night. Her personal desire to see community control of schools began after first pushing for integrated schooling earlier in the 1960s. It became clear at the time that real integration would be too politically and practically painful to pull off, so Edwards and others began seeking to turn around troubled schools through locally empowered boards that could hire and fire the school staff. For a while, angry parents around the city felt as if they were about to be empowered to fight for their children for the first time in their lives. "It was an amazing evening," Edwards said of the controversial board meeting. "Parents from all over the city took it seriously until we were carted off to jail."[11]

But the real fight for people like Edwards was about giving parents power to control their children's destiny, not about decentralization. New decentralized community school districts were created a short time later but were taken over by political machines and the teachers unions, thus assuring that parent voices would continue to be silenced. Essentially, community control never translated into parent power because other special interests seized the power first. By 1976, frustration with the poor quality of public schooling in Harlem led a group of parents to pull their kids out of the system while demanding that they get their money back in the form of vouchers. That demand got them nowhere with school officials, who instead gave them warnings that they would be reported to the proper authorities for child neglect, even though they were being tutored by a group that Edwards had put together. Nonetheless, Edwards's group of Harlem parents empowered themselves, understanding that desperate times demanded desperate measures. "Parents yanked them out of school," Edwards said, and enrolled them in the Harlem Tutorial and Referral Project, a sort of freedom school she ran at the time.[12] The program had math experts teaching math and English majors teaching English. They took field trips to cultural institutions and prepared some students for eventual enrollment in private schools where their needs would be better met.

Edwards, like many inner city leaders at the time, resented that poor parents didn't have the same kinds of options that more well-to-do families had. They had no recourse for the horrible public schools in Harlem at the time, schools that no one seemed to be doing anything to fix. "You're obliged to send your child to a failure-factory," Edwards said. "Could they do any worse? I'm not a knee-jerk conservative, but I had to support the concept of vouchers."[13] For Edwards, like many other 1960s-era radicals, the concept of school choice was "power to the people" come full circle.

The public can take back its runaway public school systems in a way that puts kids first, but only if it is willing to help parents wrestle power away from the special interests. The system itself has proven that as long as it has no reason to put kids first, it will never, ever do so. Parents, with help from the public, must provide a reason to change, even if it involves scaring the daylights out of those with power. As organizing genius Saul Alinsky has

---

### 12 RULES TO HELP PARENTS
### TAKE BACK THEIR PUBLIC SCHOOLS

**Rule 1** Never, ever be ashamed of the fact that you want a good education for your child.

**Rule 2** If you don't blow the whistle on school problems, no one will.

**Rule 3** If parents want to be treated like customers, they must start acting like customers.

**Rule 4** Do your homework.

**Rule 5** Don't trust PTAs to do anything other than raising cold, hard cash.

**Rule 6** There's strength in numbers.

**Rule 7** If the facts are on your side, share them with the world.

**Rule 8** Fight for transparency throughout the system.

**Rule 9** If an administrator tells you something can't be done, assume they are wrong and plow forward.

**Rule 10** Remember that school politics revolves around money.

**Rule 11** If you've tried steps 1 through 10, and your kids still aren't a priority, it's time to demand your tax money back.

**Rule 12** Be a part of the political process.

---

noted in his book *Rules for Radicals*, a true revolution will only occur if the "have-nots" steal power from the "haves." In this case, the "haves" are the members of the education cartel who hold all of the power in school systems; the "have-nots" are parents who have no power over whether their children get a good education or not.

Parents who want their kids to come first in education need to assert themselves in new ways. Too much of the pain and discomfort in today's education system is felt by parents and students alone. A true child-centered approach spreads this pain more evenly to the adults who earn healthy salaries to make sure our children are educated properly. Many people who operate in government and within school systems will find this kind of talk to be too radical, but parents have been reticent for too long and too willing to allow their own children to be hurt by school systems that aren't the least bit responsive to their needs. If parents aren't willing to take drastic measures for their kids, the status quo will surely prevail.

Parent activism can take on many forms because parents have needs and wants that run the spectrum. Such drastically different ends justify drastically different means to achieve those ends. After the collapse of the World Trade Center's twin towers on September 11, 2001, parents at several public schools near "ground zero" mobilized to make sure their kids wouldn't be returning to classes if there was any chance that the air quality was not safe. At several of the schools in Lower Manhattan, which represented some of the wealthiest schools in the city, parent associations hired lawyers and environmental engineers who could provide independent air-quality readings, which often produced different results than the official government-sponsored tests showing no danger in the air. They demanded negotiations with school leaders, organized protests, threatened legal action, and developed a disciplined media strategy; they ended up giving themselves power in deciding the dates and conditions by which students would return to their schools. They were able to demand the types of clean-up measures that would be undertaken. They were concerned, and they put their feet down and insisted that the health needs of their kids be addressed. At Stuyvesant High School, located blocks away from the towers site and the first school to call its students back in the aftermath of the terrorist attacks, nosebleeds and persistent coughs and headaches prompted parent leaders to push to have the school's air ducts and upholstered furniture cleaned with high-powered vacuums to remove asbestos and other chemicals. But they, too, had to fight for it. These parents became a powerful force at the time. As one parent leader in Lower Manhattan explained to me then: "Our parents' generation used to go to the chancellor's office and chain themselves to the desk until they got what they wanted. Our generation hires lawyers."

Parent power doesn't have to rely on lawyers, however. Sometimes old-fashioned activism will do the trick. What follows are twelve rules to help parents who care about their kids take back their public schools.

## Rule 1: Never, ever be ashamed of the fact that you want a good education for your child.

Even in so-called good schools, in which people will tell you things are much worse in other schools, you're responsible as a parent to fight to raise the bar of expectations. Always remember that no one in the school system deserves a job more than your child deserves an education.

Former Milwaukee superintendent Howard Fuller used to launch into speeches before public school parents by asking this question: "Are there any crazy parents in the house?" Often, the parents looked back at him with some suspicion, until he explained exactly what he was getting at. "You know, those crazy parents who have the nerve to go up to their schools and ask 'What's happening to my child?'" Fuller explained that he is talking about the kinds of parents who, as they approach their children's schools, cause the people inside the building to nervously declare, "Here come those crazy parents again!"[14]

Real education reform doesn't come from hiring management consultants to rearrange administrative structures, or from imposing new curriculum kits, or from making students wear uniforms. Real reform requires a transfer of power from the haves within the system to the have-nots whose children desperately require a better education.

Fuller argued that the entire school choice movement in Milwaukee (see chapter 11) was about getting better treatment for those crazy parents in the city who cared enough to demand more for their kids. Under the city's private school choice program, low-income parents aren't forced to wait around for the latest in a series of school reformers promising improvements for their children's education. If they aren't satisfied, they can take their public education dollars someplace else that better meets their needs. "Now everybody knows if you don't treat crazy parents right, not only is the child going to leave, but the money leaves too," Fuller said.[15]

Parents must make their children a "special interest" in the schools. Teachers and other employees have unions that fight for them when they are treated poorly. Parents need to fight just as doggedly for their kids—and must keep on fighting to make sure they never again slip from the top of the priority list in public education. This shouldn't be much to ask of parents. The public, for their part, should support structural reforms that allow parents to truly act like customers, so that children's needs supersede the needs and wants of the other supposed special interests.

Make school officials eat their words if they claim that parents are not involved in schools. It is up to parents to dispel such a claim by translating their interest into action. "It really astonishes me that people think that people in our community don't care about their kids' education," said Harlem's Edwards.[16]

Whether the walls that school leaders build between parents and schools are real, as in San Francisco, or theoretical, knock them down. Public schools belong to the public, and that includes parents.

## Rule 2: If you don't blow the whistle
## on school problems, no one will.

The culture of most public schools doesn't allow for risk taking on the part of employees. Teachers and administrators aren't usually lining up to put their jobs on the line by calling attention to failure. The message sent to them from the bureaucracy is clear: keep your head down, hope for the best, and if all else fails, there's still a heck of a pension waiting at the end of the rainbow.

Kathleen Gerlach spent four years trying to get leaking and nonfunctioning toilets replaced inside her son's school on Manhattan's Upper East Side. Her advocacy earned her the nickname "The Toilet Lady" at the school, but until 2003–04 she was forced to settle for excuses: there was no money to fix the toilets, the pipes were too old and couldn't fit with modern plumbing, et cetera. "They give you every reason in the world why they won't give our kids a safe, sanitary environment," Gerlach told me.[17]

Because Mayor Michael Bloomberg had introduced a "311 complaint line" for city services and pledged to fix problems as they arose, people at the school encouraged Gerlach to phone in the problem to the mayor's line. She also took pictures of the deplorable conditions in the school's bathrooms and shared them with the world. In April 2005, after the story hit the newspaper, the toilets were replaced and every single one flushed.

"Our kids shouldn't have to live with this," said Gerlach, whose advocacy was not appreciated by some parents, who felt the publicity gave the school a black eye. Some parents at the school worried that if they spoke up, vindictive educrats would torpedo their child's application to a decent middle school; others feared that middle-class parents wouldn't want to send their kids to a school where the toilets didn't flush—something that might harm the school in the long run—so they maintained their perverse code of silence.

If your child's classroom doesn't have books, fight like hell to get them, but keep fighting to make sure the teachers do something with them. Basic problems can be symbolic of larger problems—and tackling them can send a message that parents won't tolerate the way things are done. If teachers' cars are parked in the children's outdoor play area and children have no place to play, it is a sign of a larger problem. Fight to get the cars moved, but also to address the kind of adult-centered thinking that allowed the cars to be parked there in the first place.

## Rule 3: If parents want to be treated like customers, they must start acting like customers.

Parents have become too conditioned to the idea that they must accept the school system's decisions. They must shop around, learn how to recognize quality, and demand it for their kids. "If there are two grocery stores in the same neighborhood and one sells rotten vegetables and the other sells fresh vegetables, don't let anyone make you buy the rotten vegetables," said Harlem's Babette Edwards.[18]

As customers, parents are the ones who get to decide when there is a problem with their child's education. The producer doesn't get to decide whether or not the product is worth buying, the customer does. The way it works now is backwards, and parents need to be the ones to demand better.

There is a curious similarity in the positions of self-proclaimed reformers like Mayor Bloomberg and his allies on one side and the unions and education experts on the other: They both believe they know what is best for education reform and have little faith in parents' ability to make the right choices for their children. When parents are given clear signals that their views don't matter, they have no way to make their views known.

Neither New York City chancellor Joel Klein nor his predecessor Harold Levy sent their kids to public schools, which is their right as Americans. Interestingly, this is a right that many school leaders and teachers exercise. In 1999, when Al Davis was being considered for the job of running the New Orleans public schools he publicly pledged to send his children to the schools as an incentive for him to improve the school system. A year later, after he was on the job, he was forced to admit that he had pulled one of his daughters out of her school so that she could attend an all-girls private school. "People do what's best for their kids," Davis explained. "Choice is good."[19]

In 1993, news reports indicated that Washington, D.C., superintendent Franklin L. Smith was considering taking his son Delvin out of the district's Alice Deal Junior High School and enrolling him at Falls Church High School in Virginia, where Smith's older son was a resident.[20] After the ensuing hooplah from the news reports, Smith opted instead to enroll his son at St. John's College High School, a private prep school.[21]

If the public schools aren't good enough for the people running them, no one should be forced to send their own kids there. It's bad public policy.

## Rule 4: Do your homework.

Knowledge is power. One of the reasons parents in low-income areas don't demand more of their children's schools is they don't fully understand how the system works, or even how the conditions at their kids' schools compare with other schools in their cities and around the nation. Often this is because of a lack of real transparency and the education cartel's unwillingness to allow the outside world to see detailed data on school performance.

It is amazing what happens to parents when they find out what information on schools is available to them and learn how they can use it to evaluate their children's schools. It is even more amazing when they visit other schools of similar circumstances and see how much better things could be in their own schools.

One thing that school systems are particularly good at is collecting data. Find out what kind of information is available to use to compare and assess schools. In addition to test scores, parents are usually able to demand information about teacher certification, school budgets, and student suspensions and expulsions. Assume that every piece of paper that passes hands in a public school system is public and fight to see it if you think the public's right to know anything outweighs a school employee's right to privacy.

Parents should also understand the governance structure of their local schools: who is in charge of what and who can affect change at which levels.

## Rule 5: Don't trust PTAs to do anything other than raising cold, hard cash.

Chester Finn, of the Thomas B. Fordham Foundation, calls the PTA an "echo of the public school establishment, rather than a voice for parents and children." Finn is onto something, particularly when he uses the description "All T and no P." He believes the PTA's national organization has been more interested in propping up "institutional claims and employee interests."[22]

Savvy principals often exercise control over these groups, steering them to believe that he or she is doing everything possible under the circumstances to improve the schools. These compliant parents, in turn, often become apologists themselves for the problems at the school. "The PTAs are part of the system," said Jesse McDonald, of Mothers on the Move, a group of activist school moms in the South Bronx. "We didn't want to sit around a table and just do whatever the principal tells us."[23]

PTAs must be considered an entrenched part of the status quo, and are often therefore part of the problem. The very structure of the organization depends on everyone in the school getting along, a sort of big educational group hug of teachers, parents, and administrators.

Founded in 1897 as the National Congress of Mothers, the PTA has always enjoyed close ties with the teachers unions. Teachers officially joined the organization in 1899 and changed its face forever. Education writer Thomas Toch noted in a 2001 *New York Times* piece that one of the PTA's three Washington lobbyists at that time was married to a National Education Association (NEA) lobbyist, and from the founding of the PTA's Washington legislative office in 1978 through 1993, its lobbyists were housed in rent-reduced offices in the NEA's headquarters a few blocks from the White House. American Federation of Teachers lobbyist Charlotte Frass told Toch: "We often lobby together."[24]

This cozy—and organizationally incestuous—relationship has broad implications. It is very difficult to identify a single educational issue, for example, on which the PTA has broken ranks with the NEA or the AFT, the prime apologists for a system that has failed millions of students. The problem is at its worst when the subject of collective bargaining comes up. The Education Policy Institute's Charlene Haar, who has documented the history of the PTA and the organization's growing ineffectiveness over the years, notes that teachers threatened to walk out of PTAs in the late 1960s if the organizations supported management during teacher strikes. Because the issue was so explosive within individual PTAs around the country, the entire organization agreed to adopt a policy of neutrality on all issues surrounding the teachers' contracts—even parts of the contracts that directly affect parents.

So it is important to note that when we talk about applying pressure to transform—and thus save—the modern public education system, our calls for more "crazy parents" in schools tend not to include the kinds of parents who are already part of the public school blob by virtue of their PTA membership. We're talking about taking power from the haves and giving it to the have-nots. Some parents have shown an extreme interest in the work of community school councils, elected bodies throughout the city who advise the chancellor on issues but have no real power. But not all parents want to sit on councils or PTA boards: they simply want to enroll their kids in a school that works and support their child's learning once there.

## Rule 6: There's strength in numbers.

Being a crazy mom or dad is a lot easier if there are other crazies there to support you. Parents are, after all, going up against powerful forces within the school system, with direct ties to the political parties that control government. A solitary parent complaining about a watered-down reading curriculum is sure to be written off as a mere nuisance. But 100 parents complaining together make politicians sweat. The larger the crowd, the more politicians will want to side with the crowd, particularly if crowd members make it clear to politicians they will remember their support or lack of it come election time. This is how the special interests do it, parents should do the same. Quid pro quo is a good thing if it results in your child getting a better education.

Whenever possible, enlist powerful friends. The best outside agitating has a friendly connection with someone on the inside who can help. A school board member or a well-placed administrator can provide valuable inside information and assistance. Let them know you can be trusted and show them your interests are truly putting the needs of your children first. In public battles with school officials, invite elected officials to join your cause and stand with you. School systems rely on federal, state, and local governments for their livelihoods. Use whatever political leverage you can get.

## Rule 7: If the facts are on your side, share them with the world.

A good information campaign can increase the number of parents you bring to the cause. If your school has the lowest math scores in your district and the school isn't doing anything about it, create graphs and charts and hand them out in front of the school in the morning as parents are dropping off their kids. Give them to real estate agents who sell homes in your neighborhood and urge them to ask school officials why the math scores are so low. The worst thing that will happen is some ruffled feathers in the principal's office or in the math department. You can guarantee that if the information is correct, there will at least be more interesting conversations about mathematics instruction at the school than if you allowed the status quo to continue for another year.

If you're battling entrenched forces, the press can be a great equalizer. What school leader or politician wants to have to explain to a reporter why the parents at a school are so unhappy? Gather your facts, take pictures if it helps, show that you have other parents on board, select a spokesperson and a clear message, and call a local reporter. Force your school leaders to defend what you consider indefensible learning conditions for your child. The special interests within the public education cartel usually exercise their power behind the scenes. Make your battle as public as possible to level the playing field.

## Rule 8: Fight for transparency throughout the system.

There are many different battles affecting parents from school to school, but every successful battle to open up information makes the next battle that much easier for someone else to do the same. Public schools are public. In order for parents and the public to reward success and punish failure, they need to be able to see things for themselves. "It has to be open and information has to be available," said Harlem's Babette Edwards. "That's the only way people are going to make intelligent decisions."[25]

Parents can only act like customers if they are empowered with reliable information that they can use to evaluate schools and then act based on that evaluation. It is amazing what happens when parents do their homework, even so-called unsophisticated parents in central city neighborhoods, the ones who are often accused of being AWOL when it comes to their children's schools. At the start of the 2004–05 school year, thousands of New York City high school parents lined up outside regional registration centers to try to get their kids out of bad schools. Many were looking for something—anything—that was better than the school to which they had been assigned. Many were able to cite to the tenth of a percentage point the graduation rates and the pass rates on mandatory New York State Regents exams of the schools they were talking about.

When school officials make this information available, many parents begin to demand better for their kids. Parents must continue to push school leaders and politicians to increase the supply to meet this pent-up parental demand for non-failing schools.

## Rule 9: If an administrator tells you something can't be done, assume they are wrong and plow forward.

This is another way of saying don't take no for an answer when it comes to your kids. When Elnora Yarborough needed to arrange bus service from her home in rural Madison County, Tennessee, to her children's school, the

school superintendent told her to forget it—bus service was only for neighborhoods that had enough children to support a bus. The Yarboroughs
lived on a dirt road at the time, in a predominantly black neighborhood,
and the children in the area had to walk a long distance to the paved road
where a bus could pick them up. Yarborough told the superintendent that
there were 40 kids in that neighborhood; the superintendent told her he
didn't believe her.

"So my husband and I got a list of the kids, and I carried it back to the
superintendent," Yarborough said. "Then he thought I had made up the
names."[26] Undeterred, Yarborough went back to the neighborhood and
went door to door to get the names of the students' parents and their addresses. "I went door to door, walking, and asking the parents if they would
go over there in a group," Yarbrough said. "Some people were scared, they
had never done this before, and they didn't want to do it. So I said, we've
started and we're not going to stop. I got all the information and carried it
back. I had to make seven trips. I had to convince him."[27]

In the end, the Yarborough kids and their neighbors got their bus, but
because it couldn't travel on the dirt road when it rained, the parents then
set their sights on other parts of local government to get a blacktop road
built. Yarborough, who went on to become a community organizer, said she
learned that if you want anything in life, you have to fight for it. "Cause all
you've got to do is ask," she said. "And if they say no, don't take no for an
answer. Because they're going to say no—but keep going back. You'll get
something done when they know that you're a person that sticks."[28]

## Rule 10: Remember that school politics revolves around money.

If you have to hit 'em, hit 'em where it hurts—their budgets. Many parent
activists understand that when all else fails with schools, they can get action
when they threaten to cut off the public purse strings. Fourth grade parents
in El Sobrante, California, learned one month into the 2004–05 school year
that their kids still didn't have a permanent teacher in place, so they decided
they needed to do something bold. They heard stories from their children
about being locked out of class, waiting for a substitute to show up. They
were informed by school officials that the original teacher had left at the
start of the year for undisclosed reasons and that the delays in finding a replacement were caused by the district having to comply with teachers' con-

tract hiring rules. None of that seemed to matter to the parents. "We pay taxes," said parent Cynthia Herron. "That's not a lot to ask for."[29]

Herron and other parents in the class organized a mass "sick out" of students, understanding that a reduced daily attendance reduced the amount of state aid the district and school would receive, because the payments were based on average daily attendance. Many parents would argue that it is foolish to adversely impact the school's budgets, and foolish to keep your kids away from classroom learning for any period of time. But look at what we're talking about. The money was going to substitutes, who didn't appear to be teaching much anyway. In fact, at a school open house, the substitute teacher knew so little about the students in the class that it was a waste of everyone's time. "I don't need a babysitter for my son," Herron told the *Contra Costa Times* newspaper.[30] The sick out, reported in the press, caught the attention of the school administration, which quickly sprang into action to find a replacement.

In Green County, Alabama, in August 2002, hundreds of the county's students boycotted classes while their parents picketed the school board to protest what they said was gross mismanagement by their superintendent and school board. Despite a property tax increase earlier in the year, the system was $1.2 million in debt. The protest, which also threatened to affect state aid to the district, caught the attention of the Alabama Board of Education. Weeks later the state board took over financial operations of the district. By the end of October, with parents chanting "superintendent must go," superintendent Carol Morrow was relieved of her duties and placed on paid leave and the district's schools began taking steps to right themselves again.[31]

Parents don't usually want to yank their kids out of class, especially if there are financial repercussions for their kids' school. But when school leaders won't listen, it is often one of the most effective ways to get their attention. Since many parents traditionally support teachers, any time parents picket against them is also sure to turn a few heads. When a teacher strike in Benton, Illinois, hit its fourth week in 2003, parents decided to form their own picket line to picket the picketers. Parents, noting that local residents had a median income of $27,000 while the average teacher salary was $56,000, said that enough was enough. One of the 250 parent protesters, Mike Pritchard, told the Associated Press that he has always recognized the need for a union but he felt the teachers union was holding the community hostage. Union president Mike Salmo raised an excellent point that many parents in America fail to consider: "We have every legal right to picket about the issues that are involved," Salmo said. "And the parents have every right to protest and picket about their issues. That's the American way, isn't it?"[32] If more parents understood that they, too, have a right to picket and protest when their children don't come first, we likely wouldn't be in half as much trouble as we're in today with public education.

## Rule 11: If you've tried steps 1 through 10, and your kids still aren't a priority, it's time to demand your tax money back.

Because the education cartel adores tax money, its members will resist you and your money-back-guarantee talk at all costs. But the more parents demand their money back, the more the idea will catch on that public school money belongs to the public, not to the school system. If the system is unwilling to control its urges, it's time for taxpayers to cut it off. Only when this threat is a possibility can the tables be completely turned.

Choice equals power. Offering real parental choice—whether in the form of interdistrict public school choice, charter schools, or private school vouchers—is the only way to allow those who don't have power in the traditional sense to control their child's destiny. It is parents (with the help of business leaders and the general public) who just might be able to save public education in America. Milwaukee, Wisconsin, has the oldest private school voucher program in the nation, but it is a city that has also completely redefined the definition of public education as an education that *serves* the public.

While the chattering classes in other cities engage in such debates as "Which schools are better, public schools or private schools?" Milwaukee's redefinition changed the debate to "Who should decide which schools are best for each child?" Or in the words of state representative Annette "Polly" Williams: "We've tried to [fix the public schools] for years, and the best we get is, 'Well, we're the experts, you are just parents.' We're tired of that excuse. Look, if you go to a doctor and you stay sick, at some point don't you have a right to a second opinion? The choice plan is our second opinion. The folks who run the poverty industry in this town are worried that kids will get a better education at schools that cost half the amount they spend on the public schools. In their shoes, I'd be worried too."[33]

There is widespread recognition in Milwaukee that parents—not bureaucrats and politicians who owe their jobs to the special interests—are the ones most likely to seek options that truly place the needs of their children first. Leaders in Milwaukee have decided that since the adults in the school system failed to put kids first, that power should be given to parents.

## Rule 12: Be a part of the political process.

Vote. We've seen that education is a creature of politics. The unwillingness of parents to get involved as voters fighting for their kids is one of the reasons the special interests within the education cartel are able to maintain their power within the system. Refuse to support any politician who sides with the big people over the little people within the school system. Parents must make politicians understand that they are worth listening to and make them trip over each other in their quest to serve parents better.

### PARENT ACTIVISM AT WORK

These are the rules that can help parents take back their public schools in ways that their children's needs are given the highest priority. Those who believe it is only wishful thinking to suggest that parents can make a difference need only look at the work done by an unlikely group of motivated mothers in one of the poorest sections of New York City. Mothers on the Move followed many of the rules listed here and rocked the boat in their South Bronx neighborhood, playing an important part in the urban renewal that has taken place there in the last decade.

In 1991, a group of parents in a South Bronx adult literacy program participated in a research project that helped spark a parent-led ouster of a long-serving school superintendent who wasn't getting the job done in New York City's Community School District 8. The adults in the program that day were asked to look up the results for their children's schools in the school-by-school test scores that were printed in the *New York Times*. The parents all were products of the New York City public school system and had trouble with basic reading and writing, yet they were stunned when they discovered their children attended some of the worst schools in the city. Hunts Point, in the southeast corner of the Bronx, is predominantly filled with low-income African American and Hispanic residents. The neighborhood had the highest asthma hospitalization rate in New York City and nearly half the city's sludge was processed there.[34] Community School District 8 included Hunts Point to the south, but it also included the white, middle-class neighborhood of Throgs Neck to the north.

The simple research project eventually led the South Bronx parents to join forces with other parents to fight for change. Organizers from the new group, which called itself Mothers on the Move or MOMs, went door to door looking for new recruits, talking up what they had learned about their schools. Lucretia Jones's son had been in the gifted and talented program in Hunts Point's Intermediate School 52 and had earned good marks through eighth grade, but it became apparent to her when he was starting to look at high schools that he hadn't been adequately prepared for high school academics. She started poking around with the other moms and was shocked by what she discovered. "My son was taking Spanish but there were no Spanish books," Jones told me. "There was no science lab and there was no heat in the winter."

Many parents knew their own children were doing poorly, but they had no idea the schools themselves were so much worse than in the rest of the city—and in the rest of District 8. They learned that the schools in their neighborhood had a higher percentage of inexperienced teachers and special education students than the district and city as a whole. School officials blamed the discrepancies on poor parenting and bad luck.

Mothers on the Move ran workshops for parents on dealing with the system and understanding school data that was available to them. "I didn't understand how bad the school was performing until we started looking at all the numbers," said Jesse McDonald, who joined MOMs in the early days, after attending an informational workshop for parents on how the Board of Education was structured.

McDonald said she soon started going to school board meetings in District 8 and the problem became clear to her: The system was rigged against the African American and Hispanic students in the southern half of the district. "Once I got educated and I understood what was going on and I understood my rights as a parent, it got the fire burning inside me," McDonald told me.

Lisa Ortega was one of many "crazy moms" in the South Bronx who decided that serving on the school parents association at a struggling school was a waste of time if you were powerless to make radical changes. Ortega quit the parents association at Public School 75 in the South Bronx and hooked up with parents fighting for their kids in Mothers on the Move. She quickly earned a reputation as a gadfly among school administrators—the kind of parent whom administrators would prefer to have just sit back and take the substandard education the system had been dishing out. "She tries to get parents to sign petitions," P.S. 75 principal Eve Garcia complained in 1997. "She's a bright young lady, but for whatever reason, she creates a lot of dissension."[35]

What were these "crazy moms" fussing about in the South Bronx? They were frustrated that their schools had some of the worst math and reading scores in the city, that their schools didn't have crossing guards, lacked textbooks, and frequently used the schoolyard as a parking lot for teachers, leaving no place for the children to play at recess.

In addition to the generally horrible education their children were receiving compared to the rest of the city, the issues the moms were originally rallying against were so basic that they remain a damning commentary on public education in America. "It was so bad in the beginning," Jesse McDonald told me in 2004. "We were fighting for things like running water in the bathrooms and doors on the bathroom stalls. We wanted things like books that kids could take home so parents could read with them."

Organizers even arranged trips to good schools in other neighborhoods so that the parents could see for themselves how things could be a lot, lot better for their kids. It was an eye-opening experience for many of the moms. "Some got angry," said Barbara Gross, an activist who led the original research project for the parents. "In each group there was always someone who cried."[36]

The strategy pursued by the MOMs was one of research first, then education, followed by action. The organization used grant money from the Edna McConnell Clark Foundation to handle the research and parent education programs. The MOMs did the rest. They used data about school performance in the South Bronx to create flyers headlined "District 8 is Failing South Bronx Children."

Joining Mothers on the Move allowed parents like Lisa Ortega to learn how to make a difference through confrontation and education. They organized parent workshops on leadership development and parental involvement, held forums featuring school board members, and picketed outside the district office to demand better treatment for their kids. They went door to door with flyers and petitions, urging more parents to get involved in voting in local school board races.

Although only 4 of the district's 27 schools were in Throgs Neck, a majority (five of nine) of the elected members of the district school board came from the wealthier part of the district in the early 1990s when the MOMs began to organize. A common refrain in the MOMs' complaints was that the southern (and poorer) section of the district was getting short-changed at the expense of the northern section, where superintendent Max Messer held his power in the form of the board majority.

The MOMs wore buttons identifying themselves as a sign of their growing strength and to prove to school officials that while they could ignore one parent, they couldn't ignore hundreds of parents united together by their anger. "We were known as a bunch of troublemakers, a bunch of crazy mothers who were in their faces all the time," McDonald said.[37]

After the MOMs starting raising a little hell, including phone calls to reporters about their troubles, the rest of the city began paying attention to what they were saying, and the ugly underbelly of the education system was exposed for all to see.

When *Newsday* examined problems in the district in 1993, it noted that at Intermediate School 52 a leaking bathroom above the school library ruined 1,000 books (which still hadn't been replaced two years later) and described peeling paint on the ground inside classrooms. "When it rains, water pours through broken windows that have been sealed with plastic trash bags," the newspaper reported. "One classroom is sealed off for fear its broken windows could collapse."[38] In that article, superintendent Max Messer blamed the problems on student demographics. "It's societal," he said.[39]

The same *Newsday* story noted that most of the uncertified teachers in the district were in the South Bronx schools, and that those schools also tended to get staffed with teachers whose performance ratings at the northern schools were unsatisfactory. "I really hate to say this but our kids are being neglected because they're from the South Bronx and poor," said Gloria Medina, president of the I.S. 52 parents association.

When *Daily News* reporter Anemona Hartocollis (now with the *New York Times*) visited P.S. 62 in 1995, she found the designated Board of Education Street Parking area empty, while 27 cars belonging to teachers were parked on the playground area, making it impossible for children to play. On the same visit, Hartocollis observed the classroom of "star teacher" and union leader Robert Fernandez, and watched as he misspelled three simple words on the blackboard. He wrote "Tatanic" for Titanic, "interrior" for interior, and "defenitions" for definitions.[40] One student offered that Fernandez had coached them to say "it's good" if any of the visitors asked them about the school.

In Hartocollis' devastating article, Messer offered as one of the reasons for the school's poor student performance the fact that the school had a lot of kids from homeless shelters. "It's hard to get teachers to come to the South Bronx in the first place, and hard to get them to come to Hunts Point," Messer explained. Under the circumstances, he said, P.S. 62 is doing the best it could. "Quite frankly, after all is said and done, I don't know what different things can be done at the school," Messer said.[41]

Superintendent Messer, a former gym teacher who was named superintendent in 1976 and was widely admired in the Throgs Neck area, continued to treat the MOMs as if they were the enemy. "Who the hell are these people and what have they ever contributed," Messer fumed, denying there was any special treatment for schools in the northern part of the district. He walked out of meetings packed with parents and showed little regard for their issues. In 1994, after he was able to renew his contract despite their protestations, Messer said the parents represented an "insignificant number" of constituents and he took their views lightly.[42]

The MOMs in 1994 presented Messer with a formal (and modest) proposal for changes at I.S. 52, which included making the school a more welcoming environment, organizing tours of the neighborhood for teachers so they could understand the students better, enhancing security, and increasing books available to the students. But the proposal was a nonstarter in Messer's eyes, as he condescendingly told the *Daily News* at the time: "It doesn't look like much of a proposal. It has lots of underlying principles like motherhood and apple pie."[43]

"He didn't want to speak to us," Jones told me. "He felt he didn't have any obligation to talk to a group of parents." The more Messer dismissed the parents as pesky outsiders, the more the MOMs were determined to make an impact. "They were always telling us that they were the experts and we were just the parents," Lucretia Jones said. "They would always talk down to us like that. They didn't want to hear from the wild, crazy parents." The MOMs made it a point to let the community, elected officials, and the city's schools chancellor know that Messer was a major problem for poor kids in the South Bronx.

When it became clear that superintendent Messer had no interest in helping to improve conditions in the southern section of the district the MOMs made his ouster a top priority. They printed "Wanted" signs in the spirit of the Wild West. "Wanted: Max Messer, For Educational Neglect." The posters, which included Messer's picture, ended with this line: "Because we need a superintendent who is as committed to the educational needs of our children as we are."

Understanding that Superintendent Messer was a powerful man, the Mothers on the Move learned that desperate times deserved desperate measures. In May 1995, after chancellor Ramon Cortines skipped out on a scheduled meeting with them in the Bronx, about 50 of the MOMs decided to take the meeting directly to Cortines with a Sunday afternoon protest outside the chancellor's home in Brooklyn Heights.

The Mothers on the Move caught Chancellor Cortines's attention, but the chancellor left his job a short time later—something school leaders do

quite often in America. In Cortines's case, his departure was due to deterio-
rating relations with mayor Rudy Giuliani. Cortines's replacement, Rudy
Crew, met with the MOMs and seemed to take them seriously from the
start. Some parents felt that Cortines must have warned Crew that they
would be showing up outside his residence if he didn't take them seriously.
"He (Crew) willingly met with us and eventually even adopted some of our
views," said Lucretia Jones, pointing to that era as the time when the outsiders began to treat the MOMs as a force to be reckoned with.

Crew came to appreciate what these mothers brought to the table. As
he told researchers from New York University in 2003: "I have a very,
very clear impression of them. First of all, they were wearing particular
shirts, I think their shirts actually said 'Mothers on the Move' and they
stood up and asked some pretty probing questions about things that had
to do with a particular school. They also asked things about the system
and that was when I noticed this very, very skillful engagement process
that they had developed in which they essentially said, will you sign on
this dotted line."[44]

In early 1997, the MOMs met with Crew and reiterated their belief that
Messer should be removed as superintendent due to his inaction regarding
the schools in the southern part of the district. Later that month Messer announced that he would retire. It was not clear what sort of behind-the-
scenes pressure was put on Messer by Crew, but when Messer later tried to
rescind his retirement, it was Crew who blocked it and declared it final.
"That was a big moment for us," said Lucretia Jones.

Parents like Lucretia Jones and Jesse McDonald learned that even a
bunch of "crazy moms" can have power when they work together and have
the facts on their side. In 2003, researchers from New York University set
out to answer the question of whether or not this kind of parental activism
could make a difference in terms of reforming schools and enhancing student achievement. They found that despite some ups and downs along the
way, the MOMs exceeded everyone's expectations. Test scores in the originally organized schools increased dramatically between 1999 and 2003, but
there was even more evidence that their impact had been felt.

> The group exposed the disparity in achievement and resources between the
> schools serving the north and south in District 8, ending Throgs Neck's
> domination of the school board, forced Superintendent Max Messer out of
> the District after 20 years and influenced the selection of his replacement.
> MOM forced the district to act more transparently, and collaboratively

with parents, helped improve leadership in several Hunts Point schools, and won an increase in the number of textbooks distributed to students. . . . Their work helped legitimize community organizing as an important school reform strategy in New York City and nationally, and inspired parents across the country to organize for better schools.[45]

Perhaps the most important lesson for the MOMs, however, was the lesson each participant learned: Power was obtainable in a system that had fought tooth and nail against letting them have it. "Parents have to come together because there is strength in numbers," said Lucretia Jones. "It's hard for any one parent to march in there and get what they need, but if a whole bunch of parents do it together, it's a different story. You can't be afraid to voice your concerns and ask questions and make noise. The teachers and the administrators come and go but these are our children."[46]

Working out of a storefront office in their neighborhood, the Mothers on the Move continued to play a role in holding school leaders in the South Bronx accountable after control of the school system was given to Mayor Bloomberg in 2002. They also started to organize to address other quality of life issues for parents, such as affordable housing. This unlikely group of activists came to understand the nature of power: how to recognize who has it, how to take it away from them, and how to use it for the public good. "Even I can't believe we came as far as we did," Jesse McDonald told me. "From no respect to all the respect in the world."

## THE MORAL IMPERATIVE

Throughout this book, I've described some of the many ways that adults in American public education stack the deck against the children who most need its services. I've shown how the overall structure of the public education system puts children's interests on the table only after it has met the needs of school employees, vendors, philanthropists, and politicians. The obvious question emerges: Are we serious about putting kids first, and if so, what are we going to do about it? Unfortunately, the recent history in America shows we are not serious about altering our education system in any manner that upsets the applecart for the adults who have long been well served by the system. That doesn't mean we can't become serious about change, however. But radical change will require everyone to do their part to make children a special interest group that can compete for the attention of policymakers.

It is apparent that politics drives much of what happens in public education, which means the first step toward solving the educational problem is solving the political problem. Parents need to step forward and declare that enough is enough if their kids are not the top priority in their school systems. They must understand that they aren't doing their children a favor by politely accepting a substandard education from their school and political leaders. Like the Mothers on the Move in the South Bronx, parents need to put their feet down and demand competence from the system. Like parents in Milwaukee, they need to demand their money back if they have been sold a defective product. One reason that the members of the education cartel have been able to retain their power over the years is that no one, including the press, has called them on it. I'm convinced that major change is possible if a critical mass of individuals comes to understand that power has been in the wrong hands for too long. Parents just may be the one group left who can save public education in America.

Parents can't do it alone, however. Business leaders need to stop being so squishy on education issues and start demanding the kind of results from school leaders that they demand from their own employees. Philanthropists must understand that it is possible to reform the inside of school systems by poking and prodding from the outside and by supporting the parent-consumers who have the best chance of demanding better results for their children. If everyone plays their part, it becomes easier for spineless politicians to buck the orders of the school cartel members and do what is right for kids. Our kids have to matter this much.

The goal for those who wish to make the public schools responsive to students rather than adult employees should be parent empowerment rather than vouchers per se. Milwaukee chose to use vouchers to transfer power to low-income parents, and charter schools to empower parent-consumers of all incomes, but the focus has been on that empowerment in the broader sense. The power comes from being able to bolt from bad schools if and when it becomes necessary for parents to do so.

There are some obvious advantages, however, to including vouchers in the mix. Charter schools offer a strong opportunity to expand public school options, but they are under attack from teachers unions in many areas because they often require teachers to work without a bulky labor contract. More traditional public school choice programs often are designed and implemented in ways that favor well-off students or protect them from having to be educated alongside disadvantaged students. Alone they do not provide a kind of customer-is-right relief. Additionally, as the federal No Child Left

Behind law has shown in many communities, there simply isn't enough room in good public schools to hold all of the students who wish to be there.

If vouchers and charter schools aren't palatable in other communities, creative minds should still be able to come up with ways to put parents in charge of their children's futures so that schools can get back into the business of serving students first and foremost. Some have suggested taking a large city like New York and turning it into multiple school districts, each with its own schools scattered throughout the city. Each could offer its own curricular approach and management style, and parents could select their public schools based on their preferences, with the school tax money following them to the school.[47] It bears repeating: Relief from a system that puts children last comes from real parent empowerment, not a from a piece of paper inscribed with the word "voucher."

Real reform will require brutal honesty about the problem we have on our hands. While I wouldn't go as far as he did in saying this, *Hartford Courant* columnist Laurence Cohen in 1998 suggested that kids in struggling central city schools might best be served if society just came out and admitted that we—on the whole—don't care about them. That way, he surmised, we could at least spare them the charade of having to wait patiently year after year while reformers come and go with no success. "Instead of telling the truth, and dealing with it, we're killing these families with kindness," Cohen wrote. "School boards get dumped, superintendents get fired, school buildings get repainted, bond issues get passed—all to the beat of a Greek chorus of politicians and 'civic leaders' who cluck about how much we all care. But all we really care about is dumping enough money into the system to ensure that the union employees' paychecks don't bounce."[48]

Our inability to be honest about our education system's shortcomings is one of the reasons we aren't yet in a position to take radical steps to help change the equation in most of our American cities. There are still Americans who are foolish enough to believe that "the system" knows what is best for kids, even while the evidence continues to mount that the same system often puts kids last. Many others are convinced that with just a few more dollars flowing into the coffers, all will be right again, despite the fact that it is the structure of the education system that is as much the problem as the financial ledger.

Americans have been at the business of trying to reform dysfunctional schools for decades, with little success. Prominent educators, like Columbia University Teachers College president Arthur Levine, have reached conclusions similar to what the Milwaukee reformers came to realize about the need to free children from failing schools once and for all. As Levine put it in 1998: "Throughout my career, I have been an opponent of school voucher programs. . . . However, after much soul-searching, I have reluctantly concluded that a limited school voucher program is now essential for the poorest Americans attending the worst public schools. . . . Today, to force children into inadequate schools is to deny them any chance of success. To do so simply on the basis of their parent's income is a sin."[49]

This is serious stuff, and incremental reforms aren't going to get the job done. As former New York representative Floyd Flake testified before Congress in 1997: "It is really a question about whether or not we are going to continue to let every child die, arguing that, if we begin to do vouchers, if we do charter schools, what we in fact are doing is taking away from the public system. We say, 'Let them all stay there. Let them all die.' It is like saying there has been a plane crash. But because we cannot save every child, we are not going to save any of our children; we let them all die."[50]

That, in a nutshell, describes the concept of children last. As a society, we are dismissing the needs of individual students to protect a romantic notion of public education whose very core is consumed with meeting the needs of adults first and foremost. Changing that dynamic requires strong leaders who embrace ideas rather than institutions. Leaders such as Tommy Thompson and Polly Williams had larger-than-life personalities in Milwaukee. They thrived in battle because they knew they were on the side of real people, not of the special interests. Business leaders Richard Abdoo and Robert O'Toole put their own corporate necks on the line for poor parents—making it easier for politicians to do the same when faced with the choice between siding with parents and students or siding with the status quo. What happened in Milwaukee took courage on the part of many, and there are thousands of students today who are better off because of it.

As I wrote at the onset, public education is at a crossroads in America. We can no longer afford to continue down the path that has led us to the dismal state of education we have today. To counter the power of vested interests—unions, vendors, and bureaucrats—we, as parents, must become more engaged. Opting out is not an option. Even for those who can afford to send their children to private schools, the returns on investment in changing the education system are huge. At stake is the future of our American democracy, justice system, culture, and economy. Our kids, and our future, demand that we get serious about the problem and run our public schools in a way that makes children the number one priority.

If we want kids to come first in education, we're going to have to fight for it. And as parents such as those in places like Milwaukee and the South Bronx have shown, it's a battle than can be won.

# NOTES

## CHAPTER 1

1. Joe Williams, "Speech costs grad; valedictorian who ripped school denied diploma," *New York Daily News*, June 26, 2004, p. 3.
2. Ibid.
3. Floyd Norris, "U.S. students fare badly in international survey of math skills," *New York Times*, Dec. 7, 2004, p. 23.
4. Richard Lee Colvin, "Congratulations! You're about to fail," *Los Angeles Times*, Jan. 2, 2005, p. M1.
5. "Each day in America," The Children's Defense Fund, August 2004, available online at www.childrensdefense.org/data/eachday.asp.
6. New York City Department of Education, *The Class of 2003 Four-Year Longitudinal Report and 2002–2003 Event Dropout Rates*, March 2004.
7. Speech by New York City schools chancellor Joel Klein, New York Urban League's Second Annual Rev. Dr. Martin Luther King Jr. Symposium, Jan. 15, 2004.
8. Speech by New York City schools chancellor Joel Klein at Pace University, Oct. 4, 2004.
9. Nina Bernstein, "Promise unfulfilled; PS 113 under fire for failing scores," *Newsday*, April 16, 1989, p. 5.
10. George Archibald, "$500 billion spent on education," *Washington Times*, Aug. 5, 2004.
11. Joseph C. Anselmo, "Questions arise about war costs as Congress prepares to clear defense bill," *Congressional Quarterly*, July 21, 2004.
12. National Center for Education Statistics, *Characteristics of the 100 Largest School Districts*, 2001–02.
13. Martin Haberman, "Who benefits from failing urban school districts," published March 2003 on the Internet, http://www.educationnews.org/Who%20Benefits%20from%20Failing%20Urban%20School%20Ditricts.htm.
14. Paul Ciotti, "Money and school performance: Lessons from the Kansas City desegregation experiment," Cato Institute *Policy Analysis*, March 16, 1998.
15. David W. Kirkpatrick, "School administration part of the problem," U.S. Freedom Foundation, *School Report 681*, Aug. 19, 2004.
16. New York City chancellor Joel Klein speech at the Steinhardt School of Education, New York University, Dec. 10, 2004.
17. Bob McManus, "A school system of their own," *New York Post*, June 22, 1998, p. 21.
18. *A Nation at Risk: The imperative for education reform*, National Commission on Excellence in Education, April 1983, p. 1.

19. Albert Shanker, weekly op-ed column, American Federation of Teachers, October 13, 1995.

20. Matthew Miller, *The Two-Percent solution* (New York: Public Affairs, 2003), p. 47.

21. Tommy G. Thompson, *Power to the People* (New York: Harper Collins 1996), p. 110.

## CHAPTER 2

1. Maureen Magee, "Schools caught between weedy yards and union jobs; volunteers limited after budget cuts," *San Diego Union-Tribune*, Oct. 5, 2003, p. B1.

2. Willy Surbrook, interview with author, May 18, 2004.

3. For a good summary of the school funding adequacy movement, see Peter Schrag, *Final Test: The Battle for Adequacy in America's Schools* (New York: New Press, 2003).

4. Gary Wolf, "Steve Jobs: The next insanely great thing," *Wired*, February 1996, http://www.wired.com/wired/archive/4.02/jobs_pr.html

5. Alan D. Bersin, "Making Schools Work: From Spinning Wheels to Common Sense Reform," unpublished review of *Common Sense School Reform* by Frederick M. Hess, essay given to author by Bersin, May 2004.

6. Richard Rothstein, "Lessons: The other role for the schools," *New York Times*, June 12, 2002, p. 8.

7. Ibid.

8. Elissa Gootman, "5 Educators without duties accused of playing hooky," *New York Times*, June 30, 2004, national edition, p. C14.

9. Alison Gendar, "Repairmen need fixin': School crews spent workdays asleep—or at the gym," *New York Daily News*, June 26, 2003, p. 5.

10. The full quote: "First God created idiots. That was for practice. Then he created school boards." From Mark Twain, *Following the Equator: A Journey around the World* (New York: Ecco Press, reissue edition, 1996, p. 561).

11. Mayor Michael Bloomberg testimony before panel of special masters hearing the Campaign for Fiscal Equity lawsuit, Fordham University Law School, Oct. 13, 2004.

12. Joe Williams, "It's a red-tape jungle for schools," *New York Daily News*, Nov. 30, 2004, p. 37.

13. Brian Thevenot, "N.O. School employees plead guilty in fraud; teachers, clerks, broker admit paycheck kickbacks, shakedown," *New Orleans Times Picayune*, July 3, 2004, p. 1.

14. Ibid.

15. Ibid.

16. Karen Tumulty, "School board corruption scandal rocks New York," *Los Angeles Times*, November 30, 1988, p. 1.

17. Lydia Segal, *Battling Corruption in America's Public Schools* (Boston: Northeastern University Press, 2004), p.121.

18. Jane Perlez, "School board is assailed over nepotism," *New York Times*, Aug. 25, 1987, p. B1.

19. Wayne Barrett, "Patronage Outrage," *Village Voice*, May 5, 1998, p. 63.

20. For more information on the circumstances surrounding Diana Lam's departure from the New York City schools, see Michael Saul and Joe Williams, "She's out like a Lam: School bell tolls for scandal-scarred deputy," *New York*

*Daily News*, March 9, 2004, p. 3, and Joe Williams, "Lam link lops 2nd ed head," *New York Daily News*, March 11, 2004, p. 7

21. Joe Williams, "Ed Board faces steep building costs," *New York Daily News*, Feb. 5, 2002, p. 16.
22. Joe Williams, "Through the roof school costs hit," *New York Daily News*, May 3, 2002. p. 8.
23. Joe Williams, "Builders: Schools a hassle; add 20% to contracts," *New York Daily News*, Aug. 30, 2002, p. 45.
24. Ibid.
25. Michael Saul and Joe Williams, "Ed enthusiasm building," *New York Daily News*, May 7, 2004, p. 30.
26. Joe Williams, "Klein's plan: Build cheap," *New York Daily News*, Nov. 3, 2003, p. 6.
27. Joe Williams, "Student plan tops bids for new school," *New York Daily News*, July 15, 2004, p. 8.
28. From the United Federation of Teachers website, http://www.uft.org/about/history/strike_1960/index.html
29. Stephen Dyer, "Teachers using leverage," *Akron Beacon Journal*, Oct. 9, 2003, p. 1.

## CHAPTER 3

1. Kevin P. Chavous, *Serving our Children: Charter Schools and the Reform of American Public Education* (Sterling, Va.: Capital Books, 2004), p. 38.
2. David W. Kirkpatrick, "The superintendency: neither inevitable nor necessary," U.S. Freedom Foundation, *School Report # 681*, Sept. 23, 2004.
3. Marc Fisher, "What DC Got From the Wizard of Long Beach," *Washington Post*, July 8, 2004, p. B1.
4. Chavous, p. 37.
5. Martin Haberman, "Who Benefits from Failing Urban School Districts," March 2003, http://www.educationnews.org/.
6. Ibid.
7. Wilbur C. Rich, *Black Mayors and School Politics* (New York: Garland Publishing, 1996), p. 5.
8. Haberman.
9. Joe Williams, "MPS officials spurn plan by School Board: Administrators committee offers its own options on attendance," *Milwaukee Journal Sentinel*, Feb. 4, 1999. p. 1.
10. Ibid.
11. Joel L. Klein, weekly e-mail to principals in the New York City Schools, Aug. 24, 2004.
12. Rebekah Marler interview with author, Sept. 13, 2004.
13. Joe Williams, "Innovative school faced many hurdles: Congress Elementary is now offered as an example for the future of MPS," *Milwaukee Journal Sentinel*, June 21, 1999. p. 1.
14. School Report Card, South Shore High School, 2002–03.
15. Ibid.
16. Christine MacDonald and Brad Heath, "Metro schools pad rankings," *Detroit News*, Aug. 30, 2004, p. 1A.

17. Paul T. Hill, *School Boards: Focus on School Performance Not Money and Patronage* (Washington, D.C.: Progressive Policy Institute, 21st Century Schools Project, 2003).

18. Michael Hirsch, "UFT Victory Bans '4 in a Row,'" *New York Teacher,* June 1, 2004.

19. Both the reading rugs and rocking chairs became widely recognized symbols for Klein's Children First classroom reforms in 2003–04. Administrators stressed that the requirements for both the rugs and the chairs represented the standardization of the most effective instructional practices. See Joe Williams, "He's really strict; teachers need management, says Klein," *New York Daily News,* Oct. 24, 2003, p. 46. Critics charged that it represented an unprofessional form of top-down micromanagement. See Joe Williams, "Off their rockers; wacky new rules for teaching class," *New York Daily News,* Sept. 17, 2003, p. 5.

20. Official transcripts of the New York City Council Education Committee hearing on school custodian contract and work rules, Nov. 12, 2003.

21. Celeste Katz, "Ed Dept called on carpets," *New York Daily News,* Feb. 13, 2004, p. 3.

22. Ibid.

23. Joe Williams, "Schools are called on carpet—again," *New York Daily News,* April 26, 2004, p. 23.

24. John Merrow, "Can D.C.'s search make the grade?" *Washington Post,* Aug. 8, 2004, p. B1.

25. Ibid.

26. Jake Wagman, "Schools audit may focus on who gets what jobs: Some contracts go to those with political connections," *St. Louis Post-Dispatch,* Oct. 6, 2003, p. C1.

27. Ibid.

## CHAPTER 4

1. Liz Willen, "Lending a touch of class: Teaching fellows test new skills in city schools," *Newsday,* Sept. 8, 2000, p. A7.

2. Joe Williams, "Slap at young musicians hits sour note," *New York Daily News,* June 18, 2002, p. 8.

3. Official transcripts of the New York City Council Education Committee hearing on teacher retention, Oct. 30, 2002.

4. Ibid.

5. Ibid.

6. Ibid.

7. Joe Williams, "City teachers go beggin' on the web," *New York Daily News,* April 17, 2004, p. 4.

8. Official transcript of the New York City Council Education Committee hearing on teacher retention, Oct. 30, 2002.

9. Lorri Helfand, "Class acts: Answering the call to teach," *St. Petersburg Times,* Aug. 18, 2002, p. 1.

10. Julie Blair, "Teaching prospects show mixed SAT scores," *Education Week,* May 19, 1999.

11. Matthew Miller, *The 2% Solution* (New York: Public Affairs Books, 2003), p. 119.

12. Darrell S. Pressley, "Teaching the teachers," *Boston Herald,* July 8, 1998, p. 4.

13. Joel Klein, Weekly e-mail to principals, New York City Department of Education, Sept. 1, 2004.

14. Abraham McLaughlin and Gail Russell Chaddock, "The perils of testing teachers," *Christian Science Monitor,* July 3, 1988.

15. Joe Williams, "Miami school offers Milwaukee Tech a model to aspire to," *Milwaukee Journal Sentinel,* May 26, 1998, p. 1.

16. Joe Williams, "Teachers union gives ground on seniority," *Milwaukee Journal Sentinel,* Jan. 19, 1999, p. 1.

17. Terry Pesta, "Changes Abound, SDEA Offers '03-'04 Guidance," Sept. 2003, available online at http://www.sdea.net/column_pres/2003/0903.html.

18. Joe Williams, "The Labor-Management Showdown in San Diego," *San Diego Review,* Sept. 2004.

19. William Celis, "Minnesota's teacher of the year is laid off in budget crisis," *New York Times,* Jan. 27, 1991, p. A20.

20. Peter Schweizer, "School daze; firing offenses; why is the quality of teachers so low?" *National Review,* Aug. 17, 1998.

21. *Chicago Tribune,* "She loses the job, but keeps the vest," May 11, 2003, p. MC2.

22. Douglas McGray, "Working with the enemy," *New York Times,* Jan. 16, 2005, Education Life, p. 28.

23. "An Institution at Risk," a report prepared by the Kamber Group, Washington, D.C., for the National Education Association, Jan. 14, 1997.

24. Ibid.

25. For detailed information on 30 years of collective bargaining for teachers in one urban school district, see Howard L. Fuller, George A. Mitchell, and Michael E. Hartmann, "Collective Bargaining in Milwaukee Public Schools," in Tom Loveless, ed., *Conflicting missions? Teachers unions and educational reform* (Washington, D.C.: Brookings Institution, 2000).

26. Author's background interview with a New York City charter school operator, conducted on condition of anonymity, December 5, 2002.

27. Joe Williams, "Flap over fingerprint fee," *New York Daily News,* Nov. 9, 2004, p. 19.

28. Willy Surbrook, interview with author, May 18, 2004.

29. David Herszenhorn, "New York's obstacle course," *New York Times,* Jan. 16, 2005, Education Life, p. 31.

30. Curtis Lawrence, "New teachers union president still crossing traditional lines," *Milwaukee Journal Sentinel,* May 5, 1997, p. 1.

31. Bruce Murphy, "One bad apple," *Milwaukee Magazine,* February 1998, p. 88.

## CHAPTER 5

1. Alec MacGillis, "Schools chief took junket paid for by seller of software; Prince George's considers big contract with sponsor," *Baltimore Sun,* Sept. 25, 2004, p. 1A.

2. Ibid.

3.  Ibid.
4.  Erin Kennedy, "Lying, obstruction cited in sanctions for law firm," *Fresno Bee*, Jan. 18, 2005, p. A1.
5.  Larry Parsons, "School district law firm in Monterey County, Calif., sanctioned by judge," *Monterey County Herald*, Jan. 20, 2005, p. 1.
6.  Joe Williams, "Ya got to shop around as education department overpays for supplies, there is proof . . . ," *New York Daily News*, April 16, 2004, p. 5.
7.  Ibid.
8.  Sam Dillon, "Waste and fraud besiege U.S. program to link poor schools to Internet," *New York Times*, June 17, 2004, p. 20.
9.  Paul Davidson, Greg Toppo, and Jane O'Donnell, "Fraud, waste mar plan to wire schools to net," *USA Today*, June 9, 2004, p. 1A.
10. Ken Foskett, "Crackdown on E-Rate waste demanded," *Atlanta Journal-Constitution*, June 18, 2004, p. 1A.
11. Davidson et al.
12. Ibid.
13. Ken Foskett and Paul Donsky, "Congress presses for E-Rate details; panel focuses on APS spending on computers," *Atlanta Journal-Constitution*, June 9, 2004, p. 8C.
14. Foskett, "Crackdown on E-Rate waste demanded."
15. Davidson et al.
16. Joe Williams, "School funds hung up in scaffolding," *New York Daily News*, Sept. 1, 2003, p. 9.
17. Carl Campanile, "School de-construction; Mayor and Klein hack 600 jobs in overhaul," *New York Post*, November 1, 2002, p. 4.
18. Joe Williams, "Divided ed board OK's trimmed building plan," *New York Daily News*, December 15, 2001, p. 10.
19. Comments by New York City Mayor Michael Bloomberg on his weekly radio show, WABC, May 9, 2003.
20. Joe Williams, "School funds hung up in scaffolding," *New York Daily News*, September 1, 2003, p. 9.
21. Austin Fenner and Paul H.B. Shin, "Ex-school honcho indicted for graft," *New York Daily News*, Nov. 2, 2000, p. 2.
22. Merle English, "Payback for bribes; ex school supe, others must give ed board $4.85M," *Newsday*, Oct. 19, 2002, p. A6.
23. Greg B. Smith, "Feds bag food sellers in price-fix scam," *New York Daily News*, June 2, 2000, p, 27.
24. Joe Williams, "Schools out to lunch on food costs," *New York Daily News*, Feb. 5, 2004, p. 28.
25. Todd S. Purdum, "Police seeking more witnesses in baffling case," *New York Times*, Aug. 14, 1987, p. B2.
26. Mark A. Uhlig, "Tapes link Genovese group to murder of a union chief," *New York Times*, July 24, 1988, p. 21.
27. Lydia Segal, *Battling Corruption in America's Public Schools* (Boston: Northeastern University Press, 2004), p. 9.
28. Toni Heinzl and Jennifer Autrey, "Pair get 8 years for school fraud," *Fort Worth Star-Telegram*, June 26, 2004, p. 1.
29. Ibid.
30. Ibid.

## CHAPTER 6

1. Joe Williams, "MPS school for deaf immersed in problems; board member says trouble indicates district 'out of control,'" *Milwaukee Journal Sentinel*, June 22, 1998, p. 1.
2. Ibid.
3. Ibid.
4. Ibid.
5. Ibid.
6. Terry M. Moe, *Reforming Education in Texas* (Stanford, Calif.: Hoover Institution, Koret Task Force on K–12 Education, 2003), p. 82.
7. Alan Bersin, interview with the author, May 21, 2004.
8. Sol Stern, *Breaking Free: Public School Lessons and the Imperative of School Choice* (San Francisco: Encounter Books, 2003), p. 107.
9. *Form LM–2 Labor Organization Annual Report*, filed with U.S. Labor Department, for fiscal year 2003.
10. Rick Berg, "With 'friends' like these, schools don't need enemies," *Wisconsin State Journal*, Oct. 30, 1995, p. 5A.
11. David M. Herszenhorn and Elissa Gootman, "City's new system delays suspensions of violent students," *New York Times*, December 12, 2003, p. 1.
12. Alan G. Hevesi, *Legislative Politics in New York State: A Comparative Analysis*, (New York: Praeger, 1975), p. 49.
13. The University of Wisconsin-Milwaukee eventually granted two charters to schools that would be run by Edison Schools but they were delayed until 2000–01.
14. Frederick M. Hess also refers to "threats that UWM's ties with the school system and with (Milwaukee Teachers Education Association) members would be severed," in his book *Revolution at the Margins; The Impact of Competition on Urban School Systems*, (Washington, D.C.: Brookings Institution, 2002), p. 128.
15. From Nov. 27, 2002 letter to Alan D. Bersin from National Education Association staff counsel Cynthia Chmielewski on NEA stationary. Wayne Johnson's handwritten remarks at the top margin are dated Jan. 22, 2003.
16. Perry Link, "The anaconda in the chandelier: Chinese censorship today," *New York Review of Books*, April 11, 2002.
17. Joe Williams, "MPS teachers win big pay raise," *Milwaukee Journal Sentinel*, Sept. 3, 1998, p. 1.
18. Jennifer Radcliffe, "Romer's uphill battle: LAUSD's chief faces pressure from UTLA," *Daily News of Los Angeles*, May 30, 2004, p. N1.
19. Joe Williams. "Parents get timed chat with teach," *New York Daily News*, Nov. 20, 2003, p. 8.
20. Joseph Dolman, "Blowing lid off schools doesn't win pals," *Newsday*, Nov. 19, 2003, p. A32.
21. David Saltonstall and Joe Williams, "Labor big hits Miller on ed probe," *New York Daily News*, Nov. 22, 2003, p. 8.
22. Lizzy Ratner, "Taking on unions and paying a price," *New York Observer*, Dec. 8, 2003, p. 5.
23. Joe Williams, "Mayor rips councilmen for goin' easy on union," *New York Daily News*, Nov. 15, 2003, p. 8.

24. Carl Campanile, "Teachers aim to torpedo Eva," *New York Post*, Jan. 30, 2004, p. 21.
25. *An Institution at Risk: An External Communications Review of the National Education Association* (Washington: Kamber Group, 1997).
26. Ibid.
27. Ibid.
28. Ibid.
29. Carol Innerst, "NEA follows scripts to alter image," *Washington Times*, May 30, 1997, p. A1.
30. Joe Williams, "Local teachers resist peer review," *Milwaukee Journal Sentinel*, July 10, 1997, p. 1.
31. Ibid.
32. Ibid.
33. Randi Weingarten, speech to New York City Teaching Fellows, June 21, 2004, Avery Fisher Hall, Lincoln Center, New York City.
34. Joe Williams, "Teachers union votes against merit pay," *Milwaukee Journal Sentinel*, July 6, 2000, p. 1.
35. The advocacy group People for the American Way put out a press release on February 23, 2004 entitled, "Paige smears group as 'terrorist'; Bush education chief takes White House intolerance of dissent to absurd level."
36. Joe Williams, "Religious schools see racial mix; study says integration rises in parochial schools." *Milwaukee Journal Sentinel*, June 26, 2000, p. 1B.
37. Alex Molnar, Philip Smith, John Zahorik, et al, "Evaluating the SAGE program: A pilot program targeted pupil-teacher reduction in Wisconsin," *Educational Evaluation and Policy Analysis*, Volume 21, 1999, pp. 165–177.
38. Celeste Amalfitano, "UFTers' voting power decides elections," *New York Teacher*, June 2, 2004, p. 6, city edition.
39. Ibid.
40. Nick Anderson, "Standing Bush in a corner," *Los Angeles Times*, June 26, 2004, p.1.
41. The states where the ads aired were Florida, Arizona, Nevada, Pennsylvania, and Ohio.
42. Anderson.
43. Brian Friel, "An apology for the teachers," *National Journal*, July 10, 2004.
44. Ibid.
45. Steve Bousquet, "Democrats hang hats on minimum wage push," *St. Petersburg Times*, July 31, 2004. p. 1B.
46. Linda Chavez, "As Democrats look away, unions flout campaign finance laws." *Los Angeles Times*, July 2, 2004, p. B11.
47. Ibid.
48. Martin Peretz, "It's John Kerry, stupid: bad messenger," *The New Republic*, Nov, 22, 2004, p. 10.
49. Dan Gerstein, "More muscle, more God, less Shrum," *Wall Street Journal*, Nov. 11, 2004, p. A16.
50. Joe Williams, "MPS candidates battle at news conference," *Milwaukee Journal Sentinel*, April 1, 1999, p.1.
51. David M. Herszenhorn, "Promotion rate for third graders looks stable," *New York Times*, August 19, 2004, p. 1.

## CHAPTER 7

1. Transcript of the Democratic Presidential Debate at Harlem's Apollo Theater, February 21, 2000, Cable News Network.
2. *Economist*, "Teachers pet," April 1, 2000.
3. Vincent Morris, "Al won't be voucher grouch—downplays split with Lieberman," *New York Post*, Aug. 10, 2000, p. 6.
4. *Washington Post*, "Peter Milius," by the editors, Jan. 12, 2002, p. A20.
5. Howard Fuller, comments at 2004 National Charter School Conference session on "The importance of political leaders," June 18, 2004, Fountainbleau Hilton, Miami, Fla.
6. Charles Mahtesian, "Payback is hell," *Campaigns and Elections*, Feb. 2000, p. 22.
7. Kevin Chavous, comments at 2004 National Charter Schools Conference session on "The importance of political leaders," June 18, 2004, Fountainbleau Hilton, Miami, Fla.
8. Peter Schrag, "The voucher seduction," *American Prospect Online*, http://www.prospect.org/print/V11/1/schrag-p.html.
9. *Economist*, "Teachers pet," April 1, 2000.
10. From comments made by Antonio Riley (D-Milwaukee) during a visit to Milwaukee by the Geo Foundation, audio can be found at: www.geofoundation.org/ milwaukee_tour_pg3.html
11. Sam Schulhofer-Wohl and Steven Walters, "Democrats caught in choice net; many constituents support program, even as party shuns it," *Milwaukee Journal Sentinel*, June 15, 2001, p. 1A.
12. "Feinstein's school choice," *Orange County Register*, July 24, 2003, commentary.
13. Andrew J. Rotherham, "Impotent liberalism," Progressive Policy Institute, *21st Century Schools Project Bulletin*, Feb. 10, 2004.
14. Based on 2005 U.S. population of 295,000,000. There are approximately 2.5 million members of the National Education Association and 1 million members of the American Federation of Teachers.
15. David Boldt, "Convention speech by NEA president actively skirted the truth," *Philadelphia Inquirer*, August 19, 2000, p. 16.
16. Ann Coulter, "No teachers union left behind," *FrontPageMagazine.com*, July 29, 2004.
17. David S. Broder, "SEIU chief says the Democrats lack fresh ideas," *Washington Post*, July 27, 2004, p. A2.
18. *Washington Post* Web site, http://www.washingtonpost.com/wp-srv/mmedia/politics/072604–12s.htm
19. "Spend your summer helping dump Bush," *New York Teacher*, June 16, 2004, p. 6.
20. Ibid.
21. Sylvia Saunders and Kara Smith, "Unionists work to elect pro-education Kerry Nov. 2," *New York Teacher*, Aug. 2, 2004, state edition, p.2.
22. Ronald Brownstein and Maria L. LaGanga, "Kerry proposal would boost teachers, but with a price; the $20-billion plan would increase hiring and pay but make it easier to fire faculty," *Los Angeles Times*, May 7, 2004, p.1.
23. Ibid.

24. Mike Antonucci, "NEA memo: Kerry backs away from pay for performance," Education Intelligence Agency, *Communique*, May 24, 2004.
25. Ibid.
26. Ibid.
27. Mike Antonucci, "Kerry and Edwards get beamed into the convention," Education Intelligence Agency, *NEA Convention Coverage*, July 7, 2004.
28. Brian Friel, "An apology for the teachers," *National Journal*, July 10, 2004.
29. Mike Antonucci, "Kerry promises no dollar left behind," Education Intelligence Agency, AFT Convention Coverage, July 16, 2004.
30. David Broder, "Fold education into labor," *Washington Post*, June 7, 1995, p. A21.
31. Frederick M. Hess, *Revolution at the Margins: The Impact of Competition on Urban School Systems*, (Washington, D.C., Brookings Institution, 2002), p. xi.
32. Carrie Sturrock, "Bush highlights education in Rock Hill trip," *Charlotte Observer*, February 11, 2000, p. 1Y
33. Siobhan Gorman, "Pro choice: How Democrats can make vouchers their secret weapon," *Washington Monthly*, Sept. 1, 2003, p. 18.
34. Brian Friel, "An apology for the teachers," *National Journal*, July 10, 2004.
35. Craig Gilbert, "Norquist says Bush retreated on choice plan; he hasn't made the case for school vouchers, mayor charges," *Milwaukee Journal Sentinel*, May 4, 2001, p. 16A.
36. Andrew Rotherham, "No pundit left behind," *New York Times*, January 12, 2005, p. 21. See also, Greg Toppo, "White House paid journalist to promote law," *USA Today*, January 7, 2005, p. 1.
37. Ray Hagar, "Teachers, advocates blast education law," *Reno Gazette Journal*, Aug. 13, 2004, p. 1C.
38. Neal McCluskey, "A lesson in waste, where does all the federal education money go?" Cato Institute *Policy Analysis*, July 7, 2004.
39. Adam Cohen, "The courts: The supreme struggle," *New York Times*, Jan. 18, 2004 Education Life Supplement, p. 22.
40. Sol Stern, "Yes, the education president," *City Journal*, Summer 2004.
41. Ibid.
42. Ibid.
43. Joe Williams, "School's failing? Be patient, says Mike," *New York Daily News*, Sept. 26, 2002, p. 7.
44. Joe Williams, "Failure to communicate; word doesn't get out on free tutoring," *New York Daily News*, Oct. 6, 2003, p. 6.
45. Ibid.
46. Joe Williams, "Council rips ed dept.'s tutor goof," *New York Daily News*, Oct. 22, 2003, p. 10.
47. "How to rescue education reform," *New York Times*, October 10, 2004, p. 10.

## CHAPTER 8

1. Estimates of philanthropic contributions to K through 12 education from The Foundation Center, *Foundation Giving Trends*, 2004.
2. Richard Rothstein, "Lessons: Of gift horses and close looks," *New York Times*, Oct. 16, 2002, p. 9.
3. Barbara Dudley, "It's time to rein in the power of the biggest donors," *Chronicle of Philanthropy*, Oct. 21, 1999, p. 50.

4. James Conant, *The American High School Today* (New York: McGraw Hill, 1959), p. 23.
5. Conant, p. 27.
6. Walter H. Annenberg, remarks at the White House, December 17, 1993, as archived by the Brown University News Bureau.
7. Frederick M. Hess, "Re-tooling K–12 Giving: New funders with new strategies seek success where others have failed," *Philanthropy Roundtable*, Sept-Oct. 2004.
8. C. Quinn Hanchette, "Report issued from Annenberg Challenge," *Chronicle of Philanthropy*, June 1, 2000, p. 39.
9. *Can Philanthropy Fix Our Schools?: Appraising Walter Annenberg's $500 Million Gift to Public Education* (Washington, D.C.: Thomas B. Fordham Foundation, April 2000).
10. Neil Weinberg, "Good intentions gone nowhere," *Forbes*, Oct. 6, 2003, p. 108.
11. The State of New York, in exchange for a sizeable increase in state aid to the city, had required that the massive school system be reorganized.
12. Richard Magat, "Tensions of the Shanker era: departed foes on decentralization," *Education Week*, March 26, 1997.
13. Fernando Ferrer, testimony before the New York State Task Force on Community School District Reform, Dec. 10, 2002.
14. Magat, "Tensions."
15. Hess, "Re-toolings."
16. For a complete list of grants awarded by the Wallace Foundation, see www.wallacefunds.org.
17. Maureen Magee, "Schools in S.D. to get grant worth $5 million; money depends on Bersin keeping job," *San Diego Union Tribune*, Feb. 12, 2002, p. B1.
18. Chris Moran, "Private money in public schools," *California Journal*, March 3, 2003, p. 14.
19. Hess, "Re-tooling."
20. Ibid.
21. Ibid.
22. Ibid.
23. Ibid.
24. Ibid.
25. Hess, *Philanthropy Roundtable*.

## CHAPTER 9

1. Joe Williams, "Biz bigs push state for school aid," *New York Daily News*, May 7, 2004, p. 30.
2. Jerry Butkiewicz, interview with the author, June 30, 2004.
3. John O. Norquist, interview with the author, November 10, 2004.
4. Joe Williams, "Transforming an education system: Milwaukee's private sector catalyzes major change," from *Seven Studies in Education Philanthropy*, a collection of papers published by the Thomas B. Fordham Foundation, December 2001.
5. Ibid.
6. *Milwaukee Public Schools in an Era of Choice*, (Milwaukee: American Education Reform Council, Oct. 2003).

## CHAPTER 10

1. Gallup USA poll based on telephone interviews with 1,004 national adults, age 18 and older, conducted Jan. 12–15, 2004. Margin of error is +–3 percentage points.
2. Gallup Canada poll based on telephone interviews with 1,003 national adults, age 18 and older, conducted April 28-May 4, 2004. Margin of error is +- 3 percentage points.
3. Washington Post–ABC News poll conducted by telephone June 17–20, 2004, among 1,201 randomly selected adults nationwide. The margin of error is +- 3 percentage points.
4. Kevin Chavous, *Serving our Children: Charter Schools and the Reform of American Public Education* (Sterling, Va.: Capital Books, 2004), p.12.
5. Joe Williams, "It's time for schoolwork; Cleveland, mayor to begin rebuilding system," *Milwaukee Journal Sentinel*, March 12, 1998. p. 1.
6. Peter Schrag, "The voucher seduction; the issue liberals can't ignore," *American Prospect*, Nov. 23, 1999, p. 46.
7. Terry Pesta, "Voters are anxious to hear from you," *San Diego Education Association Advocate*, Oct. 2002.
8. Alan D. Bersin, "Making schools work: from spinning wheels to common sense school reform," unpublished review of *Common Sense School Reform*, by Frederick M. Hess. Essay given to the author by Bersin, May 2004.
9. Raphael Sugarman and Stephen McFarland, "Kids'll be no. 1, Crew promises," *New York Daily News*, Nov. 9, 1995, p. 6.
10. Ibid.
11. Alison Gendar, "Ed board perks under fire: $580G per member for staff and cars," *New York Daily News*, February 12, 2002, p. 4.
12. Paul H.B. Shin, "Mayor slaps UFT ed bd. plan," *New York Daily News*, June 5, 2001, p. 17.
13. Dave Saltonstall, "Rudy: It was a great 8," *New York Daily News*, December 20, 2001, p. 25.
14. Michael Cooper, "Mayor assails school and tax policy critics," *New York Times*, March 13. 2002, p. 3.
15. Carl Campanile and David Seifman, "Silver will give Mike schools in exchange for teacher raise," *New York Post*, April 27, 2002, p. 2.
65. Stephanie Gaskell, "Teachers union says contracts 'held hostage' by Bloomberg," *Associated Press*, March 9, 2002.
17. From speech by Diane Ravitch, at New York University, Oct. 29, 2004.
18. Joe Williams, "High hopes for class act," *New York Daily News*, Sept. 3, 2002, p. 10.
19. Carl Campanile and David Seifman, "Parents flunk Mike's no-promotion plan," *New York Post*, Feb, 11, 2004. p. 2.
20. From speech by Diane Ravitch, at New York University, Oct. 29, 2004.
21. New York City's third grade reading and math tests were tainted by reports that students in parts of the city had used practice tests with the same questions and reading passages as the real version. Later, when a retest was given, the scoring sheets did not correspond with the questions, prompting Mayor Bloomberg to admit, on his weekly radio show on WABC-AM, that it made the city's Department of Education look "like the gang that couldn't shoot straight."

22. Diane Ravitch, New York University.
23. Joe Williams, "Tab's 33G (a month) for Klein's extra PR," *New York Daily News*, March 1, 2004, p. 12.

### CHAPTER 11

1. Joe Williams, "Tide first turned when justices upheld choice," *Milwaukee Journal Sentinel*, June 10, 1999, p. 1.
2. "Ahead of the curve," *Education Week*, January 13, 1999.
3. James A. Barnes, "Banker with a cause," *National Journal*, March 6, 1993, p. 563.
4. Rogers Worthington, "Tax funding for private schools faces test," *Chicago Tribune*, July 23, 1990, p.1.
5. Mikel Holt, *Not Yet Free at Last: The Unfinished Business of the Civil Rights Movement* (Oakland, California: Institute for Contemporary Studies, 1999), p. 56.
6. This hit close to home, as mine was one of those white families whose children benefited from such a school. My son is attending Elm Creative Arts Elementary School, an arts-based school in a beautiful building on 10th and Walnut Streets. The year my son applied for the 4-year-old kindergarten program, every white student who applied was granted a spot. Because of quotas established back in the 1970s for integration, however, several dozen black students were placed on the waiting list for the popular school.
7. Ira J. Hadnot, "Annette Polly Williams," *Dallas Morning News*, March 15, 1998, p. 1J.
8. Dan Allegretti, "Black school district voted: defeat of budget amendment expected in Wisconsin Senate," *Chicago Tribune*, March 19, 1988, p. 3.
9. Ibid.
10. Ibid.
11. Tommy G. Thompson, *Power to the People: An American State at Work* (New York: Harper Collins, 1996), p.90.
12. John O. Norquist, interview with the author, November 10, 2004.
13. William H. Honan, "Looking back at forward thinkers," *New York Times*, Education Life supplement, November 2, 1997, p. 24.
14. Ibid.
15. Program guide to the Fordham Prizes in Excellence in Education, 2004, Thomas B. Fordham Foundation.
16. Comments made by Howard Fuller at a community meeting held December 8, 1998, at Gray's Child Development Center, 6618 N. Teutonia Avenue, Milwaukee, Wisconsin.
17. Ibid.
18. Thompson, p. 93.
19. Thompson, p. 107.
20. Tommy Thompson left office in 2001 to join the cabinet of president George W. Bush, as Health and Human Services secretary. He was replaced by Republican lieutenant governor Scott McCallum, who went on to lose to attorney general James Doyle in 2002. Doyle was supported by the teachers union and did not support school choice, though he said he would not try to end it in Milwaukee.

21. Quentin L. Quade, "The automatic benefits of school choice," paper published by the Virgil C. Blum Center for Parental Freedom in Education, Marquette University, March 16, 1998.

22. John O. Norquist, interview.

23. Ibid.

24. John Norquist left office in January 2004 to join the Congress for New Urbanism. Voters elected Tom Barrett, a former Democratic congressman, who was endorsed by the teachers union and who didn't support school choice.

25. Susan Mitchell, "Developing strategic coalitions: lessons from Milwaukee's school choice coalition," *Heritage Foundation Insider*, June 2000.

26. "Teachers get a chance for change," *Milwaukee Journal*, April 1, 1994, p. A10.

27. Alex Molnar, "Tommy Thompson: Riding the corporate highway," *Capital Times*, Sept. 18, 1995, p. 1C.

28. Thomas W. Still, "Just one choice: Milwaukee schools need fix," *Wisconsin State Journal*, July 5, 1995, p.1B.

29. Daniel Bice and Richard P. Jones, "Choice ruling ushers in new era: religious schools open up for up to 15,000 pupils," *Milwaukee Journal Sentinel*, June 11, 1998, p. 1.

30. There were varying estimates of the projected cost to the Milwaukee Public Schools system if all 15,000 student allowed under the Milwaukee Parental Choice Program opted to enroll in private schools. While superintendent Alan Brown estimated that the cost would be $100 million, the Wisconsin Department of Public Instruction estimated the cost at $75 million. Governor Thompson said both estimates were wrong, but did not provide an estimate of his own. School board member John Gardner, meanwhile, predicted that the per-pupil spending in the Milwaukee system would rise after the students left. History has proven Gardner correct.

31. Joe Williams, "Choice ruling ushers in new era," *Milwaukee Journal Sentinel*, June 11, 1998, p. 1.

32. Eugene Kane, "Ruling pleases the mother of school choice," *Milwaukee Journal Sentinel*, June 11, 1998, p. 1.

33. Daniel Bice and Joe Williams, "Public backs Norquist on school choice, residency rule," *Milwaukee Journal Sentinel*, Aug. 9, 1998, p. 1.

34. Alan J. Borsuk and Joe Williams, "Choice, voice, basics, and values: That's what people demand in their schools, according to poll," *Milwaukee Journal Sentinel*, Oct. 17, 1999, p. 1.

35. *Milwaukee Public Schools in an Era of Choice*, School Choice Wisconsin, October 2004.

36. Paul E. Peterson, "A choice between public and private schools: what next for school vouchers?" *Spectrum: The Journal of State Government*, Sept. 22, 2003, p.5.

37. Laurence D. Cohen, "If we love our children, set them free," *Hartford Courant*, Nov. 26, 1998.

## CHAPTER 12

1. Dave Weber, "Accused teacher drew complaints; parents say they raised concerns about the veteran teacher but were ignored or shut down," *Orlando Sentinel*, Nov. 18, 2004, p. B1.

2. Letter reproduced on November 18, 2004, on the Internet at: http://images.ibsys.com/2004/1118/393067.pdf.

3. Sandra Tan, "School allows banned mom to come back," *Newport News (Va.) Daily Press*, Jan. 20, 1999, p. C1.

4. Ibid.

5. Ray Delgado, "Parents storm Ackerman's office; angry over S.F. school enrollment," *San Francisco Chronicle*, May 20, 2003, p. A13.

6. Heather Knight, "$38,200 wall irks schools chief," *San Francisco Chronicle*, June 11, 2004, p. B4.

7. Ibid.

8. Robert Maranto, "No class: Why are 'public' schools closed to the public," *Wall Street Journal*, Sept. 16, 2004, Opinion Journal.

9. Ibid.

10. Diane Ravitch, *The Great School Wars* (New York: Basic Books, 1974), pp. 307–8.

11. Babette Edwards, interview with the author, November 22, 2004.

12. Ibid.

13. Ibid.

14. Joe Williams, "2 rallies, 2 views on school choice," *Milwaukee Journal Sentinel*, December 9, 1998, p. 3.

15. Ibid.

16. Babette Edwards, interview.

17. Joe Williams, "It's their potty . . . and parents cry for mayor to fix broken school toilets," *New York Daily News*, April 12, 2004, p. 7.

18. Babette Edwards, interview.

19. "Orleans public school boss moves daughter to private school," *Associated Press*, Sept. 15, 2000.

20. "Who gets to choose a school," *Washington Times*, Nov. 19, 1993, editorial page.

21. Sari Horwitz, "D.C. Superintendent transfers son, 15, from public school to St. Johns," *Washington Post*, Oct. 4, 1994, p. B1.

22. Chester Finn, "Not all parents are fools," *Educational Gadfly*, Oct. 21, 2004.

23. Jesse McDonald, interview with the author, October 31, 2004.

24. Thomas Toch, "The plight of the PTA," *New York Times*, Jan. 7, 2001.

25. Babette Edwards, interview.

26. Brenda Bell and Elnora Yarborough, "Don't take 'No' for an answer: a poor community organizes," published by the New England Literacy Resource Center, located on the Internet at: http://hub1.worlded.org/docs/vera/noanswer.htm

27. Ibid.

28. Ibid.

29. Shirley Dang, "Parents pull their kids from school over teacher," *Contra Costa Times*, Oct. 3, 2004. p.4.

30. Ibid.

31. Charles J. Dean, "Interim school chief named to guide troubled Greene," *Birmingham News*, Oct. 22, 2002.

32. "Parents picket striking teachers," *Associated Press*, Sept. 11, 2003.

33. John H. Fund, "Champion of choice," *Reason Online*, http://reason.com/williamsint.shtml.

34. Kavitha Mediratta and Jessica Karp, *Parent Power and Urban School Reform: The Story of Mothers on the Move* (New York: Institute for Education and Social Policy, Steinhardt School of Education, New York University, Sept. 2003), p. 3.

35. Joanne Wasserman, "Mothers fight to upgrade schools; they find persistence overcomes bureaucratic resistance," *New York Daily News*, Sept. 21, 1997. p. 6.

36. Marjorie Coeyman, "Moms on the move," *Christian Science Monitor*, June 16, 1998, p.B1.

37. Jesse McDonald, interview with the author, October 31, 2004.

38. Ray Sanchez, "Learnin' the hard way; in diverse Bronx district, schools are worlds apart," *Newsday*, Jan. 24, 1993, p. 18.

39. Ibid.

40. Anemona Hartocollis, "PS Stands for Public Shame: Stunning Failure of Bx School and Turnover of Leaders," *New York Daily News*, Dec. 24, 1995, p. 5.

41. Ibid.

42. Raymond Hernandez, "Despite fight, official stays," *New York Times*, Jan. 23, 1994, p.11.

43. Rafael Sugarman, "Cortines draws fire from Dist. 8 MOMs," *New York Daily News*, December 14, 1994, p. 13.

44. Mediratta and Karp, p 18.

45. Mediratta and Karp, p.37.

46. Lucretia Jones, interview.

47. Eva Moskowitz and Eric Grannis, "Let's bring the muse of competition to city schools," *New York Sun*, April 18, 2002.

48. Laurence D. Cohen, "If we love our children, set them free," *Hartford Courant*, Nov. 26, 1998, p. A15.

49. Arthur Levine, "Why I'm reluctantly backing vouchers: a proposal," *Wall Street Journal*, June 15, 1998, editorial page.

50. Consideration of H.R. 2746 and H.R. 2616, U.S. House of Representatives," Congressional Record, 105th Congress, First Session, October 31, 1997.

# SELECTED BIBLIOGRAPHY

Alinsky, Saul D. *Rules for Radicals: A Pragmatic Primer for Realistic Radicals.* New York: Vintage Books, 1971.

Berliner, David C. and Bruce J. Biddle. *The Manufactured Crisis: Myths, Fraud, and the Attack on America's Public Schools.* Reading, Mass: Addison-Wesley, 1995.

Bolick, Clint. *Voucher Wars, Waging the Legal Battle over School Choice.* Washington, D.C.: Cato Institute, 2003.

Brennan, David L. *Victory for Kids: The Cleveland School Voucher Case.* Beverly Hills, Calif.: New Millennium Press, 2002.

Brimelow, Peter. *The Worm in the Apple: How the Teacher Unions Are Destroying American Education.* New York: Harper Collins, 2003.

Chavous, Kevin P. *Serving our Children: Charter schools and the Reform of American Public Education.* Sterling, Va.: Capital Books, Inc., 2004.

Conant, James Bryant. *The American High School: A First Report to Interested Citizens.* New York: McGraw Hill, 1959.

Cuban, Larry, and Michael Usdan. *Powerful Reforms with Shallow Roots: Improving America's Urban Schools.* New York: Teachers College Press, 2003.

Finn, Chester E., and Kelly Amis. *Making It Count: A Guide to High-Impact Education Philanthropy.* Washington. D.C.: Thomas B. Fordham Foundation, 2001.

Halstead, Ted and Michael Lind. *The Radical Center: The Future of American Politics.* New York: Anchor Books, 2002.

Hess, Frederick M. *Common Sense School Reform.* New York: Palgrave Macmillan, 2004.

———. *Revolution at the Margins: The Impact of Competition on Urban School Systems.* Washington, D.C.: Brookings Institution Press, 2002.

———. *Spinning Wheels: The Politics of Urban School Reform.* Washington, D.C.: Brookings Institution Press, 1999.

Hevesi, Alan G. *Legislative Politics in New York State: A Comparative Analysis.* New York: Praeger, 1975.

Hill, Paul T. *School Boards: Focus on School Performance Not Money and Patronage.* Washington, D.C.: Progressive Policy Institute, 21st Century Schools Project, 2003.

Holt, Mikel. *Not Yet 'Free At Last': The Unfinished Business of the Civil Rights Movement.* Oakland, Calif.: Institute for Contemporary Studies, 1999.

Ladd, Helen F. *Market-Based Reforms in Urban Education.* Washington, D.C.: Economic Policy Institute, 2002.

Lieberman, Myron. *The Teacher Unions: How the NEA and AFT Sabotage Reform and Hold Students, Parents, Teachers and Taxpayers Hostage to Bureaucracy.* New York: Free Press, 1997.

McGroarty, Daniel, *Trinnietta Gets a Chance: Six Families and their School Choice Experience*. Washington, D.C.: Heritage Foundation, 2001.

Mediratta, Kavitha and Jessica Karp. *Parent Power and Urban School Reform: The story of Mothers on the Move*. New York: New York University Institute for Education and Social Policy, 2003.

Miller, Matthew. *The 2% Solution: Fixing America's Problems in Ways Liberals and Conservatives Can Love*. New York, Public Affairs, 2003.

Moe, Terry M. *Schools, Vouchers and the American Public*. Washington, D.C.: Brookings Institution Press, 2001.

Moskowitz, Eva. *Keeping Score: Can You Judge a School by Its Report Card?* Report of New York City Council Education Committee, Sept. 30, 2004.

Peterson, Peter G. *Running On Empty: How the Democratic and Republican Parties Are Bankrupting Our Future and What Americans Can Do About It*. New York: Farrar, Straus and Giroux, 2004.

Ravitch, Diane. *Left Back: A Century of Failed School Reforms*. New York: Simon & Schuster, 2000.

———. *The Great School Wars*. New York: Basic Books, 1974.

Rich, Wilbur C. *Black Mayors and School Politics, The Failure of Reform in Detroit, Gary, and Newark*. New York: Garland Publishing, 1996.

Rochester, J. Martin. *Class Warfare: Besieged Schools, Bewildered Parents, Betrayed Kids, and The Attack On Excellence*. San Francisco: Encounter Books, 2002.

Schrag, Peter. *Final Test: The Battle for Adequacy in America's Schools*. New York: The New Press, 2003.

Segal, Lydia G. *Battling Corruption in America's Public Schools*. Boston: Northeastern University Press, 2004.

Stern, Sol. *Breaking Free: Public School Lessons and the Imperative of School Choice*. San Francisco: Encounter Books, 2003.

Thernstrom, Abigal and Stephen Thernstron. *No Excuses: Closing The Racial Gap in Learning*. New York: Simon & Schuster, 2003.

Thompson, Tommy G. *Power to the People: An American State at Work*. New York: Harper Collins, 1996.

Viteritti, Joseph P. *Choosing Equality: School Choice, the Constitution, and Civil Society*. Washington, D.C.: Brookings Institution Press, 1999.

# INDEX